D1356262

British Retail and the
Men Who Shaped It

British Retail and the Men Who Shaped It

Stephen Butt

PEN & SWORD
HISTORY

AN IMPRINT OF PEN & SWORD BOOKS LTD.
YORKSHIRE – PHILADELPHIA

First published in Great Britain in 2018 by
Pen & Sword History
An imprint of
Pen & Sword Books Ltd
Yorkshire - Philadelphia

ISBN 9781526715258

A CIP catalogue record for this book is available from the British Library.

Typeset in INDIA By Geniies IT & Services Private Limited

Printed and bound in the UK by TJ International Ltd.

Pen & Sword Books Ltd incorporates the Imprints of Pen & Sword Books Archaeology, Atlas, Aviation, Battleground, Discovery, Family History, History, Maritime, Military, Naval, Politics, Railways, Select, Transport, True Crime, Fiction, Frontline Books, Leo Cooper, Praetorian Press, Seaforth Publishing, Wharncliffe and White Owl.

For a complete list of Pen & Sword titles please contact

PEN & SWORD BOOKS LIMITED
47 Church Street, Barnsley, South Yorkshire, S70 2AS, England
E-mail: enquiries@pen-and-sword.co.uk
Website: www.pen-and-sword.co.uk

or

PEN AND SWORD BOOKS
1950 Lawrence Rd, Havertown, PA 19083, USA
E-mail: Uspen-and-sword@casematepublishers.com
Website: www.penandswordbooks.com

Contents

Chapter One

High Street Blues

Returning recently to the High Street of my childhood, I found that every one of the shops and stores I had worked in as a teenager had closed. It was some time ago when I left Littlewoods Stores to go to university, and I do not believe for one moment that I was instrumental in their decline. Most managed to struggle on for some time after I left their employment. However, that discovery prompted me to consider why some of the most well-known brands which were so prominent in the High Street for so long are no longer with us, and conversely, why other names have survived.

I accept that I am not a retail success story. At Littlewoods, I once received an early and large delivery of Easter Eggs and, due to lack of space, stacked them high up on the top shelves in the stockroom as they would not be required on the shop floor for several weeks, not noticing the hot water pipe running just above. By the time they went on sale the entire stock was not so egg-shaped, but were still sold as a special offer.

A retail store's stockroom can be a fascinating place, often haunted by staff who rarely see the light of day on the shop floor except when armed with brooms, mops and buckets after the last customer has left. They are also sometimes jealously guarded and patrolled by a long-standing member of staff who has worked for the store for longer than anyone can recall.

Across the road at John Collier Menswear, the laid-down sales procedure dictated by the headquarters management in Leeds was for the senior shop assistant to greet each customer, ascertain whether he wished to buy an expensive three-piece suit or something less, and pass the poor man to another assistant in order of rank and time 'on board' the business. It was a system established many years ago in the early department stores where 'shop walkers' undertook the same role; but this was England in the 1960s! The process meant that the most junior member of staff rarely encountered a customer. When I finally managed to meet one, all I could sell was a tie or occasionally a pair of socks. As a considerable proportion of the wages were made up of commission on sales, I did not do well. I do remember one eventful day when instead of the monotonous parade of middle-aged men, several young women entered the premises. They had been taken on by a local holiday camp which had sent them be measured up for blazers. It was the only occasion when the John Collier shop in Weston-super-Mare entered the Swinging Sixties, and there was almost a scrum to say, 'Are you being served?'

There were only a few other exciting moments. I worked with other lads to open a brand-new supermarket, one of the Keymarkets chain, successor to the more famous David Greig grocery stores. I remember stacking the shelves for the first time, sticking a price label on every tin and jar, and stopping the traffic in one of the town's busiest shopping streets as we man-handled and trundled a very large and ancient *Kelvinator* fridge from one of the old Greig shops nearby.

This was the seaside, so alongside the familiar shops were numerous fish and chip outlets, souvenir shops and other retailers specifically serving the day-tripper. For one memorable summer season, I worked for a beach photography studio. Endless postcard-size black and white photographs of tourists walking along the promenade or riding a donkey were developed and printed here. I was not proficient enough to take the photographs, nor did I have the charm that was necessary to coax passers-by to pose. My role was to transport, on my bicycle, the exposed film from the photographers on the beach to the studio and to return the prints to the kiosk one hour later. The 'laboratory' was on the first floor, and the process involved washing the newly-exposed prints in the bath. On the ground floor was one of the first 'hippy' boutiques in the town, full of kaftans and other strange gar-ments and inhabited by young women with long hair and short skirts, and young men wearing granny specs and even longer hair. It was the first shop I encountered which played 'canned' music to establish a mood – but the proprietor only had one long-playing record. I remember to this day every word of every track of Sonny and Cher's Greatest Hits.

It is easy and good to reminisce, and it is important because we all have memories of shopping, of distinctive stores and shop assistants with per-sonality and character. Indeed, some newer brands have capitalised on that rose-tinted view of the past which we all have at some time. Nostalgia is sel-dom out of fashion. We are upset and feel a sense of loss when a nationwide brand disappears from the High Street and we lament its passing but often fail to see the irony that, if we had all patronised that 'wonderful shop' more regularly, it might still be in business.

The term 'High Street' originally described the principal or most important street in a town, which may have gained that status because of the importance of the people living there or due to it being a significant route, perhaps connecting with a market or other public area. It was later to become known as the street where the most useful or important shops could be found, and many of these 'High Street names' were originally market stalls. The smallest High Street in the United Kingdom is said to be in Holsworthy in Devon, and has just three shops along its 100-metre length. Across the country, High Street is the most common street name, with over 5,000 occurrences.

British people seem to enjoy the description of their country as 'a nation of shopkeepers', a phrase popularly attributed to Napoleon Bonaparte but originally used by Adam Smith in his famous *Wealth of Nations*, first published in 1776 when Bonaparte would have been all of eight years old. Whether the rise and fall of High Street brands fits with Smith's underlying belief in an economic system that is automatic and self-regulating is a matter which will occupy the time and attention of financiers and economists for many years, but Smith's words from the eighteenth century still have a powerful resonance today:

> To found a great empire for the sole purpose of raising up a people of customers may at first sight appear a project fit only for a nation of shopkeepers. It is, however, a project altogether unfit for a nation of shopkeepers; but extremely fit for a nation whose government is influenced by shopkeepers.

Just as resonant are comments by the present business and retail entrepreneur, Theo Paphitis:

> Napoleon said Britain is a nation of shopkeepers and a shopkeeper is an entrepreneur; he or she is a small business person. That's exactly what we are.

The currency of the High Street

The retail trade needs currency. The Celtic tribes that populated Britain before the Roman Invasion began using coinage in about 150bc. These were mostly minted in France and were probably brought across the English Channel by immigrant settlers and merchants and as a by-product of the slave trade that existed at that time. The first coins to be minted in Britain were those of the Cantii in Kent in about 80–60bc. A hoard of more than 2,000 of these coins, known as *potins*, from the bronze alloy from which they were cast, was found in a pit in West Thurrock in Essex in 1987.

Possibly the most advanced of the Celtic tribes in terms of a coin-based economic system were the Corielatauvi who occupied the region approximating to the modern East Midlands. Producing coinage indicates people with a sense of being a society and with a hierarchy. The Corielatauvi reproduced the names and images of their leaders on their coins, which supports this theory of an organised community already trading widely before the arrival of the Romans.

The network of roads laid down by the Romans was principally for military and administrative purposes but also became the new trading routes. Even towns on the edge of the Empire were in reach of merchants bringing exotic spices, fashions and food. The forum became a focus for trade as well as the place where news was exchanged, deals were struck and all manner of services and entertainments were available, as brought to life in Seneca's famous account of the marketplace from the first century ad:

> Imagine all kinds of uproar, fit to make you hate your ears. The hearties are put through their paces, throw their hands about laden with leaden weights, and when they exert themselves, or pretend to, I hear their grunts and their whistling, raucous breathing. If the umpire of a ball-game makes an appearance, and starts to count the tosses, I am done for. The picture is not complete without some quarrelsome fellow, a thief caught red-handed, or the man who loves the sound of his own voice in the bath – not to mention those who jump in with a tremendous splash. Besides those whose voices are good, think of the strident call of the barber, continually advertising his presence, never silent except when he plucks someone's arm pit and forces his customers to cry out on his own behalf, or the assorted cries of the pantry-cook, the sausage-seller, the confectioner, and the hawkers of refreshments selling their wares each in his own distinctive sing-song.

No marketplace was busier and more expansive than those in Rome itself. Trajan's Market was probably built at the beginning of the second century ad and can be described as the world's first shopping mall, containing over 150 different shops. Mostly these retail establishments were formed from one room which was open to the street, goods being displayed on stone counters. The shopkeeper would live behind the shop or above on a second floor, and wooden shutters would be fitted at night to deter thieves.

Many High Streets were the main routes through a town or city, and often led to or from the market place. Along these routes, coaching inns were built to service the passengers travelling from town to town. In towns that date to the Roman period, taverns stood along these streets, serving a diverse community of local militia, visiting merchants and passing soldiers. They were houses that were 'public', that offered refreshment and respite from the toils and labours of the day, and they no doubt served a selection of liquid refreshment to appeal to the wide range of clientele visiting from distant areas of the Roman Empire. Pub signs were invented by the Romans to show that a roadside building was a taberna. In Rome, vine leaves were hung at the front of the house to indicate that the landlord sold wines. In Britain, where vines were rare, the landlords used evergreen leaves instead. Some of today's pub names such as 'the Bush' may well have their roots in this early improvisation of a brand name.

The earliest High Street hostelries were described by the name of their owners, such as 'Stephen Gifford's tavern', or 'the Tavern of Roger of Glen'. The later pubs which became coaching inns, offered accommodation. Like the motorway service stations of today, they provided a range of services for weary travellers with other relevant trades such as blacksmiths, and even hatters, located nearby. The number of such inns in one street may seem surprising, often out-numbering the shops and other establishments.

Some of the landlords of these inns were notorious larger-than-life characters. In Market Harborough, the landlord of the *Three Swans* coaching inn in the latter half of the twentieth century was a particularly interesting man who recorded his opinions on the activities he saw around him along the High Street, and in his attitudes harked back to an earlier age. His name was John Fothergill.

His inn was originally known as *The Sign of the Swanne*. There are indications that the present wrought-iron inn sign depicting three swans in silhouette, although old, has been re-engineered so that two of the swans are newer. Of the many interesting and famous people who have passed through its doors is King Charles I, who lodged there on the night before the Battle of Naseby on 13 June 1645, and Queen Anne, who as Princess of Denmark, visited Market Harborough in 1688 and was accommodated along with her sizeable entourage which included the Bishop of London and the Earl of Dorset.

When Fothergill arrived in Market Harborough he was not impressed by either the town or the hotel. He called it 'the foulest little pub possible with dirty sheets.' and continued at length:

Inside the inn, whatever the dirt, not always apparent, the awful furniture, beds, the rat-holes, the wall papers coming away from the walls, the tiny, unventilated lavatory on the first floor, used by the entire house, the bars and people of the town, and the strange stillness throughout, for no one seems to come in, you could see at once, the building had a loveable character.

He was less than enthusiastic about the rest of Market Harborough's High Street, noting that:

Most of the town wants paint and those who do paint want ideas. The big sundial on the church tower is peeling away.

He wrote that the graceful curve of the road which passed in front of the *Three Swans* led visitors to anticipate a more interesting view around the corner, but the only satisfying vista was the one seen as you left the town in the direction of Leicester. There are many stories of hauntings and ghostly encounters at the *Three Swans*. Most seem to be related, not surprisingly, to John Fothergill or to a portrait of him. It is said that after his death, Fothergill's widow removed the portrait from the bar and put it in the cellar. The next day, heavy rain led to flooding, but the rising waters stopped just short of the portrait. It is also claimed that mishaps (and even premature death) occurs to anyone who moves or even touches the portrait. It was reported that on one occasion when the portrait was taken down, all the computers in the building crashed, and on other occasions, paint turned from blue to green, and the electricity supply failed. Even as recently as October 2013, the current owners of the *Three Swans* during a planned redecoration of the bar named after Fothergill, decided to work round the portrait and leave it in place. There are similar inns throughout the country where the former stabling areas can be seen, but have found a new use as conference rooms or lounges.

Supply and demand

Even at this early time in the history of shop keeping, the success of a business was clearly dependent upon being able to acquire the right product at the right price. No doubt the arrival of a new merchant would generate considerable interest and a bout of competitive bartering and negotiation. The relationship between the supplier or manufacturer and the retailer is one which has major financial implications, and changed over time with each new transport revolution: the stagecoach, the improvement of roads through turnpike acts, the canals and the railways. Different types of goods presented different logistical challenges. Suppliers of perishable goods needed to be situated close enough to a market to ensure that the goods were still saleable after a journey along rough roads. Transporting heavy goods such as coal ran the risk of cart wheels sinking in mud during the winter months and after a period of sustained rainfall.

The early cottage-based textile industry was heavily reliant on this mobility of goods and raw materials. Garments were made on frames located where the raw material came from, on farms in the countryside. The industry required 'middle men' to collect these garments and sell them. In 1815, Nathaniel Corah, the son of a Leicestershire farmer, incorporated an element of quality control by setting up an arrangement by which framework knitters would bring their goods to an upper room in the *Globe Inn* in Leicester's Silver Street, where he would select the best, negotiate a price and then transport his purchases to a regular market in Birmingham. Corah was later to bring the manufacture into the town under one roof, and went on to create a textile business which became, in the 1960s and 1970s, the largest supplier of fashion garments to Marks and Spencer.

Many of the nineteenth-century retail entrepreneurs realised that relying on others to transport your stock was a risk that could harm your business, even if you were only selling pots and pans in a corner shop. Some bought their own vans and travelled to nearby cities to obtain stock. Others went into partnership to increase their buying power. A few realised that they could partly cover the cost of keeping a van on the road by offering to transport goods on behalf of other shopkeepers and suppliers thus ensuring that no journey was made by an empty vehicle.

Others, such as Frederick Rushbrooke, founder of Halfords, began as a manufacturer selling bicycle components to shops before deciding to sell direct to the public. An advertisement for the original Rushbrooke company provides an insight into his marketing strategies:

A few words of advice to small makers. Keep well to the front with new ideas. If you would be in the front rank you must keep in constant communication with Rushbrooke & Co. [...] Spare no pains to give entire satisfaction to your customers. Study well your customer's requirements [...] No firm on earth can beat the cycle agent that buys from Rushbrooke & Co.

All these strategies, often the result of a flash of inspiration or of a canny mind, have percolated down through the centuries and are at the heart of the complex multi-billion-pound retail operations of the present day. More retail floor space means less room for storing stock, so a reliable supply chain is essential. Ensuring that each store holds a minimal quantity of each of tens of thousands of items, but does not run out of any line has only become possible with modern technologies that can monitor sales 24/7 and even anticipate the customers' actions. Even with such complex monitoring, it can still go wrong. Fashion retailers face serious financial consequences if they are still selling winter coats when the country may be enjoying a heatwave.

There were two further major monetary events in the post-war history of shopping. The first was the abolition in the UK of Resale (or Retail) Price Maintenance (RPM) in 1964. As the phrase implies, RPM prevented shops from reducing prices below a level set by the manufacturer. The general view is that this practice reduces competition between brands, and maintains profit margins and is not therefore in the interest of the consumer. Supporters of RPM argue that the system protects the entire supply chain and provides stability of prices, that it ensures a fair return on investment for manufacturers, and that Governments have no right to in interfere in what were regarded as legal contracts.

The second landmark in the UK's post-war financial development was the conversion to decimal currency in February 1971. The move towards decimalisation had begun as early as 1841 with the founding of the Decimal Association, but it was in 1966 that the Decimal Currency Board was set up by the Government. The first decimal coins, the 5p and 10p, were introduced in April 1968, being the same size and having the same value as the existing shilling and two-shilling pre-decimal coins. For several months before 'Decimal Day', shops displayed prices in both forms.

On and after the changeover, shops accepted the old currency but gave change in the new coinage. The older coins were returned to banks and were taken out of circulation remarkably quickly. The transition went smoothly due to the strict timetable of publicity which made decimalisation a talking point long before the day. In hindsight, it did fuel inflation because some retailers took advantage of the event to raise prices. As the lowest denomination of decimal currency (1/2p) was 1/200th of a pound whereas the corresponding value of the lowest old currency coin (1/2d) was 1/240th it also meant that future price rises would be by greater steps, especially when the decimal halfpenny was abolished in 1984, leaving the 1p as the lowest value coin at 1/100th of a pound.

The corner shop

It was traditional until the advent of out-of-town shopping centres to make a weekly journey 'into town', probably by bus, to do the family shopping, often walking from one end of a High Street to the other, armed with a shopping list and a basket. In the post-war period, this would involve buying pharmaceuticals from Boots or Timothy Whites, who were adjacent to one another, perhaps a pair of tights from Littlewoods or Marks and Spencer, and some essentials from Woolworths. Sometimes, one crossed the road to buy a puncture repair outfit from Currys or Halfords, cheese and butter at Maypole and tea or coffee from Home and Colonial.

However, although less packaging meant less bulk, shoppers in the 1950s were still exercising restraint in their buying habits, remembering the years of rationing which only ended completely in July 1954 when restrictions on the purchase of meat and bacon were lifted, fourteen years after limits on the sale of butter, sugar and bacon had first been imposed.

Although the High Street shops were now retailing without such limitations, there was still the need for a corner shop in your neighbourhood where you could buy most of the basic commodities needed between the larger weekly shopping trips. Many of these neighbourhood retail outlets were designed into housing estates as early as the mid-Victorian period, such as at Weston-super-Mare in Somerset where a major housebuilding programme on land south of the town incorporated several convenient shopping areas. In the days before most families could afford a motor car, these shops were vital for obtaining fresh fruit, vegetables, meat and fish.

The 1830 Beer Act led to the setting up of small outlets brewing and selling ale in neighbourhoods. The concept was an attempt to reduce public drunkenness by encouraging the working classes to drink beer in their home environment rather than in the bawdy and somewhat lawless establishments in the towns. These were often one-room bars created by converting a front room into a public area, but developers began incorporating them as purpose-built end-of-terrace dwellings. Many of these also sold other commodities and some became corner shops.

Today, after a decade or more of supermarket expansion with the construction of large out-of-town shopping centres, the concept of the corner shop is returning, although now more commonly described as a 'convenience store'. These principally sell what the retail trade refers to as FMCG, an abbreviation for 'fast-moving consumer goods', being those items that most shoppers need to buy on a regular basis and which are comparatively low-cost. Another description of this sector is 'low margin–high volume'.

Several of the largest supermarket groups now have an expanding chain of smaller stores, and the companies that own former newsagents and tobacconists are prospering. Waitrose are opening 300 'Little Waitrose' shops, and Tesco has over 1,600 small stores operating. The single trader – the shopkeeper of the past – has been revived through companies that do not own any shops or retail outlets but simply supply goods under a certain brand name or 'symbol'. The world leader in the 'symbol group' is SPAR, which began with one shop in the Netherlands in 1932 and is now the world's largest food retail chain across thirty-four countries. SPAR has more than 2,400 shops in the United Kingdom employing over 50,000 staff and with a turnover of £3 billion. Premier Stores has nearly 3,000 independently-owned shops and stores in the United Kingdom branded as Premier Express, Happy Shopper and Euro Shopper. Other similar franchise operations include Londis, Costcutter, Budgens and Nisa. In 2014, the Institute of Grocery Distribution reported that the symbol group market was worth £15.5 billion and had a 42 per cent share of the UK convenience market through 17,080 stores. Another area of convenience expansion has been the service stations supplying drivers and passengers with a range of essentials both on the UK motorway network and on many other major roads across the country. Here, the High Street brands have moved in alongside the fast-food outlets and coffee shops.

Setting out your stall

Few retailers began in the High Street in the nineteenth and twentieth century, though most aspired to opening a store in that respected location. Many began with a more modest retail arrangement such as a market stall. It was not only the famous Michael Marks who launched his retail career in a market, but also William Morrison of the Bradford-based supermarket chain, David Greig at Brixton Market, and Bill Adderley of Dunelm, formerly Dunelm Mills, in Leicester. It was in all winds and weather that these men and others discovered if they could sell their goods. It was all too easy for a customer to walk on by. Each stall must be eye-catching and offer real bargains; and customers never like to be duped so selling something damaged or below par was, and is, bad business practice.

The move from temporary market stall to permanent shop is reflected in the buildings that surround some of Britain's oldest market places. For the sake of management convenience, there was (and is) a distinction between regular traders who will be on the market in the same location every day for many years, often paying a premium for holding onto the same pitch, and the casual trader who may stay only for a day or a few weeks at the most. Those who populated the permanent end of the market began to make their stalls more permanent too, rather than dismantling the structure and removing the goods every night. Over time, these fixed stalls became buildings and the transition to the High Street began.

Shop windows on the past

Kelly's Directory, more accurately known as the *Kelly's, Post Office and Harrod & Co Directory*, opens a fascinating window on the types of trades available in the High Street in the past. It was founded in the middle of the nineteenth century by Frederic Festus Kelly, a senior official with the General Post Office (GPO), who had responsibility for compiling the London telephone directory. There were other directories, including *Wright's*, established by C.N. Wright in 1854, which contained similar information. Directories were first published around the beginning of the nineteenth century, initially covering larger centres of population. The first county directories that included smaller towns and villages were published around 1820. Their purpose was to provide information for travellers and visitors. They gave a general description of the town with details of public transport, postal collections, churches, schools, shops and businesses. As most of the directories were reissued annually, they are now a valuable source of information for local historians. Many of them also carried advertising to offset the printing costs which give a further and more detailed insight into the variety of goods and products available at that time.

John Hollingworth, one of the larger wine and spirits merchants in the Midlands, was thriving at the end of the nineteenth century, and took out full page advertisement on the inside board covers of directories. He was selling 'Scotch Whiskey, finest blend, very old' at twenty-one shillings per gallon, as well as Guinness's Dublin Stout and India Pale Ale 'in cask and bottle'.

By turning the pages of any of these directories it is possible to 'walk' along the High Street and discover the shops and traders of more than a century ago. To take one example at random, from one location and year, Leicester's High Street in 1892 accommodated milliners, haberdashers and drapers next to tobacconists and wine merchants. There was a watch and clockmaker, a hardware dealer who also undertook 'bell-hanging', a confectioner, an upholsterer and cabinet maker, a hatter, a bookseller and a printer, together with several banks. Tradesmen such as decorators, worked from premises next to fishmongers and butchers, leather bag manufacturers, chemists, willow and bamboo workers and musical instrument makers.

On one side of the *Hare and Pheasant* public house was George Pink, a dyer and cleaner, and on the other side were the premises of a tailor and clothier. At the heart of this bustling street, which led to one of the town's earlier market locations, was the grand façade of the Co-operative Society store, the largest single building in the street; and within its red-brick walls were different departments dealing in groceries, boots, tailoring and drapery, each with its own manager who is identified by name in the directory.

What is striking is the wide variety of crafts and trades that were available in a relatively small area. Many were independent family businesses, and of those, a significant number included the suffix 'and son' to the family name, indicating that these were either established businesses or newer enterprises with aspirations. Occasionally, one notices a partnership which suggests a business which is broadening its product range. In Leicester, an example of this is R.F. Swain and company at 19, 21 and 27 Highcross Street, the town's earliest High Street, listed as cigar makers, with Swain, Almond and Goodliffe at 25 Highcross Street, who are described as cheese factors and provisions merchants. In later years these amalgamated to become Swain and Latchmore, who then united the four addresses by rebuilding the entire site. This was a partnership that recognised an early 'niche market', selling cigars, wine and cheese to the wealthier citizens of the town who lived nearby.

The joining together of separate smaller businesses into one larger store created the department stores. With the possible exception of the Co-op, these were the establishments that in later times deliberately held to their traditions, almost to the point of providing a 'retro' shopping experience, when all the other shops around them were modernising. Instead, old-world courtesy and social etiquette were the order of every day.

In Leicester, entrepreneur Joseph Johnson combined his various separate retail operations, which included millinery, groceries, furniture and funeral services, to create a department store of great character in a building designed by Isaac Barradale, one of Britain's finest arts and crafts architects and which even included a mortuary in the basement and accommodation for the single female members of his staff several storeys above. Johnsons were eventually taken over by Fenwicks, which traded in the same building until 2017.

Across the country, the Co-operative Societies also built rambling retail mansions drawing together their many services from funeral parlours to butchery, bakeries to pharmacies. These were grand buildings speaking eloquently of the pride of the wider Co-operative Movement; but the Co-op was also the corner shop with smaller retail outlets in neighbourhoods and outlying areas of large towns and cities. For the working-class housewives watching the pennies in their purses, the dividend or 'divi' was all-important, probably more important than knowing they were part of a larger and powerful working-class movement.

Brand identity and self-belief

The psychology of branding and retail identity is subtle and complex. Each shopper holds an affinity to certain stores, but a dislike, mistrust and even at times a strong aversion to others. Most shoppers will say that they seek quality at a good price; that they patronise shops that sell what they want, when they need it; but this is not the full story. We like to be seen in certain stores, and we linger, forgetting the pressure of time; whereas in other shopping environments we are frustrated by even a minimal queue at a checkout.

It is true that many of the early retail pioneers built their businesses on developing a reputation as a man or woman who gave customers a fair deal. James Kemsey Wilkinson, founder of the Wilko chain, was often quoted as saying 'I always like to look people in the eye and know in my heart that they are getting a good deal.' In fact, Wilkinson was probably not a 'people' man, but he established a business with high ethical standards which have continued to the present day.

Branding is about clearly positioning a business in the eyes of the customer. Barring external factors, if a shop or store can achieve a strong bond and connection with its target customer, then it will succeed; but narrowing the focus too much will reduce the appeal of its products, while blurring that focus, perhaps by trying to appeal to too broad a spectrum of customers' tastes, will also be prejudicial to success. Woolworth may be one of the latter group of once-great brand names whose brand identity evaporated sometime in the 1980s.

As early as the 1870s, American marketing practices were becoming an influence in the United Kingdom. Thomas Lipton chose to work as a shop assistant in a New York grocery store so that he could bring new marketing and sales techniques back to his native Glasgow. It is said that his first shop, in the Gorbals district of the city, was the most brightly lit in the neighbourhood each evening to create a presence, and so that passers-by knew what he was selling. It is recorded that when Lipton opened a store in Edinburgh, he hired two 'crowds' of people, one group notably thin and the other of broader physical proportions. The former group marched along the street carrying banners announcing that they were to shop at Liptons. Sometime after the store had opened, the second group left by the same entrances carrying banners explaining that their increased volume was because they had just shopped at Liptons.

Lipton was an example of the sheer determination of some of the retail pioneers. Some held a conviction that they 'knew' how to sell and that they would be successful, come what may. Others inherited a knowledge of manufacture or retail from parents or other family members. It is said that Lipton, as a young man of twenty-one years 'lived and breathed' his shop, often working for more than eighteen hours a day and sometimes sleeping on a makeshift bed behind the counter.

James Kemsey Wilkinson's father described his occupation as a 'brass founder's assistant', and as an 'ironmonger and china dealer'. James gained further retail experience by working for Timothy Whites on the South Coast, which at that time sold hardware as well as pharmaceuticals, and then followed in his father's footsteps, first working for an architectural ironmonger in Birmingham before moving to Leicester to be employed by the wealthy ironmonger Herbert Pochin. Pochin was a successful businessman from a longstanding landowning family. The company is still trading, but the young Wilkinson walked out and away from what was probably a promising career with the firm because his innovative ideas were not taken on board. Instead, he opened his own small shop in a working-class neighbourhood and founded the Wilko chain.

William 'Bill' Adderley is another man who believed he could do better than the big-name company that employed him. On being told by Woolworths that they wanted him to uproot his family and move to another store over one hundred miles away, he refused, bought some redundant stock returned by Marks and Spencer and proved his personal conviction that he and his wife could sell by working on a market stall. The Adderleys went on to found Dunelm Mills.

At times, the lives and stories of these men and women intertwine. In 1870, William Wheeler Kendall walked from Market Harborough to Leicester intent on making his fortune in the 'big town'. It may have been raining on the way because he chose to manufacture umbrellas. By the 1960s, Kendall and Sons had over one hundred stores, mostly in High Streets. In 1981, the business was bought by Hepworths, the Leeds-based men's outfitter, with the intention of creating a womenswear chain. Instead, George Davies, who had been recruited to manage the project, proposed a total rebranding. The result was NEXT. Davies had begun his retailing career with Littlewoods Stores, based in Liverpool as a graduate trainee in the buying department, sourcing white ankle socks. The purchase by Hepworths was a shrewd move financially. The entire Kendalls chain was acquired for just £1.75 million which included the freehold on prime High Street land across the country.

NEXT was a roaring success, but seven years later, Davies was sacked. His single-minded approach to business was seen by some as egotistical and the very fast growth of the company had taken it near to bankruptcy. His next project was the George brand selling through Asda, which became the UK market leader in 2009, overtaking Marks and Spencer. Several brands later, Davies is a member of the 'super-rich'. His lifestyle is epitomised by the Cessna Citation X, the world's fastest commercial private jet aircraft, one of which he owns. Incidentally, just thirty years before Kendall walked his way from Market Harborough to retail success, Thomas Cook had his vision of worldwide travel for the working classes on the very same road.

Steam – the means of production and distribution

Without question, the development of the steam engine provided an important, and in most cases, the vital catalyst in converting a manufacturing or trading concept into reality. In every single story in this book, every business had to make that leap from being a homely cottage family industry to being mechanised. Most would not have survived had they not made that change and embraced the new technology.

We can all remember being taught about James Watt and his first experiments with steam involving a kettle, and many of us were taught about his later collaboration with Matthew Boulton which led to his engines being able to be produced with a fine degree of engineering precision and therefore efficiency. It made the difference for manufacturers who could transfer processes such as dipping cake into molten chocolate from being a hand process to an automated one, but it also enabled, through the railway networks, those retail pioneers to have their raw materials delivered to their loading bays regularly, and to be able to send their goods far and wide to distant markets.

Steam is still an essential power supply in the twenty-first century. All power stations, whether coal-powered or nuclear, have, at their heart, the same process of heating water to generate steam that powers the turbines which generate electricity. Without James Watt, none of the High Street brands of today would exist.

Incentives to buy – stamping their mark

The principles of the Co-operative movement in sharing the profits of their businesses with their customers required a means of recording each customer's purchasing history. In the latter years of the system, this was achieved electronically. Many people still remember the number that was assigned to them, or to their parents, probably because it was repeated so often. This was not a 'loyalty scheme' as such, but could have been developed into a scheme which gave tangible rewards shopping at a store or retail chain in the same way that loyalty cards operate today. With the computer technologies that the Co-op never had, loyalty cards can enable a retailer to build up a picture of how customers make purchases, which in turn feeds into more efficient stock management.

The first major incentive scheme was launched as early as 1896 by Thomas Sperry and Shelley Hutchinson in the United States, who created the famous S&H stamps. Stores and gas stations would purchase stamps from the company to give to customers, who collected them in books. These were then redeemed for household goods. The scheme became so popular that at one time, the company claimed their gift catalogue was the largest printed publication in the United States, and that they issued three times as many stamps as the US Postal Service.

The concept was introduced to Britain by Granville Richard Tompkins in 1958. Tompkins was born in Islington in north London in 1918. He worked as an engineering draughtsman during the First World War and then became a printer, setting up his own business in 1945. Whilst on holiday in Chicago in the 1950s, he witnessed the success of the American S&H scheme, and consequently created his own Green Shield Stamp Trading Company in England. Tompkins was able to register the 'green shield' as a UK trademark which meant that when S&H introduced their own scheme to Britain in the early 1960s, it was branded as S&H Pink Stamps.

Customers who shopped in affiliated stores were rewarded with stamps which, when saved in books, could be exchanged for gifts at special shops. Originally, shop assistants had to issue the stamps manually, but when Green Shield was adopted by the large retailers including Tesco, machines linked to the checkout tills would dispense the required quantity.

The competition between Tompkins' Green Shield stamps and the S&H Pink Stamps became fierce, and inevitably led to a form of inflation, offering customers double and then quadruple numbers of stamps on special promotions. By the early 1970s, when inflation began to take off in the real world of the economy, shoppers were bringing home many hundreds of stamps each week, and were faced with the somewhat tedious duty of sticking them into the books. The two companies addressed this issue by introducing higher 'value' stamps worth ten or forty single stamps. It was inflation which led to the demise of the schemes, as the value of the rewards steadily diminished, and customers began to find the process too time-consuming.

S&H survived in the USA but with very few retail outlets using their stamps. With the rise of internet shopping, they switched from paper-based incentives to a 'Greenpoints' online system. This was later sold on to a company pioneering electronic touch-to-pay technology which closed suddenly, some years later.

Tompkins' Green Shield business took a different turn by changing its identity. The entrepreneur had introduced an arrangement by which customers could redeem their stamps for more valuable rewards by paying the balance in cash. He realised that he could phase out the stamp element completely if his reward shops sold the sort of goods that customers wanted to buy. This development of the original concept came to Tompkins while he was holidaying in the Greek city of Argos in 1973, and it was this name that he chose for his new enterprise.

However, although Tompkins began opening his new Argos stores, Tesco was still using his Green Shield stamps. It was not until 1977 that Tesco, facing growing competition from other retailers offering grocery items at discounted prices, made the decision to abandon the stamps, using the more than £20 million of savings to cut the price on a wide range of products. The chain stayed closed for an additional day following the Queen's Silver Jubilee weekend so that the prices in their stores could be changed.

The Tesco decision was the trigger for Tompkins to transfer his energies to the Argos brand. Although the two companies were separate, Green Shield's transport fleet, redemption shops and administrative buildings were gradually rebranded as Argos. The original glossy gift catalogue remained the basis of the Argos business, with only a small selection of goods being on display at Argos stores. Tompkins sold Argos to BAT Industries in 1979 for £30 million. In 1983, the stamps were withdrawn entirely, although an attempt to revive them in a small number of retail outlets was made in 1987. In 2011, the company printed more than twenty million catalogues, but more recently, the emphasis has switched to online and electronic browsing.

Tompkins was awarded the CBE in 1992 but died the same year. Ironically, the Argos association with the supermarket giants has continued. Faced with growing competition from online retailers such as Amazon, the business was sold, and was eventually acquired, with its 739 stores, by Sainsbury's in 2016 for £1.4 billion. Sainsbury's then commenced the roll-out of Argos shops within their supermarkets in locations where there was no nearby Argos outlet.

The digital age

Internet shopping and the result of the 2016 EU Referendum on the future relationship of the United Kingdom and the European Union has put into focus the concept of worldwide trade and the challenges of cross-border control of taxation. Behind many of the most familiar High Street names of the twenty-first century are international companies based in Europe, the USA, China and Asia. The click of a computer mouse or one tap of a finger on a tablet or phone screen transfers today's shoppers seamlessly across continents; but the personalities and attitudes of many of the British retail founding fathers persist and still permeate many corners of this trade.

This is the story, not of anonymous billion-dollar financial empires, but of the men and women who started from next to nothing and made the most of their abilities, ambitions and self-confidence.

My choice of words in the previous sentence has been made with care and deliberation. The social limitations of the Victorian era restricted opportunities for women to pursue business careers, and indeed careers in other fields, but they were influential in many areas of commercial and business life. There is hardly a single (male) pioneer in this book who was not supported, financed or bailed out by a female member of his family, and in many cases, the ladies of the family took a very active role and were influential in the decision-making processes.

Chapter Two

The Chocolatiers and Confectioners

The British companies that dominated the chocolate industry in the nineteenth and twentieth centuries created a myriad of brands that became household names and are still familiar, some after more than a century of trading. Their products sell in millions, part of an industry which today is worth over four billion pounds worldwide.

It began in London's Bishopsgate in 1657 when a Frenchman began selling 'an excellent West India drink called chocolate'. His enterprise would be the first of many 'Chocolate Houses', which were especially enjoyed by the gentry. Their popularity took off in the later decades of the seventeenth century leading to new plantations being cultivated in the West Indies to satisfy the burgeoning demand for cocoa beans. By 1700 there were at least 2,000 chocolate houses in London alone, and some were apparently very lively and bawdy places. In his famous diary, Samuel Pepys describes a visit he took to a chocolate house and records: 'went out with Mr Creed to drink our morning draught, which he did give me in chocolate to settle my stomach'.

In England, grocers began to sell chocolate as a food, and it was one enterprising grocer in Birmingham who realised the potential of cocoa and its derivatives. John Cadbury had witnessed the thriving import and export businesses of the London docks and had explored the giant warehouses of the East India Company. He knew, even as a teenager, that there was big money to be made if he could find a new and palatable way of presenting and selling the derivative of the cocoa plant. Cadbury used a pestle and mortar to grind his cocoa beans, equipment more commonly used by chemists and apothecaries. In time, they too would use their knowledge of blending substances in developing our taste for chocolate.

Joseph Storrs Fry began selling cocoa in 1759, convincing his customers of its health-giving properties. This was a pertinent and relevant marketing strategy because his shop was in the gentrified spa town of Bath in Somerset which many wealthy people visited and stayed for extended periods because of concerns for their health. Cadbury and Fry were to merge in the early years of the twentieth century to become the world's largest chocolate manufacturer. Joseph Rowntree was also a grocer who, like Cadbury, learned much about the cocoa trade when he stayed in London.

The competition between the big brands led to much innovative marketing, especially after the advent of independent television in England in 1955, from chimpanzees banging drums and the adventures of the bespectacled Milky Bar Kid, to Turkish delights promising experiences 'full of 'Eastern Promise', and the even more seductive promises in the commercials for Cadbury's Flake. Today, for many chocolate lovers and marketing experts, Cadbury's purple-wrapped core product remains the most iconic of all confectionery brands, the 'CDM', with 'a glass and a half of real dairy milk' in every bar.

One of many fascinating facts about the big names in British chocolate is that most of them came from longstanding Quaker families. This led to high ethical standards as employers which is most vividly demonstrated in Cadbury's 'garden city' at Bournville. Cadbury, Fry and Rowntree had very similar *curricula vitae*, being grocers, cocoa and chocolate manufacturers, social reformers and philanthropists. Joseph Terry, also of York – where Rowntree was based – was, like Joseph Fry, an apothecary who sold cough sweets and other confectionery produced by other companies before manufacturing his own. Terrys, like Cadbury and Fry's, is now a part of the American multi-national Mondelez International.

It is said that one of the reasons for the Quaker involvement in chocolate was that they were keen to promote it as a healthier replacement for alcohol. There is some evidence to support this view. Certainly, in comparison with alcoholic beverages, in drinking chocolate, which is the form in which the commodity was consumed before the chocolate bar was invented, the Quakers saw a wholesome product. It is more likely though, that because Quaker beliefs of the time prevented their young men from either going into university (so therefore denied them careers as physicians and scientists) or entering military service (because of Quaker pacifist ideals), it was most likely that they would go into business. Their high motivation to work hard and to treat people in a decent way, meant that they were more likely to succeed.

Roald Dahl described the emotional experience of eating chocolate so succinctly and with tremendous sensuality in his novel *Charlie and the Chocolate Factory*:

He turned and reached behind him for the chocolate bar, then he turned back again and handed it to Charlie. Charlie grabbed it and quickly tore

off the wrapper and took an enormous bite. Then he took another…
and another… and oh, the joy of being able to cram large pieces of
something sweet and solid into one's mouth! The sheer blissful joy of
being able to fill one's mouth with rich solid food! 'You look like you
wanted that one, sonny,' the shopkeeper said pleasantly. Charlie nod-
ded, his mouth bulging with chocolate.

Just talking (and writing) about chocolate can be a pleasurable experience,
and its powerful feel-good factor has led to much research about its alleged
beneficial properties. It raises energy levels, can act as an aphrodisiac, (especially, perhaps, when produced in the shape of hearts and sold just before
Valentine's Day!) and increases serotonin and endorphin levels in the brain.
Sadly, most of the effects on our bodies are temporary excepting those
involving fat and sugar, which is why we go back so frequently to the shop,
supermarket, service station and so many other retail outlets for another
dose.

The history of sweet-making is much older than our love of chocolate.
Ancient Egyptians and Greeks dipped fruit and nuts in honey, and it was
believed that these had medicinal qualities. The ancient science of the apothecaries has been a part of the history of sweets and chocolate from earliest
times through to the establishment of the brands we are familiar with today.
Sugar was a relatively expensive raw material until the nineteenth century,
by which time the cultivation of sugar cane had moved from the Islamic
world to the West Indies and South America. It was added to liquorice-
based sweets to make them more palatable.

It was the industrial revolution that enabled the mechanisation of the
chocolate and confectionery processes, and provided the answer to the challenge of finding efficient means of transporting both raw materials and the
finished products, which greatly reduced the cost of making sweets and
reduced the price of confectionery, making it affordable to the working
classes. In every case, except perhaps for Trebor, the big brands began in the
kitchens and back rooms of men and women who used their hands and their
creative abilities to make something new, and products that people wanted
to eat.

John Cadbury

John Cadbury was the fifth child and third son of Richard Tapper Cadbury,
a wealthy Quaker who had been born in 1768 in Devon, later moving to

the Birmingham area. John attended Uxbridge Infants School in Burton on Trent and the Joseph Crosfields Quaker School on the outskirts of Nuneaton, coincidentally just three miles, crossing the ancient Roman Watling Street and passing the Roman settlement at Mancetter, from the village of Fenny Drayton where George Fox founded the Quaker movement.

Quakers in the nineteenth century were not allowed to go to university which meant they were unable to enter professions such as law or medicine. Also, as pacifists, any type of military career was out of bounds. The sons of Quaker families therefore tended to enter business, so at the age of fifteen John Cadbury was sent as an apprentice to John Cudworth, a Quaker businessman in Leeds, to learn the retail tea trade. His upbringing had already instilled in him the Quaker commitments to sobriety, responsibility and hard work, and within a short time his employers felt comfortable in leaving the young man to run the business while they travelled. John later moved on to the bonded tea warehouse of Sanderson Fox in London where he learned about the prosperous trade in tea, coffee and cocoa centred around the nearby East India Company warehouses.

He was convinced that there was an economic future in cocoa, and in 1824, with financial assistance from his father, he decided to strike out on his own to become a tea dealer and coffee roaster, selling from his own small grocery shop at 93 Bull Street in Birmingham. Here, the Cadbury connection with chocolate began, with John selling cocoa and drinking chocolate that he prepared himself with a pestle and mortar. The shop stood out from others in the street because of its remarkable décor and John's innovative approach to retail, which included a Chinese clerk who would wear oriental clothes whilst serving customers. Large blue Chinese vases and oriental chests created an atmosphere of affluence and quality. Cadbury used the ever-present aroma of roasting coffee beans to add to the customers' experience. It was no surprise when customers flocked to his doors, making his business eminently profitable, and attracting many wealthy patrons.

John began making chocolate in 1831 when he purchased a large warehouse in Crooked Lane, not far from his shop. From the outset, he was committed to developing new products and offering his customers a wider choice. By 1842, the date of the earliest surviving Cadbury product list, he was marketing eleven types of cocoa and no less than sixteen varieties of chocolate. By then, cocoa could be purchased in several forms, including cakes, powder and flakes. Four years later, he invited his brother, Benjamin, to become a partner in the firm, which changed its name to Cadbury Brothers. Within a further twelve months, the brothers had moved to a larger factory in Bridge Street in the centre of Birmingham, and in 1853, they received a major boost, being honoured by their appointment as cocoa manufacturer to Queen Victoria.

A further milestone in the Cadbury business was the introduction of a new processing technique which resulted in the launch in 1866 of 'Cadbury Cocoa Essence', the first unadulterated cocoa to be sold in the UK. The famous Cadbury Dairy Milk chocolate bar was conceived in 1897, primarily as a means of using up the cocoa butter left over from the Cocoa Essence process.

Their Quaker beliefs not only influenced their personal lives but meant that the Cadbury family were socially-responsible employers. To this end, John Cadbury became involved in the temperance movement, whilst Benjamin Cadbury focussed on the welfare and wellbeing of their employees. John believed in total abstinence, and like other businessmen such as Thomas Cook, he felt that providing other healthy activities and pursuits was a means of persuading young men not to patronise the many gin shops and ale houses. Even today, the area around the Cadbury factories is 'dry'. Not even the local Tesco store has been allowed to sell alcohol until recently.

In 1829, John was appointed to the Birmingham Board of Street Commissioners, which was later to become the municipal corporation. He was closely involved in the 1851 parliamentary bill that transferred power from this self-appointed board to the democratically-elected council. Between 1830 and 1840 he was an overseer and guardian of the poor, and was a leader of the campaign against the practice of using small boys as chimney sweeps. He also fought for animal rights, founding the Animals Friends Society which later became the RSPCA.

In 1850, his son Richard joined the business and maintained the family's reputation for diligence and hard work, soon becoming trusted enough to take charge of the company when his father or uncle were elsewhere. Unfortunately, John began to lose interest in the business because of his poor physical health and that of his mother. She contracted tuberculosis and died in 1855. John's deep grief led to bouts of depression, and, in a low physical and mental state, he then caught rheumatic fever. His health declined quite quickly and he handed over the reins to his sons, Richard and George, in 1861. They were just twenty-five and twenty-one years old respectively.

John's brother Benjamin's grand and famous idea for providing a healthy environment for his workforce came to fruition in an area known as Bournbrook, some four miles from the centre of Birmingham in what was at the time, open countryside. The plan was socially revolutionary, and economically sound because the new factory which was at the heart of the project was located close to railway lines and the canal, providing the company with excellent communication and distribution facilities. The company was dependent upon the canals for the supply of milk. The railways were required to bring in cocoa deliveries from the ports of Southampton and London. The brothers noted the plans of the Birmingham West Suburban Railway which involved an extension from the centre of the city south along the path of the Worcester and Birmingham Canal. Hence, in 1879, they transferred their operation to Bournbrook Hall. The location fulfilled all their requirements, being cleaner, healthier and with the potential for long-term expansion.

It was John's younger son, George, who drew up the plan. The first bricks were laid in January 1879, and the estate continued to be enlarged and developed over the next two decades. The project began with sixteen houses for their workers, to which were added more homes, a school and a hospital. By the turn of the century, 'Bournville' as the Cadbury brothers had named it, had developed into a garden estate of over three hundred houses, and George had set up the Bournville Village Trust to look after the expanding community.

John Cadbury, the founder figure and chocolate pioneer, was a serious and thoughtful man who fought hard to counter many of the social 'evils' of the Victorian age, and to improve the lives of his workers and their families. There is also a sense of him being a perfectionist, of rarely being satisfied with his achievements, always yearning to do more and to do things better. Such attitudes are to be applauded and are fully in keeping with Quaker beliefs, but they can also lead to depression and physical ill-heath. He suffered tragedy early in his life. In 1828 when he was only twenty-seven years old, his first wife, Priscilla Dymond, died after a marriage of just two years. He remarried four years later, to Candia Barrow, and had six sons and a daughter. He never fully came to terms with the death of his mother, which left him without his earlier enthusiasm and motivation for life and for his business. He died on 11 May 1889 and lies buried at Witton Cemetery in Birmingham.

Joseph Rowntree

The linking themes of the English chocolatiers are present in the background and life of Joseph Rowntree, notably that he was born into a Quaker family and the first trade in which he gained experience was as a grocer.

The family's grocery business had been founded in Scarborough by his grandfather, John Rowntree, who brought two of his sons, John and Joseph into the business at an early age. Joseph moved to York on his twenty-first birthday and opened his own grocer's shop at 28 Pavement. He married Sarah Stephenson, who was from a Quaker family from Stockton-on-Tees, and it was their second son, also Joseph, who was to become the famous chocolate manufacturer.

The business in York was successful and prompted moves on two occasions to larger and better premises. As well as involving his sons, Joseph senior also brought in a manager and several apprentices. Sarah Rowntree provided meals for all of them as well as managing the firm's accounts. Joseph senior could take time away from the shop to be involved in a range of social and educational activities.

Joseph junior attended the Quaker Bootham School, the foundation of which had been proposed and supported by the Tuke family, who were also grocers by trade. The Tukes could trace their Quaker roots back to the time of George Fox, and it was a granddaughter of one of the 4,000 Quaker men imprisoned for their beliefs following the Restoration in 1660 who established their grocery business. She was Mary Tuke. Her shop went on to specialise in tea, coffee and drinking chocolate, and in time she employed her nephew William as an apprentice. He inherited the business when Mary died in 1752. William's son, Henry Tuke, followed his father, and began manufacturing his own coffee and chocolate products. Much later, the Rowntree family were to take over the Tukes' enterprise as part of their expanding confectionery company.

When the younger Joseph Rowntree left Bootham School, he too was apprenticed to the family business, but in 1857 was sent to London to widen his experience of the grocery trade at a store in Fenchurch Street. He returned to York as a partner in the Rowntree business. His father died soon afterwards, and Joseph, with his brother John, both still in their early twenties, took over. As with John Cadbury, personal tragedy struck the young Joseph Rowntree. In 1862, he married Julia Seebohm who died just a year later and only months after the birth of their daughter Lilley who died in infancy. Joseph married his second wife, Emma Seebohm, a first cousin of Julia, in 1867 and they had four sons and two daughters.

Joseph sold his share of his father's shop to his eldest brother so that he could join his younger brother, Henry, who had by then had acquired the Tukes' cocoa and chocolate business, and needed financial investment to expand. Henry had just moved the firm from Coppergate to Tanner's

Moat. The enterprise was immensely successful. Rowntrees broadened their product range, manufacturing, in association with a French confectioner, their own 'fruit gum' pastilles which had previously been imported. Joseph's two sons, John Wilhelm and Seebohm both joined the company. Rowntrees were sensitive to how their customers' tastes changed, and following much research, they introduced their 'Elect Cocoa', advertised as 'more than a drink, a food'. The success of the pastilles and the purer cocoa allowed the company to expand further. In ten years, from 1883, their workforce more than quadrupled to 804 people.

Responding to the demand for their products, the company decided to build their own factory on a new site. Tanner's Moat had by then, due to expansion and innovation, become a congested rabbit-warren of buildings, and the working environment was becoming unsatisfactory. In 1890 Joseph Rowntree bought 29 acres of land in Haxby Road for a purpose-built factory, to which raw materials could be brought by a privately-constructed branch line from the North-Eastern Railway. The project was financed with a loan of £10,000 from the York City and County Bank. In 1897, the firm became a limited liability company and its name changed from H.I. Rowntree and Company to Rowntree and Company Ltd. For many years, Tanner's Moat remained in operation, and was eventually closed in 1906. By that time, Rowntrees had over 2,000 employees.

The First World War caused a downturn in demand for Rowntrees products, which was exacerbated by the depression of the 1920s, but in the next decade, under the direction of marketing director George Harris (who was later to become Chairman), Rowntrees bounced back with many of the lines which are still sold today, including Aero, Smarties, Rolos, Polo mints, Kit-Kat, Black Magic and Dairy Box. At its peak, Rowntrees employed 14,000 people.

In 1901 Joseph bought 123 acres of land adjacent to the Rowntree factory at New Earswick for a philanthropic project to improve the city's housing stock. He believed that it was economically viable to provide well-built houses which could be afforded by men earning twenty-five shillings a week. Thirty houses had been constructed by 1904 and by 1954 there were nearly 500 three-bedroom homes, 90 cottages and 40 larger properties on the estate, providing accommodation for both larger families and single people.

His Quaker principles meant that Joseph lived a relatively undemanding life with few luxuries. He spent some money on books, travel and his beloved garden, but was concerned about his wealth and how it could be put to good use for the benefit of others. He created three separate trusts, one to ensure the development of New Earswick, one to promote social, charitable and religious activities and to finance adult education, social research and Quaker activities, and the third, to undertake various social and political work including running newspapers, which could not legally be supported by money from the other charitable trusts. Joseph had the ability to let go of the company which bore his family name and to which he had given his energies and skills, but he remained actively involved right up to the week before his death. He died at his home on 24 February 1925.

Joseph Storrs Fry

Three men, all called Joseph Fry, created and developed the famous Fry's chocolate brand. The first, born in 1728, was a printer and apothecary by trade who also set up several businesses including an experimental chocolate company. He was the eldest son of John Fry of Sutton Benger in Wiltshire, a clockmaker, writer and poet who wrote *Select Poems*, which was published in 1774. The Fry family descended from a staunch Puritan background, being Quakers who converted to the faith after hearing George Fox preach. Zephaniah Fry had been arrested in 1683 and was imprisoned in Ilchester Gaol for three months for allowing a meeting of dissenters to be held in his house, and for refusing to swear the Oath of Allegiance.

Joseph Storr Fry was educated in the north of England, and was later apprenticed to Henry Portsmouth, an eminent doctor in Basingstoke, whose daughter, Anna, he married. Fry's unusual second name was inherited from his great-grandmother, Mary Storr. He began selling cocoa from his shop in 1759, emphasising its health-giving properties. It soon became popular in Bath where the coffee houses sold it to the aristocracy.

In partnership with John Vaughan he purchased the business of Walter Churchman, the leading cocoa manufacturer, in 1761. By 1764, Fry, Vaughan and Co had agents in fifty-three towns and a chocolate warehouse in London. He was convinced of its health-giving properties and believed it to be a nutritious alternative to alcohol. In 1761 Joseph Fry and his partner John Vaughan acquired the patent for a water-powered machine that could grind the cocoa flakes to a fine powder and thus produce a superior drink. In 1777, they moved to a larger site by the side of the River Frome, which supplied the water to power the chocolate grinding machines.

His son, Joseph Storrs Fry, was the man who would develop the fledgling company into a leading manufacturer of chocolate products. His first purpose-built factory was in Union Street in Bristol. His mother, Anna, died in

1803, and for the next two decades, he took on a partner, a Dr Hunt, renaming the company Fry and Hunt. He patented a method of grinding cocoa beans using a James Watt steam engine which represented probably the first introduction of factory techniques to the cocoa business. Significantly, the water power from the River Frome was proving to be unreliable, hence the move to steam. The transition revolutionised cocoa production and attracted much interest from Fry's competitors. George III later granted him a patent to build a new machine for roasting the beans, which was installed in the adjacent factory.

After Hunt's retirement in 1822, Fry took on his sons, Joseph, Francis and Richard as partners, renaming the company once again, this time as the famous J.S. Fry and Sons Ltd., under which title it was to become the largest commercial manufacturer of chocolate in Britain. New product lines were introduced, including the addition of arrowroot to cocoa which absorbed some of the cocoa oil. It was marketed as Pearl Cocoa and because it was less expensive than normal cocoa, it became popular with less well-off families.

Their greatest innovation was the invention of the chocolate bar, well ahead of their rivals. It was produced by mixing cocoa powder, cocoa fat and sugar to create a paste which was then formed into a bar. It was the first chocolate bar to be manufactured in Britain and turned chocolate from a drink into a snack that could be taken and eaten anywhere.

Joseph Storrs Fry died in 1835. He was buried in the burial ground beside the Quaker Meeting House in Frenchay on the outskirts of Bristol, next to his wife Anna and his daughter Priscilla. His grandson, Joseph Storrs Fry II (1826–1913) eventually took control of the business as Chairman of the company in 1878, following his father and uncle's retirement. At the time, the workforce numbered fifty-six men and women. By the time he retired, he was employing more than 3,000 workers in the Union Street factory. The firm was run on austere lines in keeping with Quaker simplicity. Every day began with a meeting at which a hymn was sung and there was a period of silence.

He never married, and so his personal fortune was shared between his many relations, including no less than thirty-seven nephews and nieces. He was also a prominent philanthropist. Control of the company passed through various family members following his death in 1913 and it ultimately merged with Cadburys in 1919. Every member of the Fry family through four generations held strong Quaker beliefs. Like the Cadbury family in Birmingham and the Rowntree family in York, they were good employers, paying fair wages and treating their workforce with kindness and respect. Unlike their competitors, Fry's did not set up organised welfare support or trust funds, and the working conditions and environment in their eight factories in the Bristol area were not as modern or as comfortable. However, one fine legacy of the company was the work of the later Joseph Storrs Fry's niece Margery in prison reform, which in some ways continued the work of her more famous great-aunt, Elizabeth Fry, whose image appeared on British five pound notes between 2001 and 2016.

Margery founded the University Grants Committee and was one of the first women magistrates in Britain, being appointed in 1921. She became Principal of Somerville College in Oxford, and was a governor of the BBC from 1937 until 1939 as well as a participant in the BBC's *Brain Trust* programme. The Fry Housing Trust was established in 1959 in her memory, and in 1990, the Margery Fry Award was established in her honour.

Fry's introduced many chocolate brands that are still enjoyed or remembered today, including Turkish Delight (full of Eastern Promise!), Chocolate Cream, Five Centres and Five Boys. The latter was probably the most famous of the brands and was in production from 1902 through until 1976. On the wrapper and impressed into the chocolate were five different images of one boy dressed in a sailor suit, showing five different expressions which told of the experience of eating Fry's chocolate. These were Desperation, Pacification, Expectation, Acclamation and Realisation. The young model was Lindsay Poulton, who was five years old when his father and grandfather took the photographs. They were paid £200 for the images, an incredibly large sum of money for the time.

By 1981, the brand had disappeared from wrappers, and in 2011, the last of the old Fry's factories, at Keynsham on the River Avon between Bristol and Bath, was closed. More recently, Kraft, the owners of Cadbury, has reintroduced several of the former Fry's lines, recognising the power of nostalgia.

Joseph Terry

This is another story of a father-and-son enterprise, the father being the pioneer, and his son establishing and developing the business. Terry and Berry was the name of the original confectionery business, which was later to become the famous Terry's of York brand. Joseph Terry senior owned and managed a chemist shop in Warmgate in York, having been an apprentice to an apothecary in Stonegate. In 1823, he married Harriet Atkinson, and through her, became involved in the confectionery trade. The Atkinsons owned a small confectionery business managed by one of Harriet's relatives, Robert Berry. In time, Joseph Terry and Robert Berry's son, George, formed a partnership, Joseph Terry giving up his shop to join the Berry's in York's St Helen's Square. Five years later, George left the business and Joseph Terry became the sole proprietor.

Terry began to define his style and brands and acquired a good reputation for products that included cakes, comfits, sugared sweets, candied peel, marmalade and lozenges. He began to distribute more widely, using the fledgling railway network to transport his products across towns and cities in the Midlands, the north of England and south to the London area. His considerable business skills and shrewd thinking enabled the business to prosper and to protect itself from competition. He set up field or 'territory' agents in the areas where he sold his products, and became a leading figure in establishing a trade association in London to protect the quality of lozenges and confectionery products from inferior production standards.

He died in 1850, by which time his company was well-established and becoming a familiar brand nationwide. It was the second-largest employer in York, with over 120 workers. His son, then aged twenty-two, who had been educated locally at St Peter's School in York, was to take on his father's work and develop it into one of the most significant chocolate and confectionery businesses in Britain.

The young Joseph Terry, assisted by his younger brothers, Robert and John, began by moving the manufacturing operation to a new site near to the River Ouse at Clementhorpe. Although the railways were gaining ground as the most efficient way to transport manufactured goods from factories to markets, the river provided a link to the North Sea through the Humber Estuary, enabling steam packets to bring his raw materials almost directly to the loading bays. Not only did these ships bring foodstuffs such as cocoa and sugar, but also the coal for the steam-engines that Terry had installed. Terry had taken his father's industry into the age of mechanisation.

The number of individual products made by the company grew to around 400 within a few years, including biscuits, jams, preserves, candied peels and cakes. At that time, products in which chocolate was the main ingredient were in the minority, but Terry then set up a unit within the Clementhorpe factory to manufacture only cocoa-based products, taking on the established companies. In 1876, they applied for their first trademark as 'Joseph Terry's and Sons Ltd' and the workforce had increased to 500 employees.

The company's former base in St Helen's Square premises were retained as a shop and restaurant. The Terry name which was attached to the front of the building, was kept when it was rebuilt with a dance floor, but retaining a retail facility. The company's name can still be seen on the building today.

Joseph married twice in his life and had seven children. He was knighted in 1887. His eldest son from his first marriage, Thomas Terry, became the main partner of the business in 1880, as the other males of the family had decided to follow alternative careers and professions. Thomas Terry's own contribution to the company was to develop the international trade that established the brand as far away as Australia and New Zealand.

Joseph became an active and hardworking philanthropist. His popularity amongst residents led to a career in politics, serving first as a councillor, and then as Town Sheriff, Justice of the Peace and as the Lord Mayor of York on three occasions. He died of heart failure, which it is claimed was brought on by over-work, at the Royal Station Hotel on 12 January 1898, after fighting a by-election to become Member of Parliament for York.

There were many tributes and eulogies for Sir Joseph. The *Chemist and Druggist*, the national journal for chemists and pharmacists described his death as 'a tragic feature of the recent by-election'. The Yorkshire Herald stated that 'there was no person in the city more loved or respected, and no-one who was more possessed of the qualities that constitute a genial and amiable Englishman.' Memorials to Sir Joseph included the Terry Memorial alms-houses in the Skelderdale area of the city adjacent to the Dame Middleton Hospital. The heraldic arms of the family can be seen in a stained glass window in All Saint's Church in York, commemorating Sir Joseph's grandson, Noel Goddard Terry, who provided some of the finance to refurbish the building in 1978.

Joseph William Thornton

Joseph Thornton's family came from Leeds, where they had gained experience of the retail trade through being shopkeepers and innkeepers, as well as other professions. Joseph's father, also named Joseph, moved to Sheffield in 1832 and became a railway shopkeeper. He married Ann, from a local family, in 1868 and two years later, Joseph William was born. At the time, the family were living at 12 Edgar Street in the Brightside area of the city.

Joseph junior grew up to become a commercial traveller with the Don Confectionery Company. This business had been launched in 1878 by Samuel Meggitt Johnson, the managing director of the Bassett's confectionery company, who put the two sons of George Bassett in charge because, allegedly, he did not want them at Bassetts. Bassetts were based at Broad

Street in Sheffield, and Johnson became George Bassett's son-in-law. Don Confectionery traded until 1933 when it was absorbed into Bassett's after running into financial difficulties.

Joseph married Kate Elizabeth, and they had four children, three boys, William, Frank and Joseph, and a girl, Constance. He opened his first chocolate shop in October 1911 at 159 Norfolk Street, at the junction with Howard Street. At the time of the census of 1911, the family was living at 64 Fitzwalter Road, near the city centre, but by October, when the shop opened, they were living in rented accommodation in the village of Hathersage in Derbyshire, about twenty miles away.

Joseph continued to work for Don Confectionery, relying on the steady income to support his family should the chocolate shop fail to succeed. Instead, he decided to take his eldest son, Norman, who was just fourteen years old, out of Abbeydale Secondary School and install him as the manager. His brother Stanley, then aged eleven, joined him.

The business succeeded, partly due to Joseph's intention of selling quality products in a 'superior' environment. He created a retail experience using floor-to-ceiling mirrors to make the shop look larger than it was, and by investing in expensive fittings including brass weighing machines, and glass shelves and cases, which allowed the bright colours and attractive textures of his cakes, chocolates and sweets to look their best, the glass and brass reflecting the sunlight and the gas mantles. As well as the two Thornton boys, Joseph hired two female shop assistants who were 'of a very superior type'. In time, Thornton was bringing in over £20 every week, a reasonable income from a small retail business at that time.

Joseph finally made the decision to commit himself and his family to the chocolate business. He left the Don Confectionery Company in 1913 and opened a second shop. He decided on premises in the Moor area of Sheffield because property rents were low and there was the potential for more passing trade, as this was a busy area of the city. The new shop also had a basement which Joseph put to good use as his first 'factory', manufacturing his first products. In time, he taught his son Norman how to make basic boiled sweets with names such as Mint rock and Fish Mixtures. There was more room at the back of the shop on the ground floor which Thornton committed to chocolate manufacture. Having acquired these more spacious premises, he moved his family back into Sheffield to live in rooms above the shop so that he could reduce his financial overheads by bringing his manufacturing, retailing and living accommodation under one roof.

Joseph's youngest son, Stanley, was soon to play his part in the future of the family business. He had secured a scholarship to Sheffield University to study Physics and Chemistry, but felt that his duty lay with his family because they were short of money. A successful compromise was reached by which Stanley attended university lectures during several weekday evenings and on Saturday mornings, and worked with his brother Norman, who was managing the business, during the day. Stanley went on to study food technology, which became an invaluable source of expertise to Thorntons in later years.

In the early days, Joseph Thornton sold products from other manufacturers, and undoubtedly his experience as a travelling salesman provided him with a wide knowledge of competing brands. He sold John Mackintosh's toffee from trays. This was broken up into manageable pieces by his shop assistants, weighed and then placed into waxed bags for his customers. Mackintosh had opened his first shop in Halifax in 1890, and Thornton would certainly have visited his chain of shops as he travelled the county on behalf of Don's. Much later, Mackintosh merged with Joseph Rowntree in York, and in recent times was acquired by Nestle.

Thornton then developed their own 'special toffee'. It was the brainchild of Stanley Thornton, no doubt impressed by the best-selling Mackintosh product. The Thornton's version became so successful that in a short time it was contributing more than 50 per cent of total sales. It was the company's most well-known product for more than half a century, and in Sheffield was often described as 'the steelworker's fuel'. The basic recipe created by Stanley Thornton is still used by the company today.

One of the company's innovative marketing strategies in the 1980s was to organise toffee chopping competitions. These took place across the country to find the champion toffee chopper who could chop up slabs of toffee in the shortest possible time. Some of the original toffee hammers produced for the campaign are still to be seen today. Joseph also sold Kunzle cakes in his earliest shops, displayed in shaped glass cases and served individually to customers using tongs. These cakes were the creation of a Swiss chef, Christian Kunzle, who worked for some time at the Houses of Parliament. Some of the other palette-tempting lines of that time were caramels, cachous, his own 'curiously strong' mints, and boiled sweets.

Joseph died in 1919, his sons inheriting a very prosperous business. In 1931, they moved their manufacturing base to new premises at Stalker Lees Road in Sheffield and four years later built their own factory on Archer Road to accommodate their growing workforce, which now numbered about forty people, including those who worked in the shops. At Stalker Lees, Thorntons made their first handmade chocolate truffles. It is where they also installed their first 'enrober', a machine which coats food items in chocolate and took the place of dipping items in molten chocolate by hand. The machine cost £175. The company moved to Derbyshire in 1948, having seen an advertisement in a local newspaper for a factory in Belper, which they bought for £8,400.

An unusual fact about Thorntons is that despite the globalisation of business, they still use imperial weights and measures on their packaging. Although the metric equivalents are also displayed to meet legal requirements, the weights are still expressed in pounds and ounces, reminding customers of when they used to ask for 'a quarter' of toffee or boiled sweets.

Joseph is commemorated with a blue plaque which is located at his family's former home in Sheffield. It reads: 'Joseph William Thornton 1870–1919 founder of Thorntons resided here at 64 Fitzwalter Rd with his family in 1911, the year he opened the first Thorntons shop at 159 Norfolk St Sheffield.'

Charles and Tom Maynard

Charles Riley Maynard was born in the London district of Islington in 1857, a son of Riley and Ann Maynard. His was a large family with several elder brothers. His younger brother, Tom, was born five years later. He married Sarah Ann in 1883, and began manufacturing sweets, working with Tom, in 1880 in the kitchen of Charles' home, known as 'Dawlish', in Northfield Road, Stamford Hill. The confectionery they produced was sold in a shop next door, managed by Sarah. Their products were well-received, and in 1896, the two brothers decided to set up the Maynards Sweet Company.

By 1906, the company had grown considerably from their kitchen-table beginnings, and the Maynard brothers decide to build their own factory in Vale Road, south of the centre of Harringay and close to the 'new river' which was constructed in the seventeenth century to bring fresh spring water into the London suburbs. It was a well-considered and advantageous move because the river also provided a transport connection through which the raw materials such as gelatine and sugar could be delivered to the factory, as well as coal for the steam engines. Good railway connections also enabled an efficient system for delivering their products to retailers throughout the Greater London area.

In time, Charles Maynard's son, Charles (George) Gordon, joined the family firm. He had been born in October 1889, and by the time he invented the company's most famous line of confectionery, he was living in the Camberwell district of London. His proposal was a 'wine gum'. It is said that his father, a strict Methodist and therefore a teetotaller, was outraged at the young man's idea, especially since the names of alcoholic drinks such as claret, gin, port and sherry would be imprinted on the sweets. However, his son persuaded him to reconsider, after promising that the new sweets would never contain alcohol, and might even be used to tempt drinkers to reduce their consumption. The first Maynards wine gums were produced in 1909 and have been a best-selling line ever since. The author Roald Dahl, who wrote *Charlie and the Chocolate Factory*, kept a jar of wine gums next to his bed. The late comedy actor Bill Maynard (born Walter Williams) said he based his stage name on an advertisement for Maynard's wine gums and that his mother often tried to persuade him to switch back to his real name. In the twenty-first century, the annual worldwide sales of wine gums under the Maynards brand are estimated to be more than £40 million.

The company grew fast and became a major employer in the Harringay area. Maynards also set up manufacturing bases elsewhere in the country including Newcastle, where at Ouseburn, a toffee-manufacturing plant was built. The company also expanded its retail operation to more than 140 shops. These were sold off in 1985, and in 1990 Maynards agreed a merger with Bassetts and Trebor. Cadbury acquired the group in 1998 when the remaining Maynards manufacturing plants were centred in premises in Sheffield which had been opened in 1991. The Harringay factory was closed and is now a carpet warehouse. The Newcastle toffee factory became part of an urban regeneration programme.

George Bassett

The son of a farmer, George Bassett was born in the Derbyshire village of Ashover, near Clay Cross, in 1818. After leaving school at the age of fourteen, he made the six-mile journey to Chesterfield to be apprenticed to a confectioner and fruiterer by the name of William Haslam, whose shop was situated on Low Pavement in the town. Bassett was from a strict Wesleyan Methodist background, and he remained committed to his faith throughout his life, his background moulding him into a shrewd and diligent man. He remained with Haslam for three years, and then, some years later at the age of twenty-four, bought a small confectionery and wine business in Broad Street, Sheffield. George married his first wife, Sarah Hodgson, in the same year and they had eight children. Street directories of the period list Bassett as a ' wholesale confectioner, lozenge maker and British wine trader'.

In 1859, he took over further premises in the city and began manufacturing confectionery at the America Works near the Royal Infirmary. He took on a young apprentice, Samuel Meggitt Johnson, who was only twelve years old. The Johnsons, and the related Meggitt family were also staunch Methodists. The boy's mother had died and Samuel had moved in with the Bassett family. Samuel went back to work in his father's furniture retail business, Johnson and Appleyards, at the end of the apprenticeship, but later re-joined the Bassett company and went on, in 1863, to become a partner, Managing Director and finally sole proprietor. He also set up the Don Confectionery Company, as an enterprise for Bassett's two eldest sons as, allegedly, he did not wish them to be involved in the family firm. Samuel married George Bassett's eldest daughter in 1868, who died during childbirth in 1870. Samuel's uncle, Walter, also joined the Don Confectionery Company, moving from Johnson and Appleyards, as a director. Walter served as Lord Mayor of Sheffield, and lived in Endcliffe Crescent, the same road as George Bassett, which became a fashionable enclave of wealthy Methodism.

Before Johnson returned to the company, George Bassett had acquired more extensive premises in Portland Road and had entered a partnership with a Sheffield grocer, William Lodge, which later failed. The Portland Road factory was extended during 1876, the same year in which he became Lord Mayor of Sheffield. He had political aspirations, possibly driven by his non-conformist religious beliefs, but he suffered a stroke two years later and died in 1886 at the age of 68.

Samuel Johnson took over the helm of the company and steered it to immense success, pioneering sweets which are familiar to millions to this day. Johnson died in 1925 after which Bassetts became a public company with his grandson (and therefore George Bassett's great grandson) William Johnson as Chairman and Managing Director.

The most well-known of Bassetts' creations are liquorice allsorts which, according to the company's folklore and heritage traditions, were invented by accident. It is said that in 1899, one of the company's sales representatives, Charles Thompson, stumbled over a doormat while he was visiting a customer. The tray of individual sweet samples which he was carrying cascaded onto the floor. While on his hands and knees, attempting to gather up his carefully-manufactured and assembled products, his customer saw the potential for selling a 'mixed bag' of sweets and immediately placed an order for 'all sorts'.

In 1892, the Bassett factory had a serious fire which caused Samuel Johnson to have a nervous breakdown following a family dispute which arose because the company had inadequate insurance cover. In 1918, they invented their famous jellies in the shape of babies, original sold as Peace Babies but later as the familiar Jelly Babies.

Bassetts acquired the Don Confectionery Company that Johnson Senior had launched, in 1933, and at the same time combined their manufacturing at their factory in Beulah Road, Owlerton which for a time operated under the name of Samuel Johnson and Sons, and was where candied peel and fruit gums were made. This was later extended to become a four-storey building occupied solely in the production of liquorice allsorts. The company continued to trade until 1978, but began to suffer losses due to foreign competition and the strength of the dollar. Numerous mergers followed including with Maynards, of fruit gum fame, leading to the Cadbury-Schweppes group acquiring control for a bid of £91million. Today, Bassetts are a brand of Cadbury which is owned by Mondelez International.

Henry Walker

There is one further appetising commodity to be found alongside the chocolate bars and confectionery which is worthy of mention, and has a fascinating history.

The first potato crisp was probably fried or cooked in America in the 1850s, but the concept came to Great Britain in the first decade of the twentieth century. Carter's Crisps was first incorporated in 1900, but the first documented sale of their product was in 1913. Carter, whose first name is not known, is said to have encountered potato crisps in France.

Frank Smith, a Londoner, had noted Carter's product. He set up a business in his garage manufacturing them. His wife peeled, sliced and fried, while Smith would package in greaseproof bags, before setting off in his cart to sell around London. Within a year Smiths Crisps moved to larger premises, and employed additional staff. Smith gave his customers the option of adding salt to their crisps, included within a small twist of blue paper.

The very first potato crisp to be produced outside London was made at a butcher's shop in Cheapside in Leicester in a building close to the ancient Saturday Market and the East Gate of the town. It was fried by Henry Walker in 1948. Walker moved from Mansfield in Nottinghamshire to Leicester in the 1880s to take over an established butcher's shop in the

High Street. His business prospered, and in 1912 he moved to larger premises from which Walkers the Butchers is still trading.

Rationing after the Second World War meant meat was in short supply. It is said that Walkers would be completely sold out of their fresh meat products by mid-morning with their food preparation department running at half-capacity. Henry and his son searched for alternatives to maintain his business and to keep his factory staff employed. Walkers' Managing Director R.E. Gerrard first proposed selling ice cream, but hygiene and health legislation did not allow meat and dairy products to be processed in the same factory area or by the same workers. Consequently, Gerrard looked to potatoes, which were not rationed. Some reports suggest that customers accepted Walker's first crisps, cut thickly and deep-fat fried, as a reasonable alternative in terms of texture and colour to the poor meat cuts they had become used to during the war years.

The first crisps were cut by hand and fried in an ordinary fish and chip deep fat fryer. Gerrard cooked the first batch himself. They were an immediate success and the company soon set up a production line specifically for crisps in the empty upper storey of their Leicester Oxford Street factory. They continued to experiment, and in 1954 the first flavoured crisp was produced – cheese and onion. Leicester's Gary Lineker, the television sports presenter and former footballer whose family has been prominent on Leicester Market, just yards from Walker's shop, has been the 'brand image' of Walkers Crisps for several years, and two of the company's television advertisements have been filmed in the city.

Henry Walker's reputation for pork pies lasts to the present day. Traditionally, long queues form just before Christmas each year as Leicester people buy their pork pies as part of their Christmas Day breakfast.

Robertson and Woodcock

There is only one name in British confectionery which is known by numerous generations of boys and girls who could buy Fruit Salad and Black Jacks with their pocket money. In the 1960s, these enticing sweets could be bought, four for one (old) penny.

From the start, the men who founded Trebor were determined that their confectionery enterprise would be a success. It was not a kitchen-table enterprise which gradually developed. It was a business that was designed to be pioneering and dynamic, thanks to the energies and business acumen of the founders. They launched the company in 1907. Less than a century later, when acquired by Cadbury in 1989, it was the largest manufacturer of sugar-based confectionery in Britain.

The company's adopted brand name – Trebor – was based on a coincidence. It was the name of the building on St Peter Street in the Forest Gate areas of London, which Robertson and Woodcock chose as their manufacturing base, and it happened to spell 'Robert' when the word was reversed. Hence, Trebor House became the home of Trebor mints and many other well-known and much-loved sweets.

Robert Robertson and William Woodcock brought different but complementary skills and experience to their business. Wisely, they sought out and recognised more talent and knowledge, bringing in to their enterprise two other individuals, Sydney Marks and Thomas King. Robertson was a grocer; Woodcock was a sugar boiler; Marks was a seller of sweets, and King was a travelling salesman of margarine, one of the newest food products of that time. All four men and their families lived within a few miles of each other in Lime House, Canning Town and Leytonstone although their families' histories stretched wider.

The men were also dependent upon each other. The foreign exchange rate meant that the price of imported sugar fluctuated, and at the beginning of the twentieth century, Woodcock was no longer able to afford to buy this raw material so vital to his trade. He looked for a backer with money, and found him in the form of Thomas King. King was very much an entrepreneur who spent his life creating new business ventures. All four came from very humble backgrounds and had experienced poverty and the trauma of losing family members at an early age. Robertson's father died when he was six; Woodcock married three times, his first two wives dying young.

These were men who, though only in their twenties when they came together, were already 'streetwise' and had a determination to fight against the prevailing disabling conditions in London's East End, which for many people meant a life of poverty and low social expectation. It should be noted that all four were either teenage or young men when the eight murders ascribed to Jack the Ripper, the Whitechapel murderer, terrorised the East End, the victims being found at locations that would have been familiar to each of them.

These four men committed themselves to their confectionery project by each contributing £100 of their own money to launch the business; and this meant they were equal partners. They pioneered every aspect of the business, including replacing horse-drawn vehicles with motor vehicles at an early stage. During the First World War, Trebor launched their 'Army and Navy Paregoric Tablets'. By using the word 'paregoric', Trebor inferred that their tablets contained a camphorated tincture of opium, which was well-known for its soothing qualities, and the sweets therefore became most popular with soldiers both at the front and when returning home. In fact, the small print on the labels explained that the taste and effect of these tablets 'were similar to' the effects of opium.

Robertson and Woodcock advertised that they were the manufacturers of high-quality, craftsmen-made boiled sweets, and one of their first successes was the Trebor Mint. Twenty years on, the company built a new factory in Forest Gate, and it was here that their famous Trebor Extra Strong Mints were created. Refreshers followed in 1937 after Sydney Marks, son of the founding partner, returned from a fact-finding trip to Germany with details of a manufacturing technique using powdered sugar. Sydney went on to become Managing Director in 1941, and was respected as an outstanding businessman though somewhat autocratic in his management techniques. He was succeeded by his son, John Marks, whose Christian principles led to a rather paternalistic attitude to his employees. For instance, in 1981 the firm stopped night shifts in the belief that it was disruptive to domestic life.

From the 1930s until 1989, Trebor continued to expand and acquire. A new factory was opened in Chesterfield, Derbyshire in 1939 to serve the Midlands and the North, reducing distribution and transport costs. The chocolate manufacturer, Jamesons, was acquired in 1960. Sharps, a Maidstone-based toffee manufacturer, was bought one year later. By the early 1970s, Trebor was the largest British exporter of confectionery, selling to almost seventy countries. Their biggest market was the USA, but more Trebor mints were sold in Nigeria than in England. The acquisition of Clarnico, another confectioner, in 1969 made Trebor the fourth largest confectionery manufacturer in Britain. The expansion continued with the purchase of Maynards for more than £8 million in 1986.

When the inevitable decline took place, and Trebor was sold to Cadbury (for £120 million in 1989) the Marks family, still true to their Christian principles, gifted 15 per cent of the sale revenue to their workforce.

Chapter Three

The Supermarkets

W e often say we don't like them, but we go there every week, or we welcome their delivery drivers at our door. They dominate the British grocery retail sector.

After much research, it is generally agreed that the first 'real' supermarket opened on 4 August 1930 in the Queen's District of New York City. The store, run by Michael J. Cullen, operated under the slogan 'Pile it high, sell it low' which is probably still a useful definition of what a supermarket is, and was echoed later by Jack Cohen, the founder of Tesco. One of Cullen's significant innovations was the provision of a large car park.

The first self-service store in the world opened, not in one of the great capital cities of the world, but at 79 Jefferson Avenue in Memphis, Tennessee. It was the brainchild of Clarence Saunders. Born in Virginia, Saunders had left school at fourteen to become a clerk in a general store. He later worked in a coke plant in Alabama and a sawmill in Tennessee before becoming a salesman for a wholesale grocer, earning $30 a month at the age of nineteen. In 1902, he moved to Memphis and set up a wholesale grocery co-operative. His experiences in running this business led to the belief that many small grocers failed to survive because of high overheads and heavy credit losses.

Saunders' store was called Piggly Wiggly. He introduced the idea of customers being allowed to walk through the store with a basket, serving themselves. This enabled the business to serve more customers with fewer shop assistants, the reduced overheads allowing for lower prices. Initially, shops using this format were termed 'grocerterias', being like cafeterias, which were another new self-service concept. Saunders patented the self-service concept in 1917 allowing him to offer franchises. At Piggly Wiggly, customers entered the store through a turnstile, were provided with a basket, and then passed through four aisles with the store's 605 items on display. Every item was marked with its price, and at the end of the aisles was a cashier. Allowing customers to make their own selection of goods required improved brand identity. Saunders realised that customers needed to recognise the brands that they favoured. Packaging immediately became vitally important.

Piggly Wiggly later invented the idea of the shopping cart or trolley, which was introduced at their Oklahoma stores in 1937. Today there are more than 600 independently-owned and operated Piggly Wiggly stores across seventeen states in the USA.

If one of the concepts of a supermarket is self-service then the United Kingdom was slow off the mark compared to the United States. In 1947, there were just ten self-service shops in the country. The first true British supermarkets traded under the Premier brand and were launched by Patrick Galvani in 1951 who was the son-in-law of the Chairman of Express Dairies. His first store achieved takings more than ten times that of an average grocery shop.

The so-called 'Big Four' did not begin as supermarket chains: Tesco began as a market stall, Sainsbury as a grocer's shop in North London, Morrisons in a similar capacity in Bradford, and Asda as a consortium of dairy farmers in the north of England. Asda's conversion from dairy shops and grocery stores to supermarkets was a direct result of its founders, Peter and Fred Asquith, visiting the Piggly Wiggly stores in the American southern states.

Tesco, perhaps the biggest of the big four in terms of their presence in the United Kingdom, started life in 1919 when Jack Cohen began selling surplus groceries from a stall in the East End of London. Cohen made a profit of £1 from sales of £4 on his first day.

Sainsbury's was established as a partnership in 1869, when John and Mary Sainsbury opened a shop at 173 Drury Lane in Holborn. They began as a retailer of fresh foods and later expanded into packaged groceries including tea and sugar. Sainsbury's trading philosophy was 'Quality perfect, prices lower'. William Morrison opened his business, like Jack Cohen, on a market. He began by selling eggs and butter on Rawston Market in Bradford in 1899.

Asda began when a family butcher joined forces with a group of dairy farmers in the West Riding of Yorkshire. By the 1920's, Peter and Fred Asquith were managing seven butcher's shops in and around the town of Knottingley, which is probably most easily located in the minds of motorists as being in the shadows of the cooling towers of the Ferrybridge Power Station on the A1M. At the same time, dairy farmers in the area amalgamated under the name of J.W. Hindell Dairy Farmers Ltd. They became Associated Dairies and Farm Stores Ltd in 1949. Asquiths diversified and opened a supermarket in a former cinema in Castleford. In 1965, the two businesses merged when Asquiths invited Associated Dairies to run the butchery departments in their expanding chain of stores. The result was Asquith and Dairies, which was capitalised to become AS-DA.

Today, the grocery trade and, increasingly, other retail trades including textiles, is dominated by these familiar names. They are large businesses with worldwide interests and have diversified into very different activities such as banking and insurance. The most recent statistics indicate that the four best-known supermarket names also occupy the top four places in the list of the most successful retail brands. In fifth and sixth place are John Lewis and Marks and Spencer.

The psychology of shopping suggests that consumers still respond positively to what they see as a personal service, and this is very much the marketing approach of all the major supermarket chains. This is not the story of these somewhat impersonal brands, but of those pioneers in London and Yorkshire who faced different challenges but sought the same resolutions.

The Asquith Brothers

The history of Asda began in the village of Knottingley in West Yorkshire, and the aspirations of a family butcher called Asquith. Census records show that a Robert Asquith was trading as a butcher in Knottingley in 1911, having been born in the area in about 1888. The family name is common in Yorkshire and is probably associated with the village of Askwith in the Harrogate area. From the West Riding area came the famous family that included Herbert Asquith, who became Prime Minister in the early years of the twentieth century, and from whom descends the equally well-known Bonham-Carter family. There have been members of the Asquith families in Knottingley since at least the 1850s.

The butchers, trading as W.R. Asquith, gradually expanded to own three shops and three mobile units. In time, the two sons, Peter and Fred, took over the business, and the expansion continued from the mid-1920s until they were operating seven shops in and around Pontefract. On 11 December 1959, in time for the Christmas shopping rush, they opened a 'modern' self-service supermarket in Pontefract, next door to one of their first shops. The *Pontefract and Castleford Express* described the new Asquith store as 'shopping the modern way':

Entering the store through glass swing doors, the customer can take a basket to hold the goods which she chooses from the well-stocked shelves and display units, and pay for the items at the cash desk on the way out. Everything is on show to make things easy for the housewife in a hurry and assistants are ready to help when required. Particularly striking is the meat service counter at the rear of the supermarket. This is about 42ft in length, including 30ft of refrigerated counter, and it carries an excellent display of English meat, various cooked meats and bacon.

The Asquith brothers were always looking for new ways of promoting their business and attracting new customers. One often-recounted story involved a promotion by the soup and sauce manufacturer Crosse and Blackwell which offered a refund of 6d for each promotional sticker sent to the company. The Asquith Brothers bought one thousand cans, removed all the stickers and received the refund. They then sold the sauce for 3d less than any other retailer in the area. In later years, Peter Asquith recalled that this was the turning-point for company, commenting that after that day 'we never looked back'. The concept of food discounting had been realised.

They took the surprising step of looking to the United States to see how they could expand and modify their business to meet changing trends. On their travels, they visited Piggly Wiggly, possibly the first-ever true supermarket, and returned to the UK re-vitalised with many new ideas. Joined by Jack Hewitt as a business partner who was later to become the Managing Director of Asda, Peter and Fred converted the redundant Queen's Theatre in Castleford into a supermarket, opening the doors in 1963. They did the same in Edlington near Doncaster on the site of the old indoor market, and in 1965 constructed their first supermarket from scratch on the site of the former Palace Cinema at South Elmsall. The first two supermarkets traded under the name of 'Queens'. The Asquiths also moved away from traditional shopping hours. They were the first retailers to move into later night opening (on Friday evenings) and amongst the first to realise that shoppers were more likely to travel to their supermarkets by car rather than walk or use public transport, so they incorporated large car parks in their store designs.

Simultaneously with the expansion of the Asquith business, a group of dairy farmers in the West Riding of Yorkshire joined forces. Under the name of J.W. Hindell Dairy Farmers Ltd, and including Craven Dairies and a similar business run by Arthur Stockdale, they merged and consolidated their resources. In 1949, they broadened their operations and became Associated Dairies and Farm Stores Ltd. Arthur Stockdale was appointed Managing Director. The company ran a chain of pork butchery shops branded as 'farm stores', and café shops and cafés under the Craven Dairies branding.

In 1965, Noel Stockdale, son of Arthur, approached the Asquith Brothers and struck up an immediate rapport. He invited them to set up butchery departments inside their stores. The two businesses agreed to merge, and a new company was formed on 3 May 1965. Its name took two letters from Asquith and two from Dairies to form Asda. Peter and Fred Asquith, and Noel Stockdale therefore became the first directors of the Asda supermarkets chain.

There followed a steady expansion of the new and dynamic company. A store was opened in Wakefield followed by others in the Wortley and Whitkirk districts of Leeds. Noel Stockdale bought out the Asquith Brothers in the late 1960s, re-branding their Queen's stores to Asda, and by then the company had also established retail outlets in the north-east of England. With the abolition of retail price maintenance in 1964, Asda began a policy of lowering prices and under-cutting competitors. They also expanded by acquiring branches of the GEM (Government Exchange Mart) stores which were faltering. Asda acquired the stores without cost, and at a low rent, and simply by re-branding them, converted an accumulated loss of over £300,000 into a profit, increasing the stores' weekly income from £6000 to £60,000 in just six months.

The GEM stores came with a lot of space which Peter Asquith utilised by introducing non-grocery (dry goods) lines, the first time that his stores and shops had sold anything other than food and groceries. He was also was responsible for another 'supermarketing first', by utilising the spare land at the GEM sites to open petrol filling stations, selling fuel at discounted prices. None of the major oil companies was willing to be involved, so Asquith arranged a deal with a little-known Russian supplier called NAFTA.

Fred Asquith died in 2002. Peter remained associated with Asda for much of his long life although was at times in disagreement with the company's policies. He left Asda in 1980 but rejoined nine years later and was still playing an active role, opening new stores, in his late seventies. He served as honorary Life President of Asda as well as running a property company which acquired sites for future stores. He was also a successful racehorse owner. He died in June 2008, aged 81 years.

In 2015, in its fiftieth anniversary year, Asda, now owned by the American supermarket giant Walmart, opened its 600th store, and saw its profits pass £1 billion for the first time.

Jacob Edward Cohen

The Whitechapel area of London achieved notoriety in the late nineteenth century due to the exploits of the so-called Jack the Ripper; and just ten years after the murders had shocked the country, the man who was to found Britain's most financially-powerful and dominant supermarket chain, Jacob Edward Cohen, was born there.

For centuries, the district has been home to different immigrant groups, each bringing their own culture and traditions. Today, the Bangladeshi community is prominent, but in the nineteenth century, it was home to a large Jewish community. Jacob was born into one of those Jewish families on 6 October 1898 at 91 Ashfield Street, a five-minute walk from the Whitechapel underground station, and close to the Commercial Road, which has for centuries been the trading artery of the area. His father, Avroam Cohen, was a tailor who had come to London with his wife from Lodz in Poland. Jacob went to Rutland Street Elementary School down near the docks until he was fourteen, and then started working for his father. His mother died three years later, with Jacob, familiarly known as Jack, still a teenager. His father remarried and a rift formed when Jack announced he wanted to leave the family business and become a grocer.

Possibly to sever links with his father, Jack joined the Royal Flying Corps at the height of the First World War, using his tailoring skills to make and repair the fabric-covered early aircraft, and serving in France, Egypt and Palestine. He contracted malaria, and was demobilised in 1919, receiving £30 in demob money. It was this sum which was to set Cohen on the path towards establishing a business which today receives over £6,000 in takings every minute, and is the third largest retailer in the world, measured by profits.

Jack Cohen used his £30 to buy some redundant NAAFI grocery items, allegedly mainly tinned fish, which he sold from a barrow at a stall on Hackney Market. On his first day of trading, he took £4 and made a profit of £1. He was soon taking on more stalls which were operated by members of his family. His wife Sarah, known as Cassie, was incredibly supportive, even agreeing that their wedding gifts should be used to set up a wholesale business. The Tesco brand was created by Cohen in 1924, when he merged the initials of his local tea supplier, T.E. Stockwell with the first two initials of his surname.

He gave his brand identity by taking the market stalls into the High Street, opening shops without front doors, and laying them out like a market stall. His decision to forsake the market was also influenced by his management acumen. The various people whom he had employed to work on his stalls were all personalities, with their own styles of selling and attracting customers, and true to the transient nature of the traditional market, some would find more attractive pitches elsewhere, or would simply move on to other jobs. It was the way of life for many in the East End of London in the depressed economic conditions of the 1930s. The young entrepreneur knew that brand identity was more than a coined name that could easily trip off the tongue. Customers needed to connect positively with the name, and for Cohen that meant recruiting the right people, and ensuring a uniformity of image.

Cohen opened his first store in Burnt Oak in 1929, and a second shop in 1931. Less than ten years' later, he had opened more than one hundred, many sited in newly-constructed shopping centres, where his willingness to take risks enabled him to acquire key retailing space ahead of his more cautious competitors.

Untypical for a man who ploughed everything into his business and could make courageous decisions, Cohen at first shied away from the supermarket format, although he travelled to the United States to see how the stores operated. It was not until the early 1950s that his son-in-law, Hyman Kreitman (who had married Cohen's eldest daughter, Sybil Irene), persuaded him that it was the right step.

Tesco supermarkets opened across the country, often accompanied by much razzmatazz. The first to open outside the London area, on 12 December 1961, was in Leicester, taking up the ground floor of the first multi-storey car park in Europe which could accommodate more than 1,000 cars. 'Carry On' star Sid James, whose rough-diamond accent and style was easily associated in the minds of many shoppers with the type of East End London from which Tesco had evolved, formally opened the store at 11.00 am. Measured in retail space, it was the largest in the country, and located just off the city centre, easily accessed by the new generation of shoppers who came into town by car. Tesco's advertising in the local newspapers described their new outlet as a 'wonder store' selling everything from children's clothes to fresh meat, electrical and household goods, and even 'toys for Christmas'. The combining of grocery and non-food lines within the same floor space was one of many milestones in Cohen's development of his business. Another, which was clearly indicated in the bright Day-Glo posters across the store, was his intention to challenge Retail Price Maintenance, a controversial strategy at that time in the retail world. A few years later, he was to be a major supporter of Green Shield stamps, which Tesco issued until the weekend of the Queen's Jubilee in 1977.

The five letters making up 'Tesco' were displayed vertically on the outside of the eight-storey building, giving the impression, no doubt intended, that the company owned the entire structure. In the new age of brutalist concrete city centre skylines, it was a bold statement, and within months, it was noticed that trade at the traditional department stores in Leicester, mostly inhabiting smoke-darkened Victorian red brick structures, was diminishing.

Jack Cohen spent part of the day working at the checkouts, packing goods into customers' bags, and his daughter Shirley, later Dame Shirley Porter, walked round the store talking to visitors, modelling Tesco garments. The integrated car park meant that the white-coated Tesco staff could carry shoppers' purchases straight to their cars, under cover, and an automated barrier system allowed drivers to pay for their car parking without getting out of their vehicles. The whole event attracted the attention of the British Pathé news organisation, providing Cohen with a free fifty-five-second commercial screened in thousands of cinemas across the country.

Cohen stayed with his company throughout his life, retiring as Chairman in 1969 at the age of seventy. His often-quoted business motif was 'Pile it high, sell it cheap' but perhaps his epitaph should have been one of his other observations about the secret of sustained retail success: 'Salesmanship, showmanship, call it what you will. Every week there must be something special, something new.' Also in 1969, he was honoured with a knighthood. Known as 'The Guv'nor' and as 'Slasher Jack', which has some unfortunate overtones of that other infamous Whitechapel man who is thought to have the same first name, he died in the city of his birth on 24 March 1979 and was buried at the Willesden United Synagogue cemetery. In 2009, a commemorative plaque was unveiled at his home at 91 Ashfield Street.

John and Mary Sainsbury

The story of the Sainsbury supermarket chain and its associated businesses and operations is the best-documented of all our High Street brands. The reasons for this are several, but include the significant fact that each generation of the family has produced men and women who have become prominent in public life outside of their supermarket identity, and therefore, unlike Jack Cohen of Tesco, or William Morrison, Sainsbury's is much more than a retail brand. This does not mean that the family has not been closely involved with the business which their ancestors John and Mary set up in 1869. In fact, there was continuous 'hands-on' involvement through until 1999.

Many of the grocers who founded the big retail names of the twentieth and twenty-first centuries focussed on either a specific product or a marketing strategy, or developed a reputation for quality or value. John and Mary Sainsbury concentrated on a different concept, and one that was not always a priority in grocery and food retailing in the nineteenth century. Mary Anne Staples was just nineteen years old when she and her husband John James Sainsbury opened the doors of their dairy shop at 173 Drury Lane in London to customers for the first time; but Mary was the daughter of a dairyman trading in Euston, and John, was the son of a craftsman. They were a young couple with ambition and aspirations, and an understanding of what their customers wanted. It is claimed that they founded their business on their wedding day, 20 April 1869.

The Sainsburys paid close attention to the cleanliness of their premises and the quality of their dairy products. They stored perishable foods in the coolness of the cellar of their rented shop so that it kept fresh for longer. Mary would scrub the preparation areas regularly to prevent a build-up of germs. John sourced fresh milk from the countryside, whereas some London grocers were selling watered-down milk from cows kept in the polluted inner areas of the capital. In time, John Sainsbury introduced a milestone in retailing by asking the Dutch suppliers of his butter to put a date on their wrappers so that customers could see how long the product had been in stock, and to enable John Sainsbury to rotate his stock. The Dutch Government saw the importance of this simple innovation, and later made date-stamping compulsory. Their first slogan, displayed in all their shops, is arguably one of the best, the company's mission simply stated as 'Quality perfect, prices lower'.

In just over ten years, the Sainsburys had opened further shops, in Islington, Kentish Town and Croydon, and extended their range of fresh foodstuffs to include prepared meats such as ham and sausages. They introduced their own brand, under which they sold goods such as bacon that had been smoked in Allcroft Road in the Belsize Park area of north-west London, not far from their Kentish Town shop. Their first shop outside London was opened in Croydon in 1882 and became their 'flagship' store. It was in Croydon that Sainsbury's was later to open its first self-service store. By 1889, there were sixteen Sainsbury's shops in operation, employing 178 staff.

As they became more prosperous, John and Mary Sainsbury moved their growing family to more salubrious areas, first to Kentish Town and then to Highgate. They had six sons and five daughters who, it appears, not only became involved in their parents' work but shared their very positive outlook on life. There must have been obstacles and problems along the way, but when they arose, they were responded to, practically and successfully. They actively recruited female branch managers following the outbreak of the First World War when the young men were mobilised. They established a training school for their staff in Blackfriars. They coped with food rationing but maintained their reputation for quality at low prices.

John James Sainsbury died in 1928. All six sons followed him into the business, with the eldest, John Benjamin Sainsbury, succeeding him as the Chairman of the company. During his term, the number of stores increased to 250, and staff facilities, including libraries in every store, sports grounds, pensions and a staff hardship fund were introduced. He achieved this in just ten very active years, but after a heart attack in 1938, John Benjamin handed over the company to his two sons, Alan John and Robert James Sainsbury. They continued the family tradition of retail innovation, and seemed well-matched, one focusing on the retail operation and the other on finance. It was during their tenure that Sainsbury's moved into self-service supermarkets and introduced computer-based stock management systems.

Alan John's son, John Davan Sainsbury, remains Life President of the company today. Robert James's son, David, was to be the last member of the family to be Chairman of the company. The family still holds in the region of 15 per cent of the business.

The wider Sainsbury family, descendants of John James and Mary Anne, have been active in many areas of public life, in politics (on both sides of the political spectrum) and in commerce and education. They have created and led many philanthropic projects that include the Sainsbury Centre for Mental Health (now the Centre for Mental Health), the Sainsbury Centre for Visual Arts at the University of East Anglia, the Sainsbury Wing of the National Gallery and the Sainsbury Laboratory at the John Innes Centre in Norwich.

In Spring 2018, it was announced that Sainsburys and ASDA were discussing a merger worth £15billion responding to the increased dominance of the online retailer, Amazon.

Wallace Waite and Arthur Rose

A cast metal plaque, commissioned by the Acton History Group and the Ealing Civic Society, set into the pavement outside 263a High Street in Acton near to the busy Gunnersby Lane and Uxbridge Road interchange, commemorates the opening of the first Waitrose store. It was unveiled to mark the centenary of Waitrose in 2004 when residents met together at the nearby St Mary's Hall. The premises are now being used as a pizza shop, but in June 1904 this was where Wallace Wyndham Waite, Arthur Edward Rose and David Taylor set up as grocers, selling meats, cheeses, teas and other provisions.

Wallace Waite was born in 1881, but came to London at the age of sixteen. In the 1901 Census his occupation was that of a 'grocer's assistant' living in lodgings in the Paddington area. He married, and with his wife Kathleen, had a daughter whom they named Barbara. They set up home at 3a Stuart Road, Acton, about a five-minute walk along the Steyne Road from the High Street, and his mother moved in with them, as well as a young apprentice grocer called James Cozens.

Arthur Rose was not from a retailing background. A Londoner, born in 1879, he had trained as a clerk. He married Wallace Waite's sister, Bertha, and lived in the West Ealing area, having three children. Rose enlisted in the Army Service Corps when war broke out in 1914, serving as first a private and rising to the rank of corporal. He was injured and suffered poor health for several years after being demobbed. He left the business in 1924.

David Taylor appears to have been the outsider. Waite brought his knowledge of the grocery trade to their partnership, and Rose brought his ability to document and manage the finances. Taylor worked as the manager of the shop, stayed with the enterprise for only two years, and then returned to his former occupation.

Despite competition from other grocery businesses, the enterprise was successful, partly because of the partners' energetic advertising, and the prime location of their shop. They acquired the neighbouring premises at 265 and 267 High Street, and in 1908 rebranded their business as Waitrose Ltd. They also expanded their range of goods to include hardware and household items. The two young men were obviously entrepreneurial in their approach. In 1910, they sold certain food lines at discounted prices to a local charity that distributed free food to poor people in the area. Wallace Waite also broadened the business at the outbreak of the First World War, moving into the wholesale trade to provide provisions for the British Army camp at Catterick in Yorkshire.

By 1913, two further shops opened, the first at 65 Churchfield Road, followed by one at 190 Acton Lane, and the two principals had taken on several staff. More shops were opened in Chiswick, Ealing, Windsor and in several other London districts. Remarkably for a man who was intent on expansion, and needed income to support his plans, Waite chose to close all his shops every lunchtime between 1.15 and 2.15 pm to ensure that his staff enjoyed a full hour's break. He profiled his shops to serve an 'upmarket' clientele, but also launched a parallel chain called Wyndhams, which he located in less profitable areas.

In 1937, Wallace Waite decided to pass on his very successful business to another company. He encountered Michael Watkins, who was the Head of Trading for the John Lewis Partnership, and became convinced that this was the way forward. On 1 October 1937, the ten Waitrose shops with their 160 staff became part of the Partnership. Waite continued to be involved for three more years. He was awarded an MBE in 1940 in recognition of his achievements in the grocery retail sector, and later, in 1955, saw his first Waitrose 'supermarket' open in Streatham. He died in 1971.

Waitrose returned to the area 110 years after Waite, with his two young colleagues, opened his first shop in Acton High Street. The chain has opened a large 'virtual shop' in large warehousing at 96 Victoria Road, occupying 100,000 square feet and employing 350 staff. Waitrose customers ordering online for home delivery are now served by this facility rather than by individual stores. It is less than two miles from where Wallace Waite lived with his young family at the beginning of the Waitrose story.

William Murdoch Morrison

Scottish-born Duncan Morrison, from Alloa in Clackmannanshire, was born in about 1833, travelled south of the border and married a young woman called Mary from Doncaster. They settled in Osset, a mining town midway between Dewsbury and Wakefield in what was then the West Riding of Yorkshire. Their youngest child and second son was William Murdoch Morrison.

The Morrisons arrived in Ossett just before the town experienced the major expansion of the nineteenth century which was prompted by the opening of coal mines and the establishment of a woollen industry. It is possible that the family was attracted to the area by the efforts of several entrepreneurial businessmen to create a spa town making use of natural spring waters. Several baths were opened as well as associated pleasure gardens, but the enterprises failed. An area of the town is still known as Osset Spa.

William Morrison married Amelia, and in 1899 opened a business in Rawston Market in Bradford, selling eggs and butter and trading as Wm Morrison Limited. In the 1911 Census, he described his occupation as a 'provisions merchant'. By then, he and his family were living at 25 Athol Road in the Manningham district of Bradford, about a mile north of the city

centre and near to Lister Park, today one of the city's largest parks. Their
son, Kenneth Morrison, was born in 1931. He took over the management
of the business in 1952, although when he first left school he worked in
farming, raising cattle, and was therefore able in later years to bring to the
business an understanding of the dairy and meat supply chain.

Rawston market hall was built in 1874, an impressive structure with the
coat of arms of the town of Bradford above its grand entrance. It was, from
the start, a food market rather than one where general goods were traded.
In the twentieth century, as the expectations and requirements of shoppers
changed, the market was converted into retail units. In 2006, a new shopping
centre was opened on the site, called the Rawston Quarter, retaining the
original façade. The original market is still remembered by older residents
of the area as Bradford's finest.

The first milestone in the history of the company was passed in 1958
when Morrisons moved from the market to a small shop in Bradford city
centre. It was the first self-service store in the city, and the first to have
prices displayed on every product. The shop had three checkouts. In 1961,
the company acquired the 'Victoria', a redundant cinema on Thornton Road
in the Girlington district of Bradford, converting it into their first supermarket with over 5,000 square feet of retail space selling meat, greengrocery
and dairy products, and with a free car park.

The Victoria Palace Theatre had opened in 1914, built and operated
by Henry Hibbert's 'Hibbert's Picture Ltd'. It was refurbished in 1927,
re-opened as the 'New Victoria', and was converted to sound in 1929.
Further modernisation took place in 1955 when a wide screen was installed
for Cinemascope, but because of the growing competition from television,
audiences steadily declined and it closed on Saturday 16 December 1961.
The audience on that final day watched *Voyage to the Bottom of the Sea* starring Walter Pidgeon, Joan Fontaine and Barbara Eden.

Less than a year later, the conversion from picture house to supermarket was complete. The grand opening of the new store on Thursday 1
December 1962 was performed by Bobo, one of the popular chimpanzees
from Twycross Zoo in Leicestershire who appeared in a series of PG tea
commercials. Bobo cut a white tape stretched across the entrance and then
accompanied the media to the tea display.

Morrisons later built a larger supermarket on adjacent land, and leased
the cinema store as a furniture outlet operated by Don Valley Discounts and
later to Windsor House as a discount shoe warehouse. In 1982, the building was demolished to allow for the Morrisons car park to be increased in

size. More recently, the entire area has been redeveloped with a much-en-larged new store, the cinema's legacy surviving in the name of the Victoria Shopping Centre.

Sir Kenneth Morrison, whose tenure of the company began with just two market stalls, died on 1 February 2017. He left a business, which he had managed or influenced for sixty years, with an operating income of more than £300 million from over 500 stores employing 115,000 staff. The company's Head Office in Gain Lane, Bradford, is less than three miles from where William Morrison set up his first market stall.

Chapter Four

From Market Stalls,
Railway Stations and Corner Shops

There is a temptation to indulge in romanticism when narrating the 'rags to riches' stories of many of the men and women who founded the High Street names we are most familiar with today. It is easy to imagine a teenage Henry Curry watching the giant steam engines at work at Corah's vast textile complex in Leicester, keeping them lubricated and making sure the furnaces that powered them were supplied with coal around the clock. Then discovering the fine engineering which enabled a piston to move so smoothly and effortlessly within a cylinder, and making the sideways leap into using similarly-engineered tubes to make bicycles.

The steam engine was undoubtedly at the heart of the industrial revolution, even though its component parts had been known for thousands of years. We knew that water, when heated, produced steam, and that steam expanded to occupy more space than water. We knew how to make finely-machined cylinders because we had been making cannon as armaments for numerous wars for centuries. We knew that by attaching a rod to the middle of a wheel, we could produce a lateral (vertical or horizontal) movement. It needed a project manager to put these components together, and he was James Watt.

Henry Curry worked in the first factory in Leicester to be built with integrated steam power. Other factories had already harnessed the power and reliability of Watt's creation, but had added a steam engine to existing buildings and mills. So the movement began, and the creativity which spread out to inspire numerous inventors and entrepreneurs in very different ways.

Another romantic image is that of the market trader, selling his goods in all winds and weathers, and agreeing deals with customers, 'cutting prices until it hurts'. A market place is a place of silence until the traders arrive in the early morning to set up their pitches. Then this empty space in the heart of many of our cities and market towns comes to life. Markets exist in every country, representing the age-old custom of bartering, buying and selling.

In many areas, such as England in Roman times, smallholdings were located within a day's journey by horse-drawn cart from the nearest market. In the UK, markets became regulated in the eleventh century when royal charters were awarded to local lords to allow the creation of markets, as well as fairs. When chartered, markets could operate on certain days of the week or year, and, to provide some financial protection, nearby markets could not open on the same days. These historic market charters are still respected today, as is the protection from rival markets. Most local authorities hold a market charter which allows them to prevent any rival market being set up within six and two-thirds miles of a chartered market. This includes car boot sales and farmers' markets. Councils have the powers to grant a temporary licence to any such rival operation.

It was surely a daunting place for newcomers, setting up for the first time alongside the seasoned professionals who had worked the market for their entire lives and had inherited their business from fathers and grandfathers. Even more daunting, perhaps, for Bill and Jean Adderley. He had just lost his job with Woolworths because he had refused a transfer to another store. All he had to sell was a job lot of curtains which had been rejected by Marks and Spencer.

Not a promising start, but an enterprise which resulted in the highly-successful Dunelm Mills, which, according to most recent figures has a quarterly revenue income of more than £250 million, less than forty years since Bill and Jean set up their stall. James Kemsey Wilkinson is another author of a rags-to-riches story, being so committed to his first hardware shop that he and his bride arranged for their wedding to take place in the early morning so that they could be back home to open their shop as usual. The Wilko Group now reports sales of more than £1.5 billion, less than sixty years since that first small shop opened its doors. Perhaps the young Jack Cohen, founder of Tesco 'grew up' while he was in the Royal Flying Corps during the First World War, his wartime experiences giving him the self-confidence and determination to take £30 worth of ex-NAAFI grocery items, bought with his de-mob payment, to Hackney Market, stand alongside the seasoned marketers, make takings of four pounds and go home with a profit of one pound, and return to his stall the next day, and the next until he had built a business which had a reputation and was outselling the others.

The romanticism continues, largely generated by individuals who had a belief in themselves and their product or service. These were not conglomerates or faceless organisations, but husbands, fathers and sons who in most cases involved their families in their schemes and sometimes asked them to take considerable financial risks. They were also men who often harboured doubts about their ideas and feared that they would lead to family ruin. Unlike the chocolate pioneers, for instance, most of whom came from wealthy families and also enjoyed the social and financial support of structures such as the Quakers or the freemasons, these were, for the most part, loners.

The political canvas was so different in the past, and changed in shades so frequently; but these men and women were certainly not the archetypal wealthy capitalists. They may not have been on the breadline, although Henry Curry's family was probably close to poverty, but neither did they have the privilege of class or inherited finance. They were just men (and women) who believed in themselves, worked hard, and thus created employment and prosperity for tens of thousands of others.

William (Bill) and Jean Adderley

There have been market traders in Leicester since the Romans established a garrison along the route of the Fosse Way, for some time the road that marked the northern frontier of their occupation, by the side of the River Soar in the first century AD. In the medieval period it was a town of many markets. Leicester's High Street was formerly Swinesmarket, the horse fair was situated where the Victorian town hall now stands, and until the middle of the nineteenth century, a busy market traded at the High Cross in the very centre of the town. Except for livestock, the retail elements of all these markets became gathered together in what was formerly the Saturday Market but now trades six days every week, just behind the façades of the shops and stores which face Gallowtree Gate.

This market, now known simply as Leicester Market, has been a haven for entrepreneurs for over 700 years. The first known Royal Grant dates to 1229 although the traders mark their anniversaries from a document of 1298. Through one of the narrow alleys or 'jitties' that connect the market to Gallowtree Gate can be seen the present Marks and Spencer store. This is a 'landmark' store in the history of M&S. It is said that Lord Marks chose to build on the site having secured a major deal with Nathaniel Corah and Sons Ltd. Having left the Corah headquarters nearby, and heading in his chauffeur-driven limousine towards the London Road, Marks noticed an undeveloped building site and told his driver that he would purchase it to celebrate the move towards buying directly from suppliers.

At the time, retailers such as Marks and Spencer were willing to negotiate to gain exclusive deals with top textile manufacturers. Later, the relationship would be reversed, and many British clothing manufacturers suffered because of a new ruthlessness on the part of the big brand retailers. Like Michael Marks almost a century before, William Adderley was born in Leeds, in February 1948. Also, like his predecessor, the company he founded began as a market stall.

In 1979, Bill Adderley was a manager at the Woolworths store in Belvoir Road, Coalville, a former mining town in north-west Leicestershire. The retailer wanted him to relocate to Skegness but Bill refused, and consequently left their employment. Whilst looking for a new job, he and his wife Jean rented a stall on Leicester Market selling curtains that had been rejected by Marks and Spencer, close to where former England footballer Gary Lineker's family ran a fruit and vegetable business. From this grew a business which was focussed first on home textiles and then on furniture.

The Adderleys stayed with the market trade and expanded their presence at other markets across the region. Five years later, they opened their first 'permanent' shop in Leicester's Churchgate, trading as Dunelm Mill. In 1988, the company's first major store opened in East Street, Leicester, which also served as a warehouse, and two years later, their first store on the scale of those now operating was opened in Rotherham. Until 1999, the business was managed from a shop in Loughborough but a purpose-built headquarters was then constructed at the Watermead Business Park in Syston, near Leicester. Dunelm Mills, now the Dunelm Group, floated on the London Stock Exchange in 2006. The company now operates more than 160 stores across the UK as well as selling on line.

The store in Coalville, where Bill was once the manager, closed in 2009 following the collapse of the 807-store Woolworths chain. Woolworths had been trading in the UK for exactly one hundred years since Frank Winfield Woolworth opened his first store outside North America in Church Street, Liverpool. The Coalville store remained empty for over five years. Dunelm opened a store in Coalville, in the former Rex cinema in Marlborough Square, in June 2016.

Bill Adderley's association with Marks and Spencer, remains. In 2013, it was reported that he had become the largest private shareholder in the company with a stake valued at £250 million. Bill was also Leicestershire's first billionaire. Bill and Jean's son, Will, took over the running of the group in 1996 and was re-appointed Chief Executive in 2014.

Charles Kalms

Dixons was at one time the largest electrical retail chain in the UK, but it began as a small photographic studio in the south-east of England. Charles Kalms was born on 16 March 1897 in the Westminster district of London. He went on to sell advertising space on London Underground stations and trains where he met Michael Mindel, the owner of a small photographic studio in Oxford Street who was interested in expanding his business. Kalms opened a photographic studio at 32 High Street in Southend-on-Sea. It was registered on 27 October 1937 as a private company with a share capital of £100; Michael Mindel joined Kalms as a founder director.

Kalms chose to call his business Dixons Studios Ltd simply because the small shop front could not accommodate a name with more than six letters. He found the name 'Dixons' by looking through the local telephone directory. By the time he founded his company, Kalms had married and his son Stanley had been born in 1931. Educated at Christ's College in Finchley, Stanley joined his father in running the business at the age of sixteen.

The Second World War led to a considerable demand for portrait photography, particularly of men and women wearing their military uniforms before leaving to serve overseas. Dixons responded to this need by opening seven studios across the London area. However, at the end of the war the demand fell away as quickly as it had appeared. Kalms had to reduce his business back to a single studio in the Edgware area of north London.

In the early 1950s, small and easily-to-use cameras were being manufactured, and as wartime austerity changed gradually towards more prosperity, Stanley Kalms suggested that the business should sell simple cameras and accessories. They set up a mail order business, and within seven years, they were serving 60,000 mail order customers. A new head office and buying centre was acquired in Edgware to respond to the demand. Stanley advertised in national and local newspapers, selling both new and second-hand photographic equipment, knowing that those customers who first bought second-hand goods from him would aspire to graduating later to brand-new equipment. He also offered very flexible hire purchase arrangements which attracted customers on limited incomes. Stanley travelled widely to the Far East on many occasions in those years, personally arranging trade deals with Japanese camera manufacturers so that Dixons could offer exclusive products at low prices.

The company continued to expand. In 1962, they were listed on the London Stock Exchange, opened their sixteenth shop, and acquired their competitors, Ascotts and Bennetts. They then broadened their products base by offering developing and printing services and retailing audio and hi-fi equipment imported from Japan. In 1967 they opened a large colour film processing laboratory in Stevenage covering 85,000 square feet, bought out another competitor in 1972 and opened their main distribution centre in Stevenage in 1974.

Charles Kalms retired as Chairman of Dixons in 1971 to become Life President of the company. His son took his place as Chairman. Charles died in 1978 aged eighty. Over the past thirty years, the Dixons brand has change many times because of expansion, acquisitions, mergers and restyling. A key move was their purchase of Currys in 1984 which added more than 600 stores to their retail portfolio, many of them on Britain's High Streets. In the twenty-first century, the Dixons name disappeared entirely from the High Street. The 190 Dixon stores became part of the Currys chain, which was selling from over 360 outlets, and were rebranded as Currys Digital. Dixons became an online retailer, 'a pure play e-tailer' to quote the words of John Clare, the Chief Executive of the parent group, DSG International (which stands for Disposable Soft Goods).

The Right Hon Lord Kalms served his entire business career within his father's company seeing it become a world player in retail. As well as Currys and PC World, Dixons set up Knowhow, which provides IT servicing and support, and merged with the Carphone Warehouse in 2014, renaming it Dixons Carphone. He has been married to Pamela for over sixty years and has a large family of three children, eight grandchildren and ten great grandchildren. He was a Governor of Dixons City Academy in Bradford, its art theatre complex bearing his name, and a Director of Business for Sterling, and of the National Institute of Economic and Social Research.

David Greig

The story of David Greig's provisions stores has similarities to that of Sir Thomas Lipton's empire. In their later years, these brands, along with Maypole and Home and Colonial, had a strong presence in English High Streets, selling dairy and meat products, and competing comfortably with each other. Both companies were later to become supermarket chains and inevitably lost their family identity; both were founded by men from Scotland who came south to find their fortunes; and the founders were also leading philanthropists of their time.

The Greig family's roots are to be found in the Scottish county of Midlothian. David Greig's grandmother, Margaret, was born in about 1811 in Inveresk. Her husband died young, and Margaret was left, in her thirties, to provide for four children: two boys and two girls. She worked as a laundress, presumably taking in clothes for washing in her own home.

Margaret's youngest son was David Murray Greig. He was born in 1841, and married a local girl, Maryan. They settled in Leith but by the 1870s, they had moved south to the Islington area of London where David Murray was describing his occupation as a 'house joiner'. Their eldest son, who was born in 1866, was to give his name to the family's food empire. He married Hannah Susan Deacock, familiarly known as 'Annie' who came from the Holborn area. Her family was already in the provisions business. Her father ran a dairy in Leather Lane, Holborn, which was later to become a David Greig store; but it was Greig's mother, Maryan, who should be regarded as the founder of the business. In 1870, she opened a small shop selling provisions at 32 High Street in Hornsey. A green commemorative plaque now tells passers-by of the history of this building. By the time her son was born, David Murray was also describing himself as a provisions merchant. Their son followed suit.

The Holborn connection has a further interesting connection. It was here in Drury Lane that John James Sainsbury and his wife Mary set up their first provisions shop, just months before the first Greig store. The Sainsbury and Deacock families were both in the dairy business and were friends; but later, relations between Sainsbury's and Greigs were to become tense and acrimonious due not only to personal rivalries but because Sainsbury allegedly went back on a previous gentleman's agreements about the location of new stores.

From Hornsey and Holborn, the focus moved to Brixton where David Greig opened his first shop in 1888. It was on the corner of Atlantic Road, not far from the centre of Brixton, and it had previously been a grocer's shop. His father, using his cabinet-making and woodworking skills, helped his son with the shop fittings. It was in this small shop that Greig's famous thistle logo, acknowledging the family's Scottish ancestry, was to be incorporated into the design and décor for the first time. A second shop soon followed, located on Coldharbour Lane, and then a third store selling meat and poultry further along Atlantic Road on the opposite side of the street.

By the late 1960s, the chain had grown to over 200 stores trading in the southern part of England. The family maintained control of the business throughout its existence, David Greig's son, David Ross Greig, taking over as Chairman. He died in 1964, and several other key members of the family passed away in the following few years which led to death duties from which the family and business could not recover. The chain was sold to the long-established Fitch Lovell group, which had begun as cheesemakers in the city of London in the 1780s, and the Greig stores were merged into their Keymarket chain. Keymarkets was later sold on to Gateway, and most became Somerfield stores which in time were acquired by the Co-operative Group.

For many years and several generations, the Greig family stayed loyal to the area of south London which had brought them wealth and prosperity, but in their retirement years, David and Annie moved to Beckenham in Kent, and they had also purchased valuable property elsewhere in the country. Their holdings included the twelfth-century Oversley Castle near Stratford-on-Avon, set in sixty-five acres of the Warwickshire countryside. Nearby, in the village of Alcester, is a community facility, built in 1958 and managed by the Hannah Susan Greig Memorial Company. Called the Greig Centre, it is committed to health and fitness for people of all ages and abilities. One of this company's directors is Ross Alexander Greig, who was born in 1955 and continues the family line. Another similar charitable enterprise funded by the family in memory of Samuel Victor Greig as well as Hannah Susan, was set up in Stanmore, Middlesex. Its funds now support the Greig City Academy, a Church of England school in High Street, Hornsey. Another member of the family, Oliver Scoullar-Greig, is a governor of the company appointed by the Church of England.

Henry and Anna Smith

Henry Walton Smith was born in 1738 into a wealthy and well-connected family in Somerset. It is said that he was originally from the hamlet of Hinton St George, but Smith referred to the village of Wrington as having some significance in his family's history. It is also said that he was educated at Harrow.

He moved to London and, in the 1780s, was a personal assistant to and protégé of Charles Rogers, a high officer in the London Custom House, and Fellow of the Royal Society. It is known that the society in which Rogers, and therefore Smith, moved, included many of the leading figures of the time including Horace Walpole and Sir Joshua Reynolds.

On 27 October 1784 at Christchurch, Spitalfields, Henry Smith married Anna Eastaugh, and his life and career changed dramatically. She was a domestic servant living at 95 Watling Street in the City of London, near to St Paul's Cathedral, working for the widow of a coal merchant. Henry's family disinherited him, and he was forced, with his new bride, to find a new source of income. Henry and Anna went on to have three children, Henry Edward, William Henry and Mary Anne.

In 1792, Henry and Anna established a 'newswalk' or newspaper round selling newspapers in Little Grosvenor Street near to Berkeley Square in London's Mayfair area, but Henry died only a few months later, on 23 August 1792, leaving Anna to run the business. William Henry Smith was just two weeks old when his father died.

For eight years, Anna ran the business on her own whilst bringing up her young family, until in 1800 she went into partnership with a Zaccheus Coates which lasted until 1812. An announcement in the London Gazette on 25 November 1812 confirmed the dissolution of the partnership and stated that the business, described as 'Newspaper Agents' would be carried on in Anna's sole name. Coates died soon afterwards. The severance of the partnership was probably due to his ill-health. Anna continued to manage the business, then known as H.W. Smith until her own death in 1816. It was taken over by her youngest son, William Henry Smith, working with his elder brother, and was valued at the time at £1,280, equivalent to about £80,000 today.

This was the beginning of a golden age for the newspaper industry. By the time Henry and Anna set up their stall, there were fifty-two newspapers being published in London and more than a hundred other titles. *The Times* had been launched in 1788, becoming the most important title of the time. Stamp duty on newspapers was reduced progressively between the 1830s and 1855, when it was abolished fully, leading to a massive increase in sales and circulation figures.

William was the more able businessman of the two sons, and in 1828, the business was renamed W.H. Smith. In 1821, he opened a reading room in the Strand and defined his business with the motto 'First with the news'. In addition to retailing, he also created what was to become the backbone of his business, a country-wide distribution network based on the mail coaches and the turnpike roads, which delivered national newspapers to every town and city in the land, every morning. His son, also named William Henry, joined his father as a partner on his twenty-first birthday in 1846, when the firm changed its name again to W.H. Smith and Sons. By this time, horse-drawn mail coaches were giving way to the railways. The younger William Henry was perfectly placed to transfer the business to the new technology, realising that the age of steam offered a faster and more reliable means of delivering newspapers nationwide. He worked hard to build good working relationships with the various railway companies, using the fierce competition between them to his advantage.

The next step, which was a logical progression of thought, was to sell newspapers and other reading material to the men and women who travelled the railway routes. Passengers were making more than a million journeys every week by the 1850s, and it was much easier to read a newspaper in a train than when riding inside a stagecoach. It was not a new idea. At many railway stations, there were *ad hoc* vendors, some of them being disabled or retired railway workers, selling a variety of products, but these were largely unregulated, and much of the reading matter was of poor quality, or out-of-date, and even salacious in content. William Henry Smith saw an opportunity for a well-managed and reputable news vending operation, and opened his first stall at Euston station on 1 November 1848.

The company grew rapidly alongside the expanding railway network. Within twenty years, W.H. Smith bookstalls were a familiar sight across the entire country, not only at mainline stations but on many more rural secondary routes as well. The scruffy ill-kempt vendor selling well-thumbed second-hand newspapers was an image from the past. In its place, Smith produced inexpensive reprints of books that were out of copyright which became known as his 'yellow books'. In time, these were printed on the company's own presses. Other publishers brought out their own series of books, including travel companions and travel guides, specifically for the railway market. William Henry, a religious man with a strong sense of morality, censored every title and even vetted the advertisements that were displayed on the frontages of his stalls.

Alongside the retail operation, warehouses were acquired in Birmingham, Manchester, Liverpool and Dublin to reinforce the company's distribution network. Such was the dominance of the company, when in 1905, two of the major railway companies decided to increase the rental paid for retail sites at stations, W.H. Smith opened 150 new shops on roads leading to the stations, thus ending their reliance on their relationships with the big railway operators, and initiating their move into Britain's High Streets.

William Henry also had political aspirations. He became an MP in 1868, and served in several Conservative governments as a minister. He retired from the company in 1874 to devote more time to his political career. When he died in 1891, his widow was created Viscountess Hambleden, and his son, who took over the company, became the second Viscount Hambleden.

Henry Curry

The backbone of the nineteenth century economy of many Midland and Northern towns and cities was the textile industry. It needed other industries such as dyeing and machinery manufacture, and together they provided mass employment and acted as a catalyst for entrepreneurs who went on to apply their skills and knowledge to new businesses. In Leicester, the foundation stone of the large St Margaret's Works of Nathaniel Corah and Sons was laid in 1865. Nathaniel had begun his manufacturing career as a framework knitter on a Leicestershire farm. St Margaret's was the first factory in the town built with integrated steam power. Steam did away with the vagaries of water-powered systems but the maintenance of the steam engines and associated machinery was essential to enable uninterrupted production, and required many mechanics.

Henry Curry was born in 1850 and became one of the army of young men who took on that vital role. At that time, the company was also known as Cooper, Corah and Sons, following the appointment of John Harris Cooper, one of Thomas Corah's former apprentices, as a principal of the company.

Many of the men and women who worked at Corah and the other factories by the side of the River Soar and the Grand Union Canal in Leicester lived in a densely-populated area that took its name from Wharf Street which connected the town with the wharf. Either side of this highway was constructed a maze of streets, lanes, and courts. This was a very poor area where many families lived in extreme poverty, but a redeeming feature of the presence of the giant Corah enterprise, which by the 1800s was employing over 1,000 people, was their enlightened policy of caring for their workforce and offering wages well above those of other local companies.

Henry Curry married Constance Mitchell in March 1870 and started a family. They were to have ten children, eight surviving to adulthood. Constance's family home was in Garden Street, just beyond the Wharf Street area but still in St Margaret's ward, and she was born to a family which, like many, had travelled widely in search of work. By the age of eleven, she was working as a hose seamer with her elder sister. Her parents' occupation is described as 'stocking weavers' in the 1861 census and by then they had moved to nearby 52 Lewin Street, less than ten minutes' walk from the Corah factory.

One year after that census, in Lee Street, another of the narrow back-to-back terraces in the same area, Joseph Merrick, sometimes referred to as the 'Elephant Man' was born. Lee Street and Lewin Street were demolished in

1954 as part of Leicester's post-war slum clearance programme but Joseph Merrick was to be remembered in the 1980 film directed by David Lynch and starring the late John Hurt.

Henry Curry found it difficult to provide for his growing family solely from his wages at Corah and began taking on additional work. Making use of his mechanical knowledge, he began constructing bicycles for the Leicester Tricycle Company. His skills and apparent managerial abilities enabled him to join the company. In the 1881 census, he describes his occupation as 'fitter, tricycle works', but he went on to assume a management position at a time when the company was pushing forward the design of bicycles in a growing and competitive market.

The company developed a folding bicycle that received an enthusiastic review in the *Wheel World Advertiser* in January 1882 and provides an intriguing glimpse into the world of Victorian cycling:

We think their tricycles somewhat peculiar in appearance – nothing objectionable – far from it, only they strike the visitor as being uncommon in construction. We first noticed their 'Patent Safety Folding Tricycle.' The operation of folding or unfolding this machine occupies a very few minutes, and when closed will pass through the narrowest possible doorway. When unfolded and ready for use the machine is perfectly firm and rigid. The treadles in this machine act through what is known as ' Kirby's Patent Differential Gear' which divides the power equally between the two driving wheels, either when running straight or making sharp turns. This machine, unlike all others, is mounted from behind, and as there is a bar in front it is impossible for the rider to be thrown forwards; at the same time escape is easy from behind in case of danger, and the very step on which he treads acts as a partial brake. Mounting as well as dismounting can be performed while the machine is in motion. This machine (like all made by this firm) is fitted with 'Kirby's Patent Balanced Brake,' most conveniently situated, and which may be applied instantly to the fullest extent without upsetting the machine.

Curry was working on these technical improvements as well as supplying a steady demand for the 'ordinary bicycle', otherwise known as the Penny Farthing, and he was still working shifts at Corah. Finally, in 1884, at the age of thirty-four years, he and Constance decided to go into business as bicycle manufacturers. By this time, they had moved from Hazel Street (which led to the far more famous Filbert Street, the home from 1891 of Leicester City Football Club). They set up business in their garden shed at 44 Painter Street, close to the Corah factory in the shadow of St Mark's Church. Painter Street is now the entrance to the campus of Leicester College.

It was a hand-to-mouth operation. Curry needed payment for one bicycle to fund the purchase of parts to build the next one, and he was only completing one bicycle each week. At this stage Henry's business skills came to the fore. The potential bicycle market was massive and growing, and Leicester was at the forefront of development. There are claims that the pneumatic tyre was invented in Leicester before being developed by Dunlop. Sturgess, a major motor group in Leicestershire today, began with its founder, Walter Sturgess, selling bicycles from his corner shop off Leicester's Narborough Road, including his innovative 'Austral', which added a trailer behind the bicycle.

Curry caught the spirit and dynamism of the moment and saw the potential to modernise the bicycle, which was becoming a popular form of utilitarian and recreational transport. He secured premises at 28 Painter Street, just a few doors away from his home, where he had the space to produce up to twenty-five bicycles every week. At the same time, he brought his sons, James and Edwin, into the business. Henry, the younger son, joined in 1896. He added the new pneumatic tyres (which increased his sales ten-fold) to his products, and developed bicycles marketed for safety, just ahead of rival developers in nearby towns such as Coventry.

Just four years later, he had acquired enough capital – or perhaps the self-confidence – to open his first shop at 271 Belgrave Gate, less than five minutes' walk from his home. The move was influenced by the inconvenience of potential customers calling at his small factory. He moved to larger premises at 296 Belgrave Gate in 1900 and subsequently to 287 Belgrave Gate. When the Leicester Haymarket Shopping Centre was built in 1972/73, a plaque was erected at the junction of Haymarket and the clock tower, commemorating Curry's first retail premises.

A new company was formed in 1897 called H. Curry and Sons. James, Edwin and Henry (junior) were made directors on equal footing with their father. The youngest son, Albert, was just ten years old but was also involved at his request. Net profits in the following two years rose to the equivalent today of more than £100,000. The business expanded further, acquiring premises in Halford Street and Rutland Street, and, in 1907, setting up a head office and wholesale warehouse in Belvoir Street in the town centre.

The Halford Street association involved co-operation with Frederick Rushbrooke, a businessman from Birmingham who had set up a bicycle manufacturing business in that street. This became the Halford Cycle Company Ltd, the forerunner of today's Halfords retail chain.

The expansion continued. A new factory in Marlow Road, Leicester, was incorporated into the business in 1914 and larger office premises in Stamford Street were purchased in 1916. Another factory was established in Linden Street in 1918. In the same year, Curry's went to the capital by setting up a head office in London in the heart of the city. In less than twenty-five years, a one-man business in the garden shed of a Leicester slum had become a nationally-recognised industrial player.

Henry Curry retired in 1909. In the 1911 census, he described himself as a 'retired bicycle manufacturer'. His four sons continued to extend their father's business. He died in 1916. The sons carried the business forward, opening stores across the East Midlands in Leicestershire, Nottinghamshire and Lincolnshire.

After the First World War, the company began to broaden its product range. Currys continued to sell bicycles and accessories, although it stopped manufacturing them in 1932. Henry Curry had always purchased from companies that produced quality products, and these, such as Lucas (lamps) and Dunlop, were to become familiar household names. By 1927, they had acquired the Campion Cycle Company and were also making and selling a variety of electrical goods including wireless receivers and gramophones.

The company continued as a family enterprise until 1984 when it was taken over by Dixons. In many High Streets, the two shops had traded side-by-side and offered very similar product lines. Dixons had begun in the 1930s as a photographic studio and retailer and had also diversified into electrical goods. After many takeovers and changes in branding, the group became DSG Retail PLC. In the United Kingdom and Ireland, the group began merging Currys stores with their PC World chain, opening their first merged 'megastore' in Fulham in 2009 with the name Currys PC World.

Michael Marks and Thomas Spencer

It is a story often told, and is probably the most well-known history of any High Street brand. It begins in Russia with the mass emigration of Polish Jews to escape persecution. One of those who left was Michael Marks, who came to England in the 1880s and settled in Leeds where there was already a Jewish community. He came to an arrangement with a local wholesaler and began selling sewing accessories such as pins, needles and cotton, door to door.

In 1884, having raised sufficient finance, Marks set up a market stall in Kirkgate in Leeds, with the imaginative and simple concept of selling all his goods at one price – one penny. On his stall was the slogan 'Don't ask the price. It's a penny.' His strategy matched the concept of a market where customers expect to deal and come away with a bargain. He also realised that in England, working class wages were beginning to rise, enabling families to buy commodities other than simply food for sustenance.

Marks married in 1884. His wife, Hannah Cohen, came from the same area of Russia as his family's roots. They had two children. In the 1891 census, they are recorded as living in Great George Street in Wigan, and he was describing himself as a 'smallwear dealer'. His business developed by establishing further stalls in the markets in nearby towns, and two years later he moved his family to better accommodation in Manchester's Cheetham Hill. Here, on the ground floor beneath their living quarters, he opened his first shop in 1894. Shortly afterwards came the pivotal moment when he met Thomas Spencer. Spencer was a Yorkshireman, born in 1852 in Skipton, a market town in the heart of the Yorkshire Dales. He began his business career as an apprentice to a draper, worked his way up to becoming a manager of the business owned by Isaac Dewhirst, and later transferred his skills to being a cashier or book-keeper. They formed a partnership with joint funds of £753.

Dewhirst is a distinguished name in textile manufacturing, founded in 1880 and still producing men's and women's' fashionwear in the twenty-first century. It is claimed that Michael Marks set up his first 'penny bazaar' with a loan of £5 from Dewhirst, and it is through this connection that Marks was introduced to Thomas Spencer.

As history now informs us, the partnership flourished. The running of the business was split between Spencer, who managed the office and warehouse, and Marks, who continued to run the market stalls. Spencer had developed some important contacts while working for Isaac Dewhirst and these allowed him to get the best prices for goods by dealing directly with the manufacturers. A chain of shops followed in quick succession in Manchester, Birmingham, Liverpool, Middlesbrough, Sheffield, Bristol, Hull, Sunderland and Cardiff, followed by Bradford, Leicester, Northampton, Preston, and Swansea, seven stores in London and a warehouse which was constructed in Derby Street, Manchester. The business became public in 1903 by which time its value was £15,000 and Marks and

Spencer were trading from more than thirty-six shops. Spencer died in 1905, and Michael Marks in 1907, but the partnership continued in name as their sons took charge.

It was Simon Marks, son of Michael, who turned the business into a formidable national brand. He joined the family concern as a young man, achieving a directorship at the age of twenty-six years, and becoming Chairman just two years later. Under his leadership, Marks and Spencer became tuned in to the importance of attractive and professional window displays, and of proper stock control and sales records. He also gave the company a clear direction, and established a precedent in working with suppliers to reduce costs but guarantee the quality of the products.

The leading supplier in those days was Nathaniel Corah and Sons, a large textile company that had developed from a single cotton frame on a farm in north-west Leicestershire. Simon Marks sent Israel Seiff to Corah's to discuss a ground-breaking partnership. Seiff had married Rebecca, the daughter of Michael Marks, and was very much part of the family dynasty. Corah's were delighted to receive him. They saw a close relationship with Marks and Spencer as vital to their future business, although they were concerned at how the other retailers they supplied would react.

Seiff was also pleased that his mission to Leicester was a success. It is said that after leaving Corah's' head office, his chauffeur headed for the London Road via Leicester's principal shopping street, called Gallowtree Gate. He saw an area of derelict waste land, the result of bombing during the Second World War, and announced to his driver, there and then, that he would, in celebration, buy the land and build a store. Marks and Spencer still trade from this location, and at a time when they, in keeping with other major retail chains, began focussing on large stores in out-of-town shopping centres, M&S expanded the Leicester Gallowtree Gate building. It is further claimed, although not substantiated, that whereas the company sold off its freehold assets many years ago, it still owns the Leicester site.

The landmark agreement was the beginning of a relationship which allowed M&S to control every stage in the manufacture of a garment, from design through to even programming the machines in their suppliers' factories across the country, first by using punched tape systems, and later by sending computer programs overnight from their headquarters. It also led to serious problems for many of the company's suppliers, who had to gear their entire operation to satisfy M&S's demand, including disconnecting with many previous buyers of the products. The demands for perfection meant that whole consignments of goods could be refused by M&S, leading to loss of income and cash-flow problems. It was one of those consignments that was sold on to Bill and Jean Adderley, coincidentally on Leicester Market just behind the shop front façades of Gallowtree Gate, from which the Dunelm (Mills) chain developed. Over the years, many smaller manufacturers went into receivership because M&S had a change of heart or lost faith in their products.

Although in recent years, M&S has suffered from a lack of identity and has become an indicator of how a business can be affected critically by incorrectly predicting future fashion trends, it is still a major High Street player and remains the fifth-largest retailer in the UK.

Frederick William Rushbrooke

The inherited skills and manufacturing experiences of both his parents gave Frederick Rushbrooke the ability to found Halfords, initially as a manufacturer of bicycle parts. He was born in Willenhall, Staffordshire, on 9 December 1861, one of eleven children to be born to Joshua and Harriet Rushbrooke.

Joshua Rushbrooke had relocated to the West Midlands from Coddenham in Suffolk. A family by that name is recorded as living at Lime Kiln Farm in the village, and his father lies buried in Coddenham churchyard. In Willenhall, he was apprenticed to a miller and later worked at the steam-powered Union Mill in Wolverhampton. Deciding to establish his own business, Joshua acquired a mill at Birchells near Walsall, but was forced to abandon it when a blast furnace was built nearby. With the compensation he received, he bought another mill, located on the corner of Union Street and Stafford Street in Willenhall, which had been operated by John Austin.

Attached to this mill was a grocery and bakery business. In 1844, Austin began issuing tokens to his workers, which could be used to purchase goods at his shop and other retailers in the area. These had an exchange rate of one farthing (960 in one pound). Joshua Rushcliffe continued this practice, which was relatively commonplace at the time, selling his 'Rushcliffe farthings' to fellow traders at the rate of five shillings worth (240 coins) for 4/9d, thus offering twelve 'free' coins per each transaction. When new bronze coinage was introduced in 1860, privately-issued tokens became illegal. Rushbrooke took back considerable quantities of his farthings, melted them down and re-used the metal, allegedly without making a loss on the process. Austin left Willenhall and moved to Allscott near Wellington, where he founded a business manufacturing artificial manure.

Joshua was a Free Church preacher, first with the Baptist church and later with the Wesleyan Church in Union Street, near to his business. It was there that he married Harriett Tildesley from another staunch Methodist family. Their marriage in 1849 was the first to be solemnised in the church. They were to have eleven children. One of his sons, also named Joshua, succeeded him to run the family business in 1863. Another son, Frederick, went on to found Halfords.

Other members of the Tildesley family were locksmiths, another of the staple industries of the area. In 1830, James Carpenter and John Young of Willenhall invented a rimlock which had a perpendicular action and became the forerunner of today's mortice lock. It became known as 'Carpenter's lift-up Lock' and reinvigorated the local industry. Carpenter built the Summerfield Works, a large factory in New Road, Willenhall to manufacture this product. His daughter married James Tildesley. Tildesley later inherited the business which then became Carpenter and Tildesley, and in due course, Tildesley became the sole owner. James Tildesley's ancestor, Richard Tildesley (1798–1858), had opened the first brass foundry in Willenhall. His eldest daughter was Harriett.

Frederick became a wholesale ironmonger in Birmingham, founding his business in 1892 as 'Hardware Merchants and Manufacturers' Agents – Importers and Exporters the World Over.' From the outset, Rushbrooke placed an emphasis on the display of merchandise and a clear pricing policy.

On 16 August 1896, he married Lily Jenks Wilkinson. They had a son, Donald, who was born in 1905, and two daughters, Crystal and Janet. In 1902, he opened a branch of his business in Halford Street in Leicester, calling it the Halford Cycle Shop. Family records claim that he was often seen riding a penny farthing bicycle for leisure. By 1906, he had converted his Birmingham business of nine shops from wholesale to retail, and had adopted the trading name of Halfords. Halford Street relates to a Leicestershire family, and was probably named in memory of Sir Charles Halford who had inherited his family's estate at Wistow in south Leicestershire but died without a descendant in 1780. Halford bequeathed his estates to his cousin Henry Vaughan, whose family were for many years associated with St Martin's Church in Leicester.

With its new name, the company expanded rapidly, opening over one hundred stores by 1910. In the 1911 Census, Frederick is as living at 'Onneley', Anchorage Road, Sutton Coldfield and his occupation is 'Managing Director of a cycle company'. Donald Rushbrooke joined the Halfords business in

1923 and later, became the company's Chairman. By this time, Halfords had begun to diversify, responding to the growing demand for motor vehicle and motorbike accessories, and wireless receivers.

In 1927, Frederick bought Burcot Grange, a country house in Bromsgrove which, in 1937, he gave to the Birmingham and Midland Eye Hospital to use as a facility for treating eye infections in children caused by their exposure to the pollution caused by the heavy industries of the area. Minimal alterations were made to the house, which had been built in 1890. The rooms were spacious and were converted into wards. The butler's pantry became a surgery, and a playroom was created in the former conservatory. The facility closed in 1983 and was then used as a community hospital for older people who were waiting for places in care homes. The building is now a privately-operated care home.

Lily Jenks Wilkinson died in 1938. Frederick died in 1953. Two years' later, on 12 March 1955, the company suffered the trauma of their headquarters in Corporation Street, Birmingham, being destroyed by fire, despite being located opposite a fire station. The company was back in operation in just ten days, and returned to the site in 1959.

James Kemsey Wilkinson

In 1930, a young man of twenty-four years and his fiancée opened a small hardware shop in a Victorian-built suburb of Leicester in the English East Midlands. He was James Kemsey Wilkinson, and his shop became the first Wilkinson Cash Store. In the first week of trading, the couple managed a turnover of £23.

James Kemsey Wilkinson was born on Thursday 6 December 1906 to William and Rosetta Wilkinson, née Roebuck, at 89 Wellington Road at the family home in the Handsworth area of Birmingham. The once quiet street is now the A4040, near to the busy Gravelly Hill intersection of the M6 and the A38, more familiarly known as Spaghetti Junction. The modern Wilko store at the One Stop Shopping Centre at Walsall Road in Perry Barr is less than a mile away.

The Wilkinson family's roots for several generations were in Yorkshire, principally in the Bradford area. The men of the family were mainly employed in textile manufacturing, following the industry from its cottage-based origins into the mills and factories of the towns. Later, the family moved south to follow similar employment opportunities in the Black Country of the Midlands.

In the 1871 census, his father, William Harwick Wilkinson, described his occupation as a 'brass founder's assistant', and as an 'ironmonger and china dealer' in the 1911 census. William was born in September 1859 in Wolverhampton and died in March 1928 in West Bromwich. James's grandfather, John, came from Kippax in Yorkshire and owned a smelting business, which he sold so he could invest in property. He purchased a row of terraced houses and lived on the rent income. James's great-grandfather, also named William, came from Bradford.

James, or JK, as he was to be known familiarly by family and friends, left home at the age of sixteen, only a few years after his father's death. He gained some retail experience by working for the chemists, Timothy Whites, on the south coast, which at the time sold hardware as well as pharmaceuticals. He then followed in his father's footsteps, first working for an architectural ironmonger in Birmingham before moving to Leicester to be employed by the wealthy ironmonger Herbert Pochin, whose factory was in Granby Street near the city centre.

JK moved to Leicester because the city was ranked at the time as one of the wealthiest places in Europe. Pochin's were based first at 28 Granby Street in the city centre but by 1912 had expanded and had moved up the road to occupy 30 and 32 Granby Street, listed in the street directories as 'builders and furnishing ironmongers, cutlers, silversmiths' where they remained until the 1970s. A painted ghost sign is still visible on the side wall of No 30.

At about the time JK was employed by Pochin's, it is recorded that Redmile Parish Church in north Leicestershire purchased a set of six 'Miller' lamps from them. These very stylised lamps were invented by the famous American Miller company based in Connecticut, making use of the recently-discovered benefits and applications of Kerosene. Edward Miller licensed his products, allowing them to be manufactured and distributed worldwide. It is, therefore, possible that Pochin's were tooled up to make these products when the young JK was working there.

According to his son, JK parted company with Pochin's because his ideas for new products were not taken up by the management. Instead, JK decided to go into business in his own right.

JK and his fiancée Louisa Mary Cooper opened their first shop, the Wilkinson Cash Store, at 151 Charnwood Street in Leicester in 1930. They were married at St Peter's Church in Highfields, Leicester, on 22 October 1934. St Peter's, an impressive church, designed in the Gothic Revival style during the Victorian expansion of Leicester by the Essex-born architect

George Edmund Street, was one of two churches serving the Charnwood Street area. Although Highfields was principally a middle-class residential area, it also included a range of different manufacturing industries, including the well-known organ-builder, Stephen Taylor, and Sons Ltd, so it is possible that James and Mary heard that instrument, built just a few streets away in 1910, during their marriage ceremony. Family legend tells that JK and Mary were married at 8.00 am and were back to open the shop by 11.00 am.

Donald, JK's elder brother, had stayed with the family in Handsworth and had also set up a hardware business consisting of four shops trading as Wilkinson (Handsworth) Brothers. In the early days of JK's Leicester shop, his brothers helped provide stock. Eventually, two of the Handsworth shops would become Wilkinson stores. The family did not live above their shop, but in Scraptoft Lane on the eastern outskirts of Leicester. Later, they acquired warehousing nearby in Brighton Road and moved to a new residence in Syston, north of the city.

Charnwood Street was built in the 1870s as part of the Victorian expansion of Leicester along the Humberstone Road, the main route from the city to Peterborough and the east coast. According to local historian Cynthia Brown, the land was sold to the Leicester Freehold Land Society, which was set up to enable working men to acquire a vote in elections by becoming holders of land with a value of at least forty shillings a year. Charnwood Street was divided into 720 such lots. The land had been purchased from the Farnham family, whose seat was in Quorn in the Charnwood area of Leicestershire.

The Humberstone Road area was characterised by many rows of small red-brick terraced houses. Beyond the western end of Charnwood Street were the much-feared Union Workhouse and the Midland Railway station and its associated sidings. Although this was very much a working-class neighbourhood, it was not as impoverished as some areas such as the nearby Wharf Street where there was much poverty and where the most frequently-visited premises were those of the pawnbrokers. Every house was provided with a small garden, but outside toilets were shared, one between two houses.

A highly-successful oral history project has recorded the memories of people who lived in the network of little streets surrounding Charnwood Street, and many testify to a close-knit supportive community and to a happy if tough childhood.

Certainly, the little shops along Charnwood Street catered for all the needs of the neighbourhood. When JK opened his shop, he took over premises that had been used by Merrick Crowley who described himself as a 'hard confectioner'. Before Mr Crowley, the shop had been owned by John Elson, a milk dealer. On one side, his neighbours included a butcher, a carpenter, and a toy dealer; on the other side was a dairyman, hairdresser, a milliner and a greengrocer. Charnwood Street also boasted chemists, wine merchants, several fish and chip shops, a music shop and even a brewery. In total, in 1930 there were no less than 250 separate establishments in the street, almost all of them providing goods or services, including several which may have provided JK with competition, such as William Dalton at No 233 who was a 'hardware dealer' and Mrs Elizabeth Wood at No 182 who described herself as an ironmonger.

Behind the shop ran Occupation Road or Row, a narrow street a service lane and a place of adventure for local children. To them, it was known as 'Occy Day'. The Wilkinson's shop had a wooden floor with a counter which ran the length of the building back to Occupation Road. Customers remember that the shop always smelt of paraffin and firelighters. Tony Wilkinson, JK's son, still remembers the smells. He also recalls a hatch in the floor which led down to cellars where his father kept his stock. Pots and pans hung outside the frontage. During rationing in the Second World War, JK struck up a longstanding friendship with the owner of a nearby wholesaler, sharing petrol coupons to collect stock for their businesses.

Key to the survival of any shop in local communities such as Charnwood Street was the reputation of their owners. Shopkeepers such as JK developed a reputation for honesty and fair trading.

JK opened a second store in Wigston Magna on the outskirts of Leicester in 1932. In 1937, James and Mary's first child, Tony, was born. In the same year, JK's elder brother John joined him as a director of the company, managing the business during the war years. In 1940, JK signed up and served in the Royal Armoured Corps and later as a Bevin Boy (coal miner). Known to his staff as 'Mr John', he stayed with the company until his death in 1956.

The original shop relocated a few years later to 159 Charnwood Street. JK's new neighbours were a grocer and a hairdresser. He remained there until the street was demolished in the early 1970s, by which time the company had twenty-eight stores with an annual turnover of £2.4 million.

Tony Wilkinson was educated in Leicester and at Repton School in Derbyshire. He undertook National Service in the Royal Navy, spending two years at sea, mainly in Iceland and Norway, before returning to the United Kingdom and working for F.W. Woolworth. He returned to the family business in 1960 to become branch manager of the company's new store in Leicester's Charles Street at the age of thirty. At the time, this was the company's largest store. It relocated to even larger premises further along Charles Street in 1999, and in 2008 was one of the first Wilko stores to receive the company's corporate rebranding.

In 1963, the first Wilkinson store outside Leicester was opened in Melton Mowbray. In the same year, the original Wigston Magna shop also expanded and moved to increase its floor space. The company now has over 400 stores and a turnover close to £4 million per week.

JK was clearly a man driven by a desire to succeed in life and to achieve great things through hard work and by believing in himself and his ideas. He was not an inventor or a marketing man. He was committed to his business, and his focus was on supply and demand. The secret of his success lay in providing goods that people wanted and needed to buy, at a fair price. It seems he made very few mistakes in those early years in Leicester, setting up a wholesale business to support his shops (using his wife's maiden name, L.M. Cooper), and establishing a reputation for fair dealing. He is remembered as a shrewd businessman, good with 'numbers' but perhaps not so comfortable when dealing with people on a personal basis.

His son recalls that JK sometimes tended to shout at people, even his customers! But JK also said on record that, back in the impoverished 30s, 'I always like to look people in the eye and know in my heart that they are getting a good deal.'

Chapter Five

The Big Names

An insult is not intended by introducing some of the big names in present-day retailing as 'shopkeepers'. They could be described in many ways, reflecting their multi-faceted lives, which in some cases include research, politics, academia and even appearances on television as celebrities; but at their heart, they are shopkeepers.

Some of the big names remain remote and shadowy figures. Jeyes Fluid is sold in huge quantities in shops, garden centres and DIY stores, and is named after its inventor, but John Jeyes is a relatively unknown figure in either manufacture or retailing. He was born in 1817, became a chemical manufacturer and invented his famous disinfectant, patenting it in 1877. His name is also applied to an award for chemistry in relation to the environment, awarded every two years by the Royal Society of Chemists. He died in 1892 and his product is still sold in over sixty countries. Original Jeyes memorabilia such as tins and bottles bearing the familiar logo are sought after by collectors and command high prices.

Jeyes Chemists, a small pharmacy in the Northamptonshire village of Earls Barton, has a direct historical connection with John Jeyes. In October 2011, a Heritage and Pharmacy Museum opened which explained the link to the man who invented the fluid. The Jeyes pharmacy business was founded in The Drapery in Northampton by Philadelphus and John Jeyes. Philadelphus was John's brother and appears as an even more shadowy figure in this story, but carrying the brand name in Northampton until as recently as 1969; and in 1981 his great grandson David Jeyes opened the chemists in Earls Barton. For much of its long history, Jeyes has been based in Norfolk, but the family's roots and the pharmacy business of today remains in Northamptonshire.

Of course, there are very few individuals who are as successful as Jesse Boot, or Michael Marks and Thomas Spencer. Many thousands of men and women are shopkeepers, and are content to run a business which provides for themselves and their family, without yearning to become millionaires and to see their name in lights in High Streets and shopping malls across the country. So, what makes the difference? Was Nottingham's Jesse Boot, for instance, simply lucky, or of the right time in the right place? Or was he an exceptional person with special gifts and thought patterns?

Research has shown that shopkeepers as a defined group do regard themselves as belonging to a unique identifiable class. Although they work for a living, often enduring long hours on their feet, and, at first for a low income, they do not see themselves as 'working class'. Much of their work before their businesses are established and they can hire employees, is manual: packing and unpacking, lifting boxes, cleaning and maintaining their premises; but for many the distinction is that they are their own masters, and they have their own domain. Apart from statutory and legal responsibilities such as paying tax and meeting health and safety requirements, shopkeepers have independence. They call the tune, make all the decisions, and live with the consequences – good and bad.

Most shopkeepers describe themselves as 'middle class'. This independence of thought and action is one reason why they see themselves as separate from the working-class masses; and shopkeepers also hold their own capital, manage their own economy and keep financial records, all with a degree of autonomy.

The Victorians talked about a 'shopocracy', being a clearly identifiable group of people who shared certain political ideologies. In the nineteenth century, many were enthusiastically involved in radical politics, and supported policies that would benefit the working classes, although in some cases, the motivation was possibly the realisation that if the working-classes were paid more, they could spend more. They also espoused ideals based on self-responsibility and 'standing on your own two feet'. The same was expected of their staff, as well as total loyalty and trustworthiness. The way the shop was laid out, the window displays, even the colour of the external paintwork, were all extensions of the shopkeeper's personality; and his or her employees had to follow suit and blend in. As businesses expanded, and additional shops and stores were opened, the need to maintain the brand identity became increasingly important, and more difficult to manage. Some family businesses such as Fenwicks maintained this control by appointing family members as the overall managers of their stores. David Lewis in Liverpool connected several of his stores to his office by using radio transmissions to instil a sense of corporate responsibility.

The most successful 'big names' are highly driven and extremely motivated. Many were still in their teenage years when they launched their businesses, having ended their education at the age of fourteen years. They grew up fast. It was not uncommon for many to have worked in their parents' shop from the age of ten. They were also willing to take risks at a time when debtors could be thrown into prison and the penalties for other relatively petty crimes included transportation. As a result, the early shopkeepers often lived on the premises or even slept in their shops, and worked long into the night, keeping their financial records up-to-date, cleaning and re-stocking.

In more recent times, several of the wealthiest retail entrepreneurs remember times when they were forced to mortgage their home – or their parents' home – to keep afloat, or to go through years of experimentation and research, trial and error, to design a brand-new product.

Charles Henry Harrod and Charles Digby Harrod

In any listing of the greatest department stores across the world, which must include Le Bon Marche in Paris, Bergdorf Goodman in New York, as well as Galeries Lafayette, also in Paris, and GUM in Moscow, which predates the Russian Revolution, Harrods of London has always featured prominently, along with Selfridges.

Charles Henry Harrod began trading at the age of twenty-five, opening a draper and haberdashery shop at 228 Borough High Street in the London suburb of Southwark, perhaps making use of the proximity of the warehouses along the River Thames to procure his goods. The site of his first shop is now (in 2017) occupied by the Turkish restaurant, Tas Café, which stands in the shadow of the Shard, and within a short walk of St Paul's Cathedral. It has been renumbered to become 72 Borough High Street. It was here that Harrod married Elizabeth Digby in 1830 and the banns were published in St George's Roman Catholic Cathedral. He was born in Lexden near Tiptree in Essex in 1799 and as a young man, worked as a miller in Clacton-on-Sea, some twenty miles from his home. He moved to London in 1834.

His small business developed, and included a brief partnership, but by 1832, he had launched a new venture in Clerkenwell in the City as a grocer. Two years later, having moved to the capital, he set up a wholesale grocery enterprise in Stepney, with a focus on tea, taking advantage of the ending of the East India Company's monopoly; but by 1851, capitalising on the commercial activity generated by the Great Exhibition of that year, he acquired a small site at 8 Middle Queen's Buildings, later to be renumbered as 105 Brompton Road, which is where the famous store of today was later constructed. In preparation for the exhibition, many new buildings were erected along the Cromwell Road and South Kensington, which transformed the Knightsbridge area from slums into the fashionable district of today. Thus, Harrods began in a single room with two shop assistants and a messenger boy, and achieved a turnover approaching twenty pounds a week.

A story which was discovered by his great-great grandson, Robin Harrod, and documented in a recent account of Harrods, published in 2017, describes how Charles Henry once narrowly escaped transportation for handling stolen goods. Court records indicate that Richard Moran, a porter at another grocer's shop, Booth, Ingledew and Company, stole 112lb of currants and handed them to Harrod. A contemporary press report stated that:

Richard Moran was indicted for stealing, on April 2, 1836, 112lb weight of currants, value £3, 5s, and one bag, value 6d, the goods of John Healey Booth and others, his masters. And Charles Harrod for feloniously receiving the same, well knowing them to be the same, well knowing them to be stolen, against the statute.

Moran was convicted and transported to Sarah in Tasmania. Harrod petitioned the judiciary, and instead was given a sentence of one year's imprisonment. The petition read:

He has a wife and two children, the eldest only three years and a half and the youngest a little more than a year old, both, as well as his most unfortunate partner, in delicate health, and threatened with the most unfortunate consequences, should your unhappy petitioner be removed from this country for the term of seven years. Your unfortunate petitioner therefore, in the deepest affliction, most humbly implores of His Most Gracious Majesty's Clemency that he may not be removed from this country, but that the punishment be moderated so as to give him some hope of being restored to his family, and enable him to show his grateful sense of the mercy extended to him, by the propriety of his conduct for the remainder of his life.

While he was serving his sentence, his brother, William Harrod, who was a jeweller in Southwark, ran the grocery business.

It was Charles Digby Harrod, the son of the founder, who expanded the business and developed it into a department store by broadening the range of goods on sale. He bought the business from his father who continued to work in the store for several years. Charles Digby added perfumes, stationery and proprietary medicines to his father's fruit and vegetables.

The involvement of the wealthy businessman and philanthropist Edgar Israel Cohen must be recognised in the expansion of Harrod's business. Cohen was a sponge merchant, born and bred in London, who also imported Havana cigars. It was his business experience that helped convert Harrods into a limited company. Cohen also founded the London General Motor Cab Company which introduced the first motorised cab to the capital's streets. He became known as the 'Taxi-cab King', owning at one stage in his colourful career, no less than 2,000 taxis. He was also the financier behind such commercial retail inventions as the cigarette machine and the zip fastener.

By 1880, Charles Digby had taken over adjacent buildings and was managing a staff of more than one hundred. However, weeks before Christmas in 1883, his store was destroyed by fire. The St James Gazette on Friday 7 December published a graphic account of the incident headlined 'Serious Fires in London':

> Two serious fires occurred in London daring the night [the second] proved to be the premises of Mr. Charles Digby Harrod, who has an extensive business as general dealer and grocer at 101, 103, and 105, Brompton-Road. The fire was discovered by a policeman shortly before one o'clock this morning; but, owing to the inflammable nature of the stock, the flames spread so rapidly that the buildings, which were of four floors, were burnt out, notwithstanding that a large number of steam-engines, manuals, and stand pipes were brought to bear upon it.
>
> The back of the adjoining premises, Nos. 107 and 109, were also partly burned out; and in Queen's-Gardens, which adjoin No.109, some stabling was destroyed, but the horses were got out before the flames had reached there. At the back of Mr. Harrod's premises are cottages occupied by the poorer class of people, who hastily removed their furniture; but the damage done to these houses was not great. The fire continued to burn for some hours, but had been well got under by three o'clock.

Remarkably, Harrod Junior displayed his resilience by ensuring that all his customers' orders were fulfilled, finding temporary accommodation nearby, and generating a record profit by doing so. Fortunately, Harrod had made sure that his building and stock were fully insured. The store was rebuilt, and attracted the rich and famous who lived, worked or visited the area.

The business was floated on the Stock Market in 1889 and Harrod chose to sell his interest for £120,000. The flotation brought in a new management team which could procure the finance and investment necessary to build the business. After many decades of successful trading, it was purchased by the House of Fraser in 1959 and subsequently by the Fayed Brothers in 1985, but in 1994, it was separated from the parent company and regained its independent status.

Harrods was the first store in England to introduce an escalator. It was constructed of leather with rails of glass and mahogany. Those customers who survived the journey to the upper floors were provided with complimentary glasses of brandy to steady their nerves. During the Second World War, the store transformed itself from selling luxury goods to making uniforms, parachutes and parts for Lancaster bombers. Today, Harrods occupies in the region of one million square feet of sales space on its seven floors. At night it is illuminated by 12,000 lights. It has a higher revenue per square metre of retail floor space than any other store in the world, with 330 different departments, employing about 4,000 staff, and serves over 15 million customers every year. Charles Henry died on 31 March 1885 in Chiswick. His son, Charles Digby died on 15 August 1905 in Chelsea.

Harry Gordon Selfridge: an American in London

Harry Gordon Selfridge was the man who brought showbusiness into shop keeping, but although his name is now synonymous with wealth and considerable extravagance, he came from a family with limited means and which suffered distress and hardship. He amassed a fortune, but died penniless.

He was born in Ripon in Wisconsin, the town where the American Republican Party was founded. His father was a shopkeeper, and in 1858, just after Harry's birth, the family moved to Jackson in Michigan, where Robert Oliver Selfridge had acquired the general stores. Robert joined the Union Army at the outbreak of the American Civil War, and rose to the rank of major; but although receiving an honourable discharge, he abandoned his family and never returned home, leaving his wife, Lois, to bring up their three young sons.

More sadness followed when two of the Selfridge boys died, leaving Harry as Lois's only son. She secured work as a schoolteacher and added to her small income by painting greetings cards. She struggled at first, but later became headmistress of Jackson High School. Harry also helped to support his mother, even at a young age. He was delivering newspapers by the age of ten, and started work at a local store two years later. Remarkably, with his earnings the young boy then created a monthly magazine for boys, and made more money by selling advertising space. He left school formally at the age of fourteen to work in a local bank.

There followed a period of upheaval in which the course of Harry Selfridge's life changed on several occasions. He intended to join the Naval Academy at Annapolis in Maryland, but failed the entrance examination. Instead, he found work as a book keeper for a local furniture manufacturer, but the business closed only four months later. At this point, the young Selfridge left home, and moved to Grand Rapids where he began to work in the insurance industry.

Selfridge's acquisition of wealth began in 1876 when he asked one of his former employers to write a letter of commendation to a senior partner of one of the most successful department stores in Chicago. He began as a stock boy in the wholesale department, and rose through the ranks, finally becoming a partner in the firm. It was here that Harry Selfridge coined one of the most popular retailing catchphrases of all time, promoting pre-Christmas sales with the by-line 'only [ ] shopping days before Christmas.' It is also claimed that Selfridge or one of his colleagues created the other often-used comment that 'the customer is always right.'

Over the next twenty-five years he became a rich man, and connected to a wealthy Chicago family with his marriage to Rosalie Buckingham. They designed and built their own home by the side of Geneva Lake in Wisconsin, including extensive greenhouses and rose gardens. Throughout their married life, Lois Selfridge lived with them. It appears from his biographies that Selfridge was a restless spirit: a genius at creating wealth but easily tiring of his latest project or idea. He opened his own department store in 1904, but sold it (at a profit) only two months later. He then announced his 'retirement', spending time on his estate, and bought a steam yacht, which he very rarely used.

The retirement was short lived. Two years later, he and his wife visited London for a holiday. Selfridge saw that although London was a centre for commerce and culture, its department stores could not match the scale and stature of those in other capital cities across Europe, or even in Selfridge's own city of Chicago. He immediately invested heavily in his own store in Oxford Street, choosing a site at what was then the less-fashionable West End, directly opposite an entrance to the Bond Street underground station.

The store opened in March 1909. With it, Selfridge re-wrote the retailing text books. He viewed the process of selling from the customer's perspective, introducing the concept of 'retail therapy'. Shopping could be fun and pleasurable. Shops could be elegant. Customers could learn to identify a brand as fashionable, and even elite. Selfridge incorporated smart restaurants, reading rooms, special areas to receive American, European and 'colonial' customers, a First Aid room and even a quiet area called the Silence Room, which had gentle diffused lighting, acoustic treatment and soft plush furnishings to create a peaceful ambience. Every facet of the store was designed to encourage his customers to linger as long as possible so that his staff could assist them in their purchases. The showman in Selfridge helped immensely in creating the atmosphere that turned his store into an experience. He even persuaded the General Post Office to allocate the telephone number '1' to his store.

Selfridge had a clear view of his role as the head of a successful but complex business, which to a considerable degree relied on the competence of his staff. He often spoke of himself as 'the leader' rather than 'the boss'. In his words:

> The boss knows how it is done; the leader shows how. The boss drives his men; the leader coaches them. The boss inspires fear; the leader inspires enthusiasm. The boss says "Go"; the leader says "Let's go!"

Sadly, Selfridge's lifestyle outside of his office was to be his downfall. Rose died in the flu epidemic of 1918 and his mother, Lois, in 1924. From that time, he engaged in numerous affairs, gambled and lost a fortune, and lived to excess. In 1941, he was forced out of the company, having taken the business into debt with the banks. Harry Gordon Selfridge died on 8 May 1947 at the three-bedroom apartment which he rented in Putney, south-west London. He was 89 years old. He died destitute.

Despite his personal lifestyle problems, Selfridge was one of the great retail entrepreneurs of all time because of his never-failing ability to innovate. All present retail techniques connect to him. Some were very simple ideas such as locating the perfume counter inside the entrance establishing an immediate sense of wellbeing and comfort. He worked incessantly to stay ahead of his competitors, always watching them, and never allowing himself to relax:

> Whenever I may be tempted to slack up and let the business run for awhile on its own impetus, I picture my competitor sitting at a desk

in his opposition house, thinking and thinking with the most devilish intensity and clearness, and I ask myself what I can do to be prepared for his next brilliant move.

Many of his endless marketing projects were unusual and therefore guaranteed to catch the attention of the media and the public. These included displaying Louis Bleriot's aircraft after the first cross-channel flight in 1909, and arranging for John Logie Baird's first public demonstration of television to take place on the first floor of the store for the month of April in 1925. He also developed the roof of his store into an experience, making full use of the expansive views across London, building gardens, a mini golf course and even an all-girl fun club. In 1932, he installed a seismograph on the third floor of the building which recorded the Belgium earthquake of 1938.

Harry Gordon Selfridge was buried in the churchyard of St Mark's in the Dorset village of Highcliffe, near his wife and mother, but separated from them by two unmarked graves. A simple memorial headstone bears his name and dates. In 2013, when a television series was aired which told the story of Selfridge's life, a member of the church commented to the Daily Mail that it was 'a total shame and a disgrace that the grave of an enormously great man, be left without the due care and attention it so rightly deserves'.

Harry's grand creation in London's West End, still the second-largest retail store in the UK, was sold to David Lewis's Liverpool-based stores group, which in turn was acquired by the Sears Group. They were later purchased, in 2003, by Galen Weston in Canada for £598 million. Selfridge also opened sixteen smaller stores in Manchester and Birmingham and other towns and cities, which were acquired by the John Lewis Partnership.

Selfridge was often outspoken, and was a master at uttering quotable comments. One of his throwaway lines when talking about targeting products was wonderfully prophetic: 'All businesses need to be young forever. If your customer base ages with you, you're Woolworths.'

Harvey Nichols

The famous Harvey Nichols brand, referred to by many as simply 'Harvey Nick's', was formed by a partnership of two men, Benjamin Harvey and James Nichols, who were later to become related when Nichols married Harvey's niece. The company was founded in 1831 when Benjamin Harvey opened a linen shop at the corner of Sloane Street and Knightsbridge in London. Over the years that followed, he expanded, acquiring the neighbouring property and others, and in 1841 he took on James Nichols from Oxfordshire as an assistant, later to become a manager. It was in 1848 that Nichols married Anne Beale, Harvey's niece.

Harvey died in 1850, only three years after his son, Benjamin Charles, had been born. His wife, also named Anne, went into partnership with Nichols to form the now familiar Harvey Nichols and Co. brand. Anne Harvey died in 1872, and James Nichols one year later, leaving Benjamin Charles, still a young man in his thirties, as the sole owner of the company.

By 1874, Harvey Nichols occupied the entire block between Seville Street and Sloane Street. Benjamin decided to rebuild the properties as one large department store. The project took over five years, and shortly after completion in 1894, the area was renumbered, giving Harvey Nichols the address of 109–125 Knightsbridge. The impressive store was designed by Charles Stephens, who also designed Claridge's and Harrods. Stephens was responsible for several major redevelopments in London in the 1880s until his death in 1917, beginning with the rebuilding of Hans Place, immediately south of Harrods. He was also architect to the Belgravia Estates Ltd which was formed to redevelop the nearby area. He gained the contracts for redesigning and rebuilding Harrods, and for the construction of Claridge's in Mayfair in 1894. His grand designs, which are still impressive in scale, are described as of the Queen Anne style, and Harrods is regarded as the best example of his work.

Harvey Nichols was bought by Debenhams in 1920. Today, as well as their Knightsbridge store, close to their chief rival, Harrods, the company has stores in Leeds, Edinburgh, Birmingham, Manchester, Bristol and overseas.

John and Jesse Boot

A farmworker from beside the River Trent in Nottinghamshire founded the chain of chemist's shops which are today the market leaders in High Street pharmacies. John Boot was born in Radcliffe-on-Trent in 1815, and worked on the farms in the area until ill-health made him move to the centre of the city of Nottingham to seek a different occupation. He moved to Hockley Village, close to Nottingham's lace market, and home for centuries to the city's 'rag trade'. Although now the location of many upmarket restaurants and bars which have given it the title of 'the Soho of Nottingham', in the nineteenth century, Hockley Village was a very poor area.

John Boot's mother made herbal remedies which began to sell. He married Mary Wills, and they had two children, Jesse and Jane. It was in 1849 that the first Boots shop opened at 6 Goose Gate in Hockley, trading in medicines based on herbal concoctions. Many of these herbs and other plants he grew and harvested in the Meadows area of the city which at that time was open pastureland. Sadly, the items he made and sold were not able to improve John Boot's heath. He died in 1860 at the age of forty-five years, leaving Mary Boot to continue the business which changed its name to M & J Boot, Herbalists. Jesse Boot worked with his mother to maintain the business from the age of ten years, and left school at thirteen. However, he also began studying pharmacy part-time, and opened his own chemist's shop in 1877.

In 1885, a prolonged period of poor health led Boot to travel to the Channel Island of Jersey to recuperate, and it was there that he met Florence Rowe at the Wesleyan chapel. Despite his mother's opposition, they married in August 1886. The daughter of a bookseller and stationer, Florence had been born into retailing at her parents' shop in Queen Street, St Helier. The Rowe family lived above the shop, and Florence often worked behind the counter. In 1896, a Boots store was opened next door to the Rowes' book-shop. When Florence's father died in 1908, the two shops were amalgamated structurally. They were rebuilt in the 1930s.

In Nottingham, the existing chemists had an agreement which main-tained fixed prices. Jesse Boot decided not to join them, but to sell his goods at lower prices. He took advertising space for his 'British and American Botanic Establishment' in the *Nottingham Daily Express*, and even employed a 'crier' to walk the streets of the city with a bell, announcing that all 128 products in his Goose Gate shop were being sold at lower prices. In one month, he had doubled his takings. Interestingly, his low prices led some to regard his shop as a 'cut-price trader' that was not offering quality mer-chandise. In response, Boot announced that he would give ten pounds to any customer who had a genuine complaint about any item purchased.

Boot's trading policy was motivated also by his non–conformist Christian principles. As a Methodist, he was concerned about the poverty he saw, and into which he had been born. Health care and medicines were out of the reach of many. Boot maintained his lower prices so that more lowly-paid people would be able to afford them, and he decided to rename his shop 'The People's Store'. Later, in 1883, the business was incorporated as Boot and Co. Ltd and became the Boots Pure Drug Company Ltd in 1888.

Boot took another major step in using his commercial wisdom to provide an element of social care. Prescribed medicines and prescriptions in the pre-NHS medical care system were costly, which meant that many people on low wages could not afford the cost of the treatments and medicines necessary to their health. Doctors wrote out detailed prescriptions for which they charged, and chemists then demanded further unnecessarily high fees for dispensing. Boot broke the monopoly by employing his own chemist, Edwin Waring, to provide prescriptions. These cut the costs by a full 50 per cent, and gave Boot and his fledgling business another major financial boost.

In 1881, Jesse acquired the lease of a larger property, still in Goose Gate but nearer to the city centre. Over many months, he designed his new store, paying attention to building a truly impressive shop frontage. The windows created an illusion of a theatrical stage behind large panes of glass, where he could set up attractive displays, even employing men to sit in the windows wrapping bars of soap.

The success of the Goose Gate new store led to the first Boots stores outside Nottingham, in Sheffield and Lincoln, but he continued to expand in his home city with a store on Pelham Street in Nottingham which opened in 1891. This was certainly a 'store' rather than a shop or pharmacy, and became the model for all that followed as the business expanded rapidly. It was architecturally elegant, almost stately in design, and offered a much wider range of goods and services, including a café.

In twenty years, Jesse and Florence opened sixty shops in twenty-eight towns. Still innovating, and following their Methodist principles of encouraging education and social wellbeing, it was Florence, thinking back to her own childhood retailing background, who suggested incorporating a library into their shops. They set up the Boots' Book Lovers Library, issuing books for a flat fee of 2d a copy; and they located the bookshelves at the far end of every shop so that customers needed to pass by their products on the way. By 1914, the company was selling from five hundred shops across the British Isles.

Jesse Boot retired from his company in 1920 when he sold his business to the American United Drug Company, but the family took back ownership in 1933 following the economic slump caused by the Wall Street Crash. In that year, Florence Boot officiated at the opening of their 1,000th store in Galashiels. Jesse Boot was granted the title Lord Trent of Nottingham in 1929 and died on 13 June 1931 in Jersey, where Florence had been born. Jesse Boot was a committed philanthropist, and continued to be closely involved in charity throughout his retirement years. Florence was committed to the welfare of her staff especially since the majority were young women. She introduced many innovations, including employing welfare officers and giving her staff a hearty breakfast before the stores opened. The company went on to provide GP surgeries in their factories and lay out staff sports facilities.

The Piggly Wiggly store in Memphis, Tennessee, which opened in 1916, is regarded as the world's first supermarket.

The second Piggly Wiggly supermarket opened in Alabama. Today, a consortium of Alabama Piggly Wiggly owners operates a major distribution company.

Johnson's grocery store in Belgrave Gate, Leicester. Several well-known High Street grocery chains began as a single shop operation.

Thorncroft was built by travel pioneer Thomas Cook for his retirement, and stands on the road where he first had the idea of providing mass travel for the working classes.

Castleford High Street, epitomising the post-war shopping experience, with several of the most well-known High Street brands side by side.

A visit to the Christmas Grotto at Lewis's department stores was an exciting event for many children in the 1950s and 1960s.

James Kemsey Wilkinson, known as 'JK', who founded Wilkinsons stores. The company is still owned and managed by the family.

The magnificent 'ocean-liner' Lewis's store in Broadmead, Bristol, completed in 1955 and including a public roof garden. The store is now part of the John Lewis Partnership.

A typical between-the-wars Marks and Spencer store. This is their Birmingham store photographed in 1934.

Radio pioneer Guglielmo Marconi working on one of his historic transmissions from Flat Holm, an island in the Bristol Channel. Looking on are engineers from the GPO, predecessor of today's BT.

Staff at one of Henry Curry's first bicycle shops celebrate the coronation of Edward VII in 1901.

The now-iconic Bush 22 Television Receiver, launched in 1922 and produced in a lightweight and inexpensive Bakelite casing. Many families watched the Coronation of Her Majesty Queen Elizabeth II on one of these sets.

The Lewis's store has been demolished, but the remarkable tower, built in 1936, still dominates the Leicester skyline and has influenced more recent architecture in the area.

Leicester in the 1960s with the Lewis's department store stretching back along Humberstone Gate behind its impressive tower.

James Kemsey Wilkinson's hardware shop in Charnwood Street, Leicester, the forerunner of the Wilko chain. This was his first shop, but he had moved here from a building further along the same street.

This photograph of a shop window display at Marks and Spencer's in Marble Arch, London, in the 1930s shows how contemporary their styles and products were at that time.

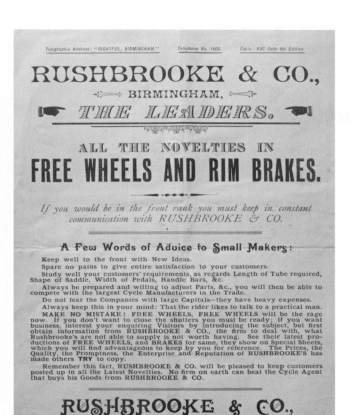

Positive and powerful marketing from Frederick Rushbrooke, founder of Halfords, who created his successful business by responding to the demand for bicycles at the end of the nineteenth century.

A British High Street in its heyday. This is Weston-super-Mare in the 1920s. Familiar names such as J. Lyons Coffee House exist alongside many local independent shops.

Television and radio personality Nicholas Parsons signing autographs in a Currys store in the early 1970s.

Queues form outside a Currys store, and a press photographer is in attendance when Nicholas Parsons visits in a horse-drawn coach.

The date of this poster is later than 1873, which is when Thomas Cook opened his Ludgate Circus offices.

Meadow Street in Weston-super-Mare preparing for the celebrations to mark the coronation of King George V in 1911. All the shops in view are local retailers, as is still the case today.

The River Soar in Leicester pictured in 1951. At that time, waterways were still synonymous with industry. Leicester City FC's King Power Stadium now stands on the site of the power station.

Weston-super-Mare's High Street before the era of the internal combustion engine. The former church on the right became the town's F.W. Woolworth store until the closure of the company in 2009.

As late as the 1980s, British textile manufacturers such as T.W. Kempton could benefit from royal patronage as in this visit by Princess Diana in 1981. Kempton no longer serves the mass market but supplies uniforms and clothing for security guards.

The Rawston Quarter in Bradford where Morrisons Supermarkets began as a market stall. Morrisons still promote their 'market roots' in their television advertising.

Many car manufacturers and agents began by making bicycles. Walter Sturgess founded a major motor vehicle franchise in the Midlands by marketing an articulated bicycle with a trailer, which he called the 'Austral'.

One of Henry Curry's first retail premises, the precursor to Curry's PC World.

Mariane Cook, beloved daughter of travel pioneer Thomas Cook. She was his confidant and supported his strong non-conformist principles, but died tragically, overcome by fumes from a water heater that her father had installed in his home.

Many nineteenth century factories have been found a new use. This is the Symington factory in Market Harborough where female underwear was once manufactured, and is now the offices of Harborough District Council.

A Safeway Supermarket window in 1973, shortly after decimalisation.

The Co-operative Movement began with humble principles but aspired to grandeur on the High Street. This is an architect's plan for a Co-op Department Store drawn in 1885.

Jesse's contributions to the city of Nottingham included the substantial donation of £50,000 to the General Hospital and the purchase of twenty acres of land along the Victoria Embankment of the River Trent for sport, recreation and as a memorial to those who fell in the Great War. He also gave to the city of Nottingham the land in the Highfields area near Lenton and Beeston that became the campus of the University of Nottingham.

John James Fenwick

The Fenwick family roots are in the Swaledale area of Yorkshire. John James Fenwick was born in Richmond on July 1846 above his father's grocers shop 83 Frenchgate, the ancient route from the Saxon settlement to the castle. Today, the building is known as The Old Sweetshop and has been refitted as a holiday cottage. A reconstruction of the house as it was when owned by the Fenwicks is on display at Richmond Museum.

John James was the fifth child of eleven born to John Fenwick and Mary (née Cooper). Mary was aunt to the racehorse trainer John Watson of Newmarket, and sister to the well-known saddler Matthew Cooper. John James was educated at the Tower Street Corporation School which was close to his home in the shadow of the castle. His first retail experience was working in his father's shop. One of his first jobs was to make up the 'farthing dips', which were small candles available to poorer families.

His mother died in 1860 when he was fourteen years old, and John Fenwick senior moved his family to Middlesbrough. John James found work in a draper's shop and subsequently gained an apprenticeship in Stockton-on-Tees. He moved to Newcastle eight years later, taking up an apprenticeship with Moses and Brown, a firm of drapers, and then with Charles Bragg & Company who were silk mercers, and where John James was appointed manager. In Newcastle, he married Mary Burnand, the daughter of a master tailor.

The family name became a retail brand on 23 March 1882, when John James opened a store in Newcastle in a former doctor's house at 5 Northumberland Street. Initially, he sold mantles, silk goods, dresses, fabrics and trimming. The business prospered and began to expand along the street, acquiring premises at Nos 37 and 38 and, after his son, Fred, had joined in 1890, No 40.

Only one year later, Fenwick made a major leap forward by opening a store in London's New Bond Street. The stock mirrored the Newcastle store, gaining a reputation for exclusive ladies tailoring, and retailing the latest fashion styles. It was Fred Fenwick who was to transform the business. He had undertaken some of his business training in France, and had been impressed by Le Bon Marche, arguably the first true department store. Fred brought the concept to England.

A hallmark of the Fenwick retail estate has been the impressive architecture of its buildings, even though several have been frequently extended. Arguably, the grandest was the company's third store in Market Street, Leicester, acquired in 1962 and closed in 2017. It was built in 1880 by Isaac Barradale, who was regarded by the architectural historian Nicklaus Pevsner as one of the finest arts and crafts architects in England, for local Leicester retail entrepreneur, Joseph Johnson. Johnson had gradually extended his small empire of shops, all in adjacent Belvoir Street, and finally decided to bring them together into one grand store, each shop becoming a department within the building.

A wide sweeping staircase led from floor to floor, which unfortunately was removed when Fenwicks took over. The front archway of the imposing building has grand classical pillars made of rare marble from a Leicestershire quarry. Barradale included accommodation for the shop girls on the attic floor, each room with an open fireplace and a fitted bed. In the basement was a mortuary, associated with Johnson's funeral service. In later years, adjoining premises were acquired, and the Barradale building was linked to them by simply knocking holes in the walls. As the floor levels of the two buildings were not the same, the overall impression for customers was a somewhat confusing but interesting 'rabbit warren' of different areas, with steps up and down in surprising places.

John James died in 1905. He was succeeded as the head of the company by Fred and later by his grandsons, first Trevor and then John. Fenwick is very much still a family business which has operated cautiously throughout its history. In some ways, it seems somewhat old-fashioned, and business analysts point to the fact that each store is run as an individual enterprise, the chain lacking a centralised stock management system. It has just ten stores, although the most recent are key 'anchor' stores in very profitable shopping centres. Its all-male top management is made up solely of family members, a complex team of cousins. The present Life President is a fourth-generation member of the family, also John James by name. His nephew, Mark Fenwick, is the company's Chairman, and the present John James's two sons, Adam and Hugo, are currently the Managing Director and Group Trading Director respectively. In Spring 2018, Fenwicks began a major reorganisation and modernisation of their business and stores.

John Spedan Lewis

London's Oxford Street has always been the home of the John Lewis Partnership. The modern department store stands on the same site as the first John Lewis drapery store which opened in 1864; but the story begins in the Somerset village of Shepton Mallett on 24 February 1836, when John Lewis, the father of the founder of the Partnership, was born.

His father, also named John, was a baker in Town Street, and his mother was Elizabeth Speed, who was born in 1797, the daughter of a milliner whose shop was next door. They had married at the Parish Church of St Peter and St Paul in Shepton Mallett.

His mother died in 1841 and his father less than three years later, leaving John, as an orphan at the age of seven, to be cared for by his aunt, Ann Speed, who brought him up. He left school at fourteen and was apprenticed to a local draper, possibly the business owned by Ann's sister Christian Speed. Still in his teens, John moved to London and by the age of twenty he was the youngest silk buyer in the capital, working for the Peter Robinson department store in Oxford Street, having worked his way up from joining as a drapery assistant. In 1864, he was invited to become a partner in the company, but instead, John Lewis opened his own drapery business nearby. The shop began trading on 2 May 1864, and it is on this site that the modern John Lewis store stands today.

The business prospered, and in time, Lewis could rebuild and extend the premises to become a department store. It is claimed that just before Christmas in 1905, he walked from his store to Sloane Square, just under three miles away, with twenty £1,000 bank notes in his pocket to buy the ailing Peter Jones store.

John Lewis married Eliza Baker, and they had two sons, John Spedan born in 1885, and Oswald born in 1887, both of whom joined their father's business, starting on the shop floor. John Spedan was named in honour of Ann Speed, and it was he who would become the founder of the John Lewis Partnership. Eliza was one of a select group, being a female graduate of Cambridge University. She was also involved in the suffragette movement, and it is certain that her attitudes towards emancipation and broadly liberal political beliefs influenced her sons.

By comparison, John Lewis Senior was known to be an autocratic employer and a somewhat ruthless man, hiring and firing staff at will. This reputation made it difficult to keep staff, and although remaining profitable, the business began to suffer, losing out to local rivals such as Owen

Owen. In 1920, during a period of economic depression, his staff went on strike. Both John Spedan and Oswald disagreed with his management style, which led to considerable family conflict. Educated at Westminster School, Spedan had joined his father's store at the age of nineteen, and had been given a 25 per cent share in the business on his twenty-first birthday.

In contrast with their father's management approach, Spedan and Oswald became aware of the difference between their wealth, which was still accruing, and the conditions of the men and women they employed. They calculated that the salaries that they and their father were paying themselves, which totalled £26,000, were far more than the wage bill for their entire workforce, which amounted to about £16,000. In addition, Spedan's quarter share in the business was worth a further £50,000.

Spedan was unable to work for a period of almost two years following serious injuries resulting from a horse-riding accident in Regent's Park in 1909. It was now that he developed his concept of sharing the company's wealth with his employees. He became convinced that the economic inequality led to lack of morale, and that if his workers felt they had ownership of their work, they would be more motivated, and would make the business more successful. The theories that evolved then were to underpin the later Partnership. Returning to work, in 1914, he asked his father if he could manage the Peter Jones store. His father agreed, providing he continued to work at the Oxford Street store until 5.00 pm every afternoon.

At Peter Jones, Spedan began testing his new ideas and trusting his theories. He employed intelligent young graduates and listened to their views. He encouraged female staff to climb the employment ladder, providing much-needed employment for women who had worked in responsible positions during the First World War, only to be displaced and made redundant when hostilities ended. One of these young women, Sarah Beatrice Hunter, started as a boot buyer, married Spedan Lewis and became a director of the company. She went on to serve as the deputy Chairman of the partnership between 1929 and 1950.

In total, around one hundred female staff joined the company in the years between the two World Wars. Spedan also worked to improve his staff's living quarters, some of whom lived in the store in purpose-built accommodation, and he displayed the store's sales figures every day so that his staff knew how the business was faring. He worked hard to foster communication between the shop floor and management, and introduced a house journal, the *Gazette*, in 1918. In 1920, some of the live-in shop girls at Oxford Street went on strike in response to his father's uncompromising management style. In the same year, Spedan offered the Peter Jones staff their first share of the store's profits. In the space of just five years, he took Peter Jones from an annual deficit of £8,000 to a profit of £20,000.

The personal psychological pressures which Spedan Lewis had to deal with at that time must have been immense. Clearly, he saw that his father's autocratic nature was damaging the Oxford Street business. He also knew how his father was likely to react if he found out about his innovations at Peter Jones. Spedan had to keep two separate ledgers of financial accounts, so that his father remained unaware that he was already sharing the company's profits with his staff, offering them shares in the business worth up to 15 per cent of their salaries, and spending money on staff welfare. It seems surprising that his father remained unaware of his son's actions. The distance between the two stores was a short walk across Hyde Park, and the employees at the two stores must have known each other and discussed their circumstances. The ledger clerks at Peter Jones were clearly very loyal and trustworthy individuals.

A measure of his father's fiery nature was the long-running legal dispute between John Lewis Senior and Lord Howard de Walden, who owned the land in Holles Street on which part of the Oxford Street store was built. The dispute continued in the courts for twenty-three years and cost John Lewis £40,000. He was sued for libel by de Walden after putting up placards in his store, and spent a short time in Brixton Jail for contempt of court.

In 1925, that great sales slogan 'Never Knowingly Undersold' was created by Spedan Lewis for his Peter Jones store. For many years it remained a powerful sales tool, providing reassurance to customers that whatever they purchased could not be bought elsewhere at a lower price. It spoke of honesty and transparency.

John Lewis Senior died in 1928, at the age of ninety-two, at his Hampstead home which he had named Spedan Towers. John Spedan then took over the Oxford Street store and formed officially the John Lewis Partnership. By this time, the business was worth more than £1million. A year later, he started sharing the company's profits with his staff. He then began rebuilding and modernising the Peter Jones store and expanding the company by acquiring further stores, the first outside the London area. In 1950, the final stage of the partnership process was completed with his employees having control of the business.

John Spedan and Sarah had three children, John, Jill and Edward. Sarah Lewis continued as deputy Chairman of the company until her death in

1953. John Spedan resigned as Chairman of the Partnership in 1955 and from then on has been known within the company as 'the founder'.

In his retirement, John Spedan lived at Longstock Park near Longstock in Hampshire until his death on 21 February 1963. He was buried at sea, in accordance with his wishes. Throughout his life Lewis was a keen and active natural historian, and was a fellow of the Linnean Society from 1933 until his death. Today, the society awards a John Spedan Lewis Medal for contributions to conservation.

John Moores and George Davies

At the age of sixteen, the author of this book clocked in and became an employee of Littlewoods Stores and so joined an empire created by Lancashire-born businessman John Moores. The store was the fifty-seventh in the chain, the first having opened in Blackpool, and the second in Brixton in south London. The author went on to work in the stockroom at Brixton, which was below ground, beneath the sales floor. When Transport for London's Victoria Line was extended in 1971, an underground river was forced up from a deep level, and flooded the basement floor. Littlewoods responded by installing catwalks. It was somewhat unnerving to see the dark waters of this subterranean watercourse beneath your feet. The stores were in fact secondary to the other and earlier business elements of Moores' empire, namely the football pools and the Littlewoods Mail Order catalogue business. Of George Davies, and his connection with Littlewoods (and indeed with the author), more in due course.

John Moores was from a working-class background. He was born in Barton-upon Irwell in Lancashire in 1896, the second of eight children and eldest of four sons. His father was a bricklayer who, because of injuries and tuberculosis, exacerbated by his fondness for alcohol, died when he was only forty-seven years old. Moores was first employed at the age of twelve years, assisting a milkman on his round. He left school at fourteen to be employed as a messenger boy for the Manchester Post office, but was dismissed. Soon afterwards, he was accepted by the Post Office School of Telegraphy as a student, and on graduating, joined the Commercial Cable Company as an operator. These skills were put to good use during the First World War when Moores served as a wireless operator.

His innate ability to see the commercial advantage in almost any situation first came to the fore when he was posted to the Waterville Cable Company station in County Kerry, Ireland. He complained about the quality of the canteen food and was therefore told to manage the Mess Committee. In response, Moores set up a supply company, buying food from more than one supplier so he could reduce purchase costs and improve the quality of the meals. In the absence of a public library in the vicinity, he established a store to sell books, which he imported in bulk. He went on to sell stationery and then golf balls, because he also realised there was no sports shop nearby. Overall, he accrued a personal income of more than £1,000 in eighteen months of trading. Then, in 1922, he was posted to Liverpool, which became his home and the headquarters of his future business empires.

The first, and most remunerative of these business ventures was Littlewoods Pools which Moores launched in association with two friends, Colin Askham and Bill Hughes, who also worked for the Cable Company; but the idea came from an encounter with John Jervis Barnard from Birmingham who had noted the country's passion for football and betting. Barnard invented a 'football pool' where people would contribute to a pool of money and predict football scores. Those who made the correct predictions received the 'pool' after Barnard had taken 10 per cent as his fee.

Moores, Askham and Hughes decided to set up a similar but more profitable enterprise. Each invested £50 in the project, a considerable financial commitment in the 1920s. A local and inexpensive printer agreed to produce the betting slips. The trio needed to run the business in secret, risking dismissal from the Cable Company if it was discovered that they were operating a business. The name 'Littlewoods' came from Colin Askham who had been born Colin Henry Littlewood, although he had been orphaned as a toddler.

The men handed out 4,000 coupons at Manchester United's Old Trafford ground before a match. They hired some young boys to help distribute them. Only thirty-five coupons were returned with the total income from bets being less than five pounds. They next printed 10,000 coupons which were distributed before a Hull match, but only one was returned as a bet. Askham and Hughes decided to abandon the project, and Moores, taking a gamble with his own finances, offered to buy them out and carry the financial burden and risk. It paid off. Despite being prosecuted under the Ready Money Betting Act, his appeal being upheld, by 1932 and still in his thirties, John Moores became a millionaire, and, as with so many retail entrepreneurs and businesspeople, he wanted to direct his energies into other areas of commerce. Next was the Littlewoods Mail Order Stores, and in 1937, the first Littlewoods department store. By 1952, the stores division had expanded to twenty-five locations across the UK, and to more than fifty by 1952. It was the largest private company in Europe in the 1980s. The company united its largely female workforce with a regular printed staff magazine called *Chainmail*, which, in each issue, featured a different store.

With the outbreak of the Second World War, Littlewoods re-equipped to support the war effort. They manufactured parachutes and barrage balloons, and later built dinghies and even munitions. They diversified quickly, re-tooling and responding with remarkable speed, manufacturing aircraft components and boats capable of travelling over land and water. Littlewoods developed an expertise in designing compact and easily-carried containers for kits that were re-assembled into vehicles near the front line. They also manufactured similar containers called 'Pacific Packs' to provide rations to soldiers in the Far East. Alongside these activities, the pools division continued to operate. Some of the experience gained during wartime, such as the scientific testing of fabric, was transferred in the post-war period to their textile retailing operation. Moores' early career in wireless was no doubt influential in the company's purchase of a computer in 1957 to manage the movement of their stock.

John Moores committed much of his free time and his money to his passion for football. He was Chairman of Everton Football Club for many years and was made a Freeman of the city of Liverpool in 1970. He was honoured with a CBE in 1972 and a knighthood in 1980. He retired as Chairman of the Littlewoods Group in 1977, when his son Peter assumed the role, but profits fell dramatically by 75 per cent in just three years. He returned in 1980 but retired again two years later. The chain of 119 Littlewoods stores was closed in 2005 and the following year some forty stores were sold to Primark. The catalogue division underwent several mergers, and a proportion of its assets, later known as 'Index' was sold to Argos.

For seven years, Moores was a Conservative councillor for the Sefton area of Liverpool. Records show that although their political views were far apart he maintained a close and friendly working relationship with the Labour MP Bessie Braddock. He died on 25 September 1993 at his home in the Freshfield district of Formby. His estate was valued at £1.7 billion. One year before his death, Liverpool Polytechnic adopted the name 'Liverpool John Moores University' in his honour. A statue now stands in the university's library. For many years, the Liverpool offices of the Littlewoods Group were known as the 'JM Centre'.

One of the former buyers – of ankle socks – for Littlewoods stores is deserving of special recognition. His name is George William Davies. It is probably not necessary to explain who George Davies is, because he is the originator of numerous highly-successful brands, including that known by his own first name. Davies was born in Crosby in Lancashire in 1941. His father was a sausage-maker, but it was his mother, Mary Davies, who, working as a seamstress was his motivation to succeed in the fashion industry. He first trained to be a dentist but left his course at Birmingham University, returned to Liverpool and became a graduate trainee for Littlewoods, moving to stock control and then becoming a buyer. Davies has stated on record that his time at Littlewoods was when he formed one of his key retailing concepts, namely the importance of effective stock control, and the need to understand local buying patterns, otherwise known, in the terminology of retailing as 'trading'. Littlewoods also provided the training that would give him the foundation for his future career.

In an interview for *The Times* in 2007, Davies recounted an early Littlewoods experience when, during the Whitsun holidays in Manchester, children dressed in white to take part in 'Whit Walks'. This local custom meant that sales of white ankle socks increased by 200 dozen in that area, but Davies had only sent 10 dozen to the store. In response to animated telephone calls from the store manager, Davies drove from Liverpool to Manchester to collect a further consignment from the manufacturer, and delivered them to Manchester. He claimed that this saved him his job, but it also taught him that stock demands were different from store to store and that regional and local differences must be recognised.

Davies joined several new retailing ventures after leaving Littlewoods, but his first big break was being hired by Sir Terence Conran to join the Hepworths menswear chain and manage their acquisition of seventy High Street stores belonging to the Kendalls group. The result was NEXT, which has become one of the most profitable High Street chains. The first NEXT shops opened in 1982. The branding is known as 'total look', encouraging customers to match various goods which, when combined, create a certain aspirational style, and prompting customers to return to add further products. It has been noted that most NEXT customers will buy five items, not only the one they had intended to purchase. Davies was made Chief Executive in 1984 and masterminded the conversion of fifty Hepworth stores to the NEXT format, later adding interior design to extend the product range. He then relocated the group's headquarters to Leicestershire from its traditional base in Leeds, to be nearer his principal textile suppliers.

Davies has a strong personality which has on many occasions led him into conflict with managers and shareholders. In December 1988 he was dismissed from NEXT by its Chairman Sir David Jones, who accused him of being egotistical and taking the company 'to the verge of bankruptcy'. Davies moved on. In the 1990s, he was approached by the Asda supermarket chain to develop a range of clothing, a project which resulted in his second household-name brand 'George at Asda'. Asda was taken over by the American giant Walmart in 2000, prompting Davies' resignation from Asda's board; but at the time of the takeover, his brand was providing an annual turnover of £600 million. The sales of the George brand goods across the USA amount to more than £2 billion annually, and in 2009, 'George' became the largest clothing retailer in the UK.

Davies' third big brand launch was for Marks and Spencer which required a specific line of clothing to appeal to the younger female market. The result was 'Per Una', literally 'For One Woman'. Less than three years after its launch, the brand was producing an annual turnover of more than £230 million, amounting to 10 per cent of Marks and Spencer's total sales, and bringing many younger customers into their stores. Its later sale took George Davies into the super-rich category. Next on the agenda was George Davies' fourth brand creation. On 13 June 2009, he revealed GIVe. The final 'e' represented e-commerce via the internet. It launched in new stores across the UK, selling Italian-styled high-quality women's' fashionwear, described by Davies himself as 'affordable luxury'. The project failed within a few years.

George Davies remains a dynamic and complex presence in the retailing world although he is now less prominent than in previous decades. Seemingly, he enjoys life, driving a silver Maserati, allegedly, owning a yacht and the world's fastest commercial private jet aircraft, which can cruise at more than 700 mph. The author of this book lives just a few miles from Davies' former residence in Leicestershire to which he moved to be closer to NEXT and his East Midlands suppliers. It is the former rectory of a small quiet village next to the little parish church which dates to Saxon times. Perhaps even the most dynamic of entrepreneurs needs, and enjoys, a peaceful retreat.

Marshall and Snelgrove

Little is known of the background to James Marshall who founded Marshall and Snelgrove. He was born in Yorkshire, and there is a possibility that his mother worked in the lace industry. He moved to London and became a shop assistant at a haberdasher at 10 Vere Street known as Burrell, Son and Toby. Sometime in the 1820s he decided to launch his own business but this ended in insolvency, and bankruptcy proceedings which continued until 1830. However, seemingly undeterred, Marshall joined forces with a Mr Wilson and in 1837 opened a shop close to his former employer at 11 Vere Street. The business opened as Marshall and Wilson, but soon gained another partner by the name of Stinton.

In 1848, on the retirement of Stinton, James Marshall formed a new partnership with John Snelgrove, whose family roots were in the village of Dulcote near Wells in Somerset, and who had worked as a shop assistant with the firm. The iconic Marshall and Snelgrove brand was formed. Marshall married Louisa Stinton, daughter of the retired partner in 1855. It seems that this was Marshall's second marriage as records show that he was first married to a Catherine Morrison from Thurso in Scotland, and by her had at least four sons. The marriage to Louisa may have precipitated a move from the family home in Cricklewood to 30 Upper Hyde Park Gardens in Bayswater, a very prestigious address, opposite Hyde Park and with extensive mews behind the property.

In the early 1850s, one of the partners visited Lyons and purchased large stocks of silk at a low price. This one action brought very large profits to the company and enabled them to pay for a new store. Premises were acquired on the corner of Vere Street and Oxford Street, and the company diversified into carpets, other floor coverings and soft furnishings as well as clothing. The store included a workroom where couturiers could alter garments, thus creating a sense of exclusivity, and was originally called the Royal British Warehouse. Similar trading resulted in the Marshall family gaining great wealth, exemplified by James Marshall's purchase of Goldbeaters Farm at Mill Hill in North London, an estate of one thousand acres. In 1865 Marshall bought the Huntingdon Brewery, including maltings, from Mr Dennis Herbert, for his sons, Arthur and Charles. Arthur became the driving force behind the business, which had been established in the eighteenth century.

Marshall retired in 1871, handing over to his eldest son, also named James. John Snelgrove died in 1903. A window in the centre of the south aisle gallery of the nearby church of St Peter's, Vere Street, commemorates James Golding Snelgrove, a son of John Snelgrove who died aged sixteen years. James C. Marshall was President of the Linen and Woollen Drapers' Institution for almost forty years till his death in 1925 at the age of ninety-five.

Marshall and Snelgrove expanded outside London, opening prestigious stores in Scarborough and Harrogate followed by Birmingham, Manchester, Southport, Leeds, York, Sheffield and Bradford. In some sites, these were not new builds but were the acquisition of existing high-class department stores with a good local reputation, such as Adderlys in Leicester.

The First World War had major financial implications for department stores, especially in the luxury market. For Marshall and Snelgrove, the war years prompted thoughts of merging with their chief rival, Debenhams. A working relationship was begun in 1916 with the merger finally taking place in 1919, but a further fifty years passed by until, in 1973, Marshall and Snelgrove was renamed as Debenhams. In this same year, work to rebuild the flagship store in the street where James Marshall had begun his career, commenced. It was completed in 1979.

Sir Thomas Lipton

Thomas Lipton was a man with remarkable reserves of self-determination. At the age of twenty-three he opened his first shop. By then he had spent five years working his way across the United States as an accountant and book-keeper at a rice plantation in South Carolina, a door-to-door salesman in New Orleans, a farmhand in New Jersey and a grocery assistant in New York.

He was born in a tenement in Crown Street in the Gorbals area of Glasgow in 1848. In the mid-nineteenth century, the Gorbals became home to many Catholic immigrants from Ireland and Italy. Lipton's parents, Thomas and Frances, were from County Fermanagh, where the family had been small-holders for several generations, and had been forced to leave Ireland by the potato famine of 1845. They settled in Glasgow in about 1847. The Liptons were Ulster Scots, descended from the migrant communities who had left lowland Scotland in the seventeenth century.

Although the Gorbals in the nineteenth century was not as poverty-stricken as it would become in the early twentieth century, the Lipton family was poor. Thomas' father undertook a variety of types of work before opening a shop at 11 Crown Street selling ham, butter and eggs, and was able to pay for his son to attend school at the cost of three pence a week. Thomas went to St Andrew's Parish School but left at the age of thirteen to support his parents, working as an errand boy for a printer and as a shirt-cutter. He also attended night school classes at the Gorbals Youth School.

In 1864, Lipton became a cabin boy on a steamer operated by the Burns Line between Glasgow and Belfast, and was captivated by the atmosphere and enthralled by the stories he heard from sailors who had travelled across the Atlantic. George Burns had earlier worked with David McIver and Samuel Cunard, and had become a co-founder of the Cunard Line, which by then was handling most of the transatlantic mail, so the stories which had such a profound effect on the young Lipton were no doubt from sailors who had retired from serving on these routes. However, Lipton's time on board was brief. He was dismissed, with one week's notice, for allowing a lamp to smoke, discolouring the white enamel of the cabin ceiling.

Clearly a young man with ambition, Thomas had saved some of his wages of eight shillings a week and, with his parents' blessing, and still only fourteen years of age, he booked a passage to the States where he lived and worked for five years. It was in New York that he learned the basics of the grocery trade, including American techniques of salesmanship and advertising which he was later to use to great effect.

He returned to Glasgow in 1870. One year later, he celebrated his twenty-first birthday by opening his first shop. Lipton's Market was situated at 101 Stobcross Street in the Anderston district of Glasgow on the north bank of the River Clyde. It has been said that he 'lived and breathed' his shop, often working for more than eighteen hours a day and sometimes sleeping on a makeshift bed behind the counter. His commitment and the techniques he had learned during his years in America paid off. By 1882 he had opened shops in Dundee, Paisley, Edinburgh and Leeds. In less than twenty years, he was managing a chain of more than two hundred shops. By 1888, his empire had grown further and Lipton had opened his 300th store. In later life, he commented that his only political ambition had been to open one new shop every week.

Lipton's involvement in tea began at this time. A staple product in his shops, he realised that due to the relatively high cost of manufacture, tea was mainly a beverage for the middle classes. By acquiring his own tea gardens, and reducing the cost of packaging and shipping, he could reach the previously-untapped working-class market. He created his famous Yellow Label tea brand in 1890 with the marketing slogan 'Direct from the tea gardens to the teapot'. Today the same blend of tea, with the familiar Lipton red shield, is sold in 159 countries.

In 1889, his mother, Frances Lipton, died. His father died some months later. With no other family, Thomas had no reason to remain in the city of his birth. He took the logical step of moving to London, where most of his business interests lay and where company decisions were being made.

As Thomas Lipton accrued great wealth, he became a well-known figure in English society, far removed from the roughness of his early years in

Glasgow. He was created a Knight Commander of Royal Victorian Order (KCVO) by King Edward VII in March 1901, and on 24 July 1902 he was created Baronet of Osidge, his adopted home in Middlesex. He was described by journalists as 'the world's most eligible bachelor', and he encouraged this public persona. His mother had been a very strong supporting and caring influence and he would often speak kindly of her, stating that no woman he had met could measure up to her. In fact, he was gay and maintained a relationship for over thirty years with William Love, who was one of his early shop assistants. After their break-up, he had other relationships including with an orphan from Crete whom he had met during a cruise in 1900.

In the First World War , Sir Thomas Lipton supported organisations providing medical aid. He placed his yachts at the disposal of the Red Cross and other groups to transport volunteer doctors and nurses and medical supplies.

At the height of a serious typhus epidemic in Serbia in 1914–15, Sir Thomas Lipton visited Serbia on his yacht *Erin*, sailing via Sardinia, Malta, Athens, and Thessaloníki. On his arrival, he visited British hospitals and medical missions in Belgrade, Kragujevac, Niš, Vrnjačka Banja, and elsewhere. He insisted that he stayed only in modest lodgings and ate the same meals, as everyone was forced to eat under war conditions. In addition to visiting many hospitals, where he encouraged doctors, nurses and soldiers, he found time to attend traditional fairs and to take a part in blackberry gathering and fishing. He was later proclaimed Honorary Citizen of the city of Niš for his philanthropy and kindness to the people of Serbia.

Thomas Lipton remained at the head of his manufacturing and retail empire until 1927 when he retired as Chairman and became Life President. It was a role without responsibility or involvement, and within months he sold his shares to the Meadow Dairy Company, which was under the control of one of Liptons' major competitors, Home and Colonial Stores. However, he maintained his interests overseas in his American company Thomas J. Lipton Inc and in his tea plantations in Sri Lanka.

Possibly, Lipton saw that the great days of his retail empire were ending, partly due to the intense competition in the High Street. In 1929 the Lipton company merged with several other major High Street grocery chains including the Home and Colonial Stores and Maypole dairies. These continued to trade under their own names and branding, often side-by-side in the same street. As a group, the combined retail operation, known as Allied Retailers, involved more than three thousand stores. The Lipton name was used for a new supermarket chain serving small towns.

Sir Thomas Lipton died at Osidge on 2 October 1931. He bequeathed most of his wealth to his native city of Glasgow. He was buried alongside his parents and siblings in Glasgow's Southern Necropolis. Allied Retailers was acquired by Argyll Foods in 1982, and the supermarkets which bore the Lipton name were rebranded as Presto.

Thomas Cook

In the early summer of 1841, Thomas Cook walked the sixteen miles from his home in Market Harborough to attend a Temperance Rally in Leicester. On the way, he had his dream of universal travel. Walking along the London Road into Leicester he passed the plot of land in the then largely undeveloped suburb of Knighton on which he would build his own retirement home, some thirty years later. A staunch and strict Baptist preacher and travelling evangelist, Thomas Cook was a religious man who believed that most Victorian social problems were related to alcohol and that the lives of working people would be greatly improved if they drank less and became better educated.

On 6 July 1841, accompanied by excited crowds and bands playing fanfares, Cook saw the first-ever railway excursion in the world depart from Leicester's Campbell Street station *en route* to Loughborough. His dream had become a reality very quickly, and his name was destined to become one of the most recognisable and well-known in the world.

Thomas's underlying reason for furthering his travel business was his non-conformist Christian motivation to broaden the horizons of the working classes and to occupy them in wholesome activities as a diversion from the curse of drink. However, his company was also a commercial success which expanded rapidly and required a high degree of business acumen in order to survive. In later years, this led to serious tensions between Thomas and his only son, John Mason Cook who took over the management of the business from his father. There were numerous disagreements on policy and strategy leading to arguments and eventually Thomas's retirement from the company and detachment from his son.

A notable example of John's skills as a manager and businessman is the Gordon Relief Expedition of 1894. He had been asked by the British Government to organise a relief expedition up the Nile to rescue General Gordon from Khartoum. Arrangements were made for the movement of 18,000 troops, nearly 40,000 tons of supplies, 40,000 tons of coal and 800 whaleboats. To transport the coal from Tyneside to Boulac and Assiout via Alexandria, 28 large steamers and 6,000 railway trucks were required. An additional 7,000 railway trucks were needed for the military stores, while on the Nile 27 steamers and 650 sailing boats were used to carry the troops and supplies. John and his Egyptian managers acted as overseers of the entire operation, which relied on the labour of 5,000 local men and boys. They completed their side of the contract in November 1884 but despite all their efforts, Khartoum fell in January 1885 and Gordon was killed.

John Cook gave his father an annual pension of £1,000, the equivalent of more than £100,000 in today's economy. With this money, Thomas commissioned Thorncroft, a substantial dwelling in the arts and crafts style on the London Road in the suburb of Knighton, for himself, his wife and his daughter Annie Elizabeth. Thomas chose the name himself and it is said to be a play on words of his birthplace, Quick Close, in Melbourne, Derbyshire. Midland Hawthorn is known as 'Quick Thorn'. Croft is another word for Close.

However, Thorncroft was to become a place of tragedy and sadness. On 7 November 1880, his daughter died of carbon monoxide poisoning caused by a faulty gas water heater. She was thirty-four years old. Thomas had always been willing to embrace new technologies. His Temperance Hotel in Granby Street, for instance, was the first building in the town to have a water supply, which came from the newly-constructed reservoir at Thornton. The water heater was one of the earliest to be installed in Leicester, no doubt on Cook's instructions. Annie Elizabeth had taken a bath before retiring to bed. Although there was a bell system in the house, it seems she was too overcome by the fumes to summon help. Thomas found her, still in the bath, on the following morning having discovered that her bed had not been slept in. At the inquest, which was held at Thorncroft, it was noted that Annie had complained of feeling dizzy and sick on previous occasions whilst taking baths.

Unlike the strained relationship with his son, Thomas had a close relationship with Annie. She had accompanied her father on several continental tours, acting at times as his interpreter. In Leicester, she had been very committed to the Sunday School and young women's sewing group at the Archdeacon Lane Baptist Chapel. Devastated by her death Cook decided to build a school house in her memory on vacant land near the chapel. Some 900 children attended the Sunday School, and she had previously, and unsuccessfully, tried to persuade her father to finance a new building. He had insisted on others contributing, but after her death he changed his mind and financed it fully himself. Thomas's wife, Mariane, died four years later. She was one year older than her husband, and they had met in Rutland when Thomas, working as a travelling preacher, had visited the village where her family farmed.

Thomas died of a stroke on Monday 18 July 1892, a few minutes before midnight, at Thorncroft. He was buried at Welford Road cemetery near to his wife and daughter. John Mason Cook did not attend his father's funeral, being overseas with one of the company's tours. He died only seven years later having contracted dysentery whilst abroad. He too is buried in Welford Road cemetery, but not near his parents and sister. He had moved in his faith away from his father's non-conformity, and chose to be buried in the area of the cemetery set aside for those of the Anglican tradition.

Despite the pension that Thomas had been paid, Thorncroft, with its furniture and fittings, was the only significant element of his estate. He bequeathed it to his three grandsons, Frank Henry, Ernest Edward and Thomas Albert ('Bert'), the sons of John Cook, who were also involved in the business. Later, the house was sold to a member of the well-known Ellis family of Leicester. It has had many owners over the century that followed before becoming the Leicestershire headquarters of British Red Cross. It was sold by them in 2016 and was acquired by Age UK to be used as a regional headquarters.

Eleven years after his famous and ground-breaking railway excursion, from Leicester to a Temperance rally in Loughborough, Thomas Cook began his plan to build an impressive Temperance Hall near to the railway station. The choice of the location was a deliberate strategy. The Hall would be used as an assembly point for his travellers, thus keeping them away from the taverns while waiting for their trains, and Cook could also provide them with uplifting literature and wholesome entertainment.

Cook's first thoughts were clearly motivated by his religious beliefs and his strong advocacy of temperance, but while the hall was still being constructed, Cook extended his plans to incorporate a hotel and business headquarters on adjacent land. So, the two buildings, built at the same time and operating as one entity, represented the two different facets of Cook's life. The balance between these two worlds, of social action and commerce, caused a rift with his son, and Cook's eventual retirement from the business he founded.

The hotel, which has the current address of 123 Granby Street, was completed before the hall, and accommodated a printing facility, tourism offices and residential quarters for Cook and his family. Although the designs were hardly 'modern', they looked to the future. They were fitted with a plumbing system a year before fresh water from the newly-opened Thornton Reservoir came on line.

The architect for the hotel and the hall was James Medland of Gloucester. Medland was the County Surveyor for Gloucestershire in which capacity he designed many of the city's public buildings of the time, including churches, chapels, a police station, a hotel and various retail stores. There is nothing in his output to suggest that he shared Cook's temperance principles or to explain why Cook appointed him rather than one of the many fine Leicester-based architectural practices.

The Hall opened on Monday 19 September 1853, amid considerable publicity, with a performance of Handel's oratorio *Messiah*. It had 1,800 seats, more than three times the number of passengers on Cook's first excursion. The main space was 100 feet in length and 58 feet in width with a balcony on three sides overlooking a stage. There was a smaller meeting room accommodating 350 people which was used for public lectures.

In time, the hotel outlived its original purpose. The Thomas Cook company expanded rapidly, and new, larger premises were required. It was converted into several retail shops which, over the years, have each been renovated and re-faced; but the upper two stories remain nearly as Medland designed them.

In recent years, a lively debate has ensued about the future of the building. Outline planning consent exists for its demolition, but there is a growing awareness that this is where the Thomas Cook company began and where many of its principles and plans were first formulated.

The entertainments staged at the Temperance Hall were, of course, subject to Cook's personal approval. They included readings by authors, including Charles Dickens, concerts by choirs, orchestras and bands, and various presentations using magic lanterns and other 'modern' technologies. David Devant, the famous illusionist, appeared here, the publicity promising that he would present his well-known Magic Kettle illusion which could pour a seemingly endless quantity and selection of alcoholic drinks. Devant, having been made aware of a clause in his contract that no intoxicating liquor was permitted on the premises, cleverly enabled his kettle to produce cocoa, coffee, water and lemonade instead.

Cook often clashed with the theatre managers in Leicester and with the landlords of nearby pubs. Unfortunately for all concerned, the hotel and hall stood between two pubs. In time, he entered in dispute with the *Nag's Head*, with Cook claiming that it had been the scene of 'orgies'. He then turned his attention to the *Black Horse*, accusing the innkeeper of allowing 'midnight tippling'. In January 1863, correspondence in the Leicester Journal referred to 'conflict and uproar' outside the premises. When attempting to stage a performance of the moral tale 'The Bottle', Cook was told that he needed to apply for a dramatic licence to perform plays. He refused, commenting that 'the hall had already sunk to the low character of a common dancing saloon, and I should be sorry it enrolled as a common playhouse.'

In the severe winter of 1855–1856, many of the poorer citizens of Leicester suffered greatly. Cook and his family responded with practical help by setting up a soup kitchen and by taking strong hot soup made in his hotel by cart to the homes of the needy. Two years later, he reacted to the failure of the potato harvest in a similar philanthropic manner.

In time, the stage presentations gave way to film, and by 1913 the hall had become a cinema, its demise as a concert hall hastened by the opening of the De Montfort Hall. It was fully converted by 1930, re-opening as the Prince's Cinema and by the 1950s, the Essoldo. It closed on 2 July 1960 and was demolished in May of the following year.

William Clark and William Debenham

The history of Debenhams is the tale of two men called William who set up draperies on opposite sides of the same London street. At 44 Wigmore Street in 1778, William Clark opened a draper's shop selling upmarket fabrics, gloves, hats and umbrellas. In 1813, William Debenham, who had been born in Alpheton in the Barbergh district of Suffolk, moved into the street. The two men became partners. On one side of Wigmore Street was Debenham and Clark, and opposite was Clark and Debenham. Intriguingly, there is a village in the mid-Suffolk area which is called 'Debenham'. It acquired its named from the River Deben. The river's name is believed to derive from *Deope* meaning 'deep'. On modern roads, Debenham is about thirty miles from Alpheton.

Later, when William Debenham retired, his son, also called William, formed a new partnership with Clark, and, in 1851, brought in a third partner, Clement Freebody. The business was then renamed Debenham and Freebody. Their first store outside London was in Cheltenham at 3 Promenade Rooms, designed as a precise replica of their Wigmore Street shop, which by then had been named Cavendish House. A second store in the similarly-upmarket town of Harrogate followed. Their principal retail lines were silks, haberdashery, hosiery, lace and – unusually perhaps – family mourning attire.

Clement Freebody brought finance and investment to the company, and concepts such as a wholesale business selling cloth to other retailers and dressmakers. Freebody also married William Debenham's sister. Various new partners were brought on board, including two trusted employees, William Pooley and John Smith, their names being added to the company's name as 'Debenham, Pooley and Smith.

The three stores maintained a group identity, selling similar goods. They also published a joint catalogue which was called the *Fashion Book*, which formed the basis of a very successful mail-order business. The company's policy of recognising their employees' abilities and commitment to the business continued with the appointment of George Hewitt, who had joined as an assistant in the drapery department of the Cheltenham store. Clement Freebody retired in 1876 and the company was re-titled again, this time to become Debenham and Hewitt. Hewitt went on to acquire the Cheltenham store, with William Debenham focussing on their London operation.

It was in the first decade of the twentieth century that Debenhams became the brand which is known today, and expanded, not by building new stores but by acquiring existing ones from other companies. By now it was led by the founder's descendant Ernest Debenham, son of Frank Debenham, as Chairman. Marshall and Snelgrove in London's Oxford Street, was the first acquisition, involving a mutual merger which was negotiated in 1919. This was followed by Harvey Nichols, in Knightsbridge, in 1920.

Ernest Debenham was born in 1865 at 42 Wigmore Street, next door to his grandfather's first shop, and joined the business after completing his education at Marlborough College and Trinity College, Cambridge. His key move when joining the company was to separate the retail and manufacturing elements, establishing the latter as Debenham and Freebody, Freebody being his grandmother's maiden name. He was particularly noted for his caring attitude towards his employees, evident in his provision of educational and medical facilities. Ernest was the last member of his family to be associated with the company. When he retired in 1927, he sold his shares and spent his retirement years farming his estates in Dorset. In 1934, the family's connections with the stores ended completely when the business became a public company.

The acquisition of other stores continued, and by the 1950s, Debenhams was the largest department store group in the UK, with 110 stores and 84 companies. It became part of the Burtons Group for thirteen years from 1985, but after demergers, it is a separate company once again.

George Newton and Thomas Chamber

Although 'big names' for what they achieved and produced, Newton and Chambers are not familiar to shoppers; but at least two of their ultimate products are very recognisable – Izal and Ronseal. A toilet paper renowned for its distinctive 'texture' and a wood preservative would appear to be household products with little in common, but Izal toilet paper and Ronseal are just two products of a major engineering group founded in the eighteenth century which had a profound if little-known effect on the British way of life until the 1960s. They are connected by the Newton Chamber Group which was formed in 1792 by two Sheffield ironmasters, George Newton and Thomas Chamber.

They had been partners in the Phoenix foundry in Sheffield, and with a third man, Henry Longden, signed a lease to extract ironstone and coal from the Thorncliffe valley near Sheffield. The mining rights were granted to them by the Earl Fitzwilliam and allowed them to construct works on the Thorncliffe site near the district of Chapeltown, north of Sheffield town centre. Newton and Chamber thus built the Thorncliffe Ironworks near to the Blackburn Brook, and above the wooded valley slopes which was where the minerals were to be extracted. Their first blast furnace was powered up in April 1795, followed by another in the following year. Together, these worked non-stop for nearly eighty years until being replaced in the 1870s.

In 1815 the partners met one of the greatest names of the industrial revolution, William Murdoch, the man who invented gas lighting. Coke ovens known as 'beehives' were built in the Thorncliffe foundry to produce gas from the coal being mined. By the end of the nineteenth century, the foundry was a major driving force in heavy engineering, a crucible of the later part of the industrial revolution, still mining coal and ironstone, constructing blast furnaces and coke ovens, operating a chemical plant, and forging heavy iron sections including those used in the construction of London's Tower Bridge and the Eddystone Lighthouse.

One of the several strands of research undertaken by Newton and Chambers was in the use of the by-products of their other manufacturing processes. This led to the production of disinfectant from coal tar by a distillation process, the product being bottled and retailed. By 1890, the company had created an emulsified form, and in 1893, Izal was marketed as a non-poisonous disinfectant. Over the years that followed, no fewer than 137 different products, used in hospitals and homes, contained Izal.

The infamous toilet paper, impregnated with Izal disinfectant, and with every sheet printed with the instruction 'Now wash your hands' was at first given away to any local authority who bulk-purchased other hygiene products from the company until it was promoted and sold as a product in its own right. Many of Izal's health-giving claims about the various infections it could prevent would not be acceptable by today's advertising standards. Tighter control of and legislation on the use of chemicals and poisons reduced Izal's market position, and competition from manufacturers of more modern and acceptable products gradually led to Izal's demise, but it was still a big money-earner for Newton Chambers until the 1970s.

During the Second World War, sheets of Izal toilet paper were produced which were overprinted with cartoon characterisations of Adolph Hitler. Understandably, these were immensely popular in certain quarters, but publicly disapproved of by government as being not quite 'British'. W. Heath Robinson, the renowned cartoonist of the nineteenth century, famous for his zany and laughingly complicated machines for achieving simple objectives, had been employed during the inter-war years to provide illustrations of the various stages of production, for use on posters and postcards. Whether he was responsible for the Hitler toilet paper images is not known.

However, the company's relationship with Hitler became very serious when William Joyce, otherwise known as Lord Haw Haw, threatened in one of his propaganda broadcasts to 'dot the 'I' on the Izal name with a bomb. This was not in retaliation for bringing Hitler's image into disrespect, but because the Thorncliffe Ironworks had come under the control of the Admiralty. Nearby, in an annex to the complex, army vehicles were being built, and the works became the largest supplier of Churchill tanks for the war effort. The site was bombed by the Luftwaffe, but despite a near miss, the buildings were not damaged and production continued.

Back in 1896, a company called Ronuk was founded in Brighton, which launched Ronseal in 1956. The company was bought by Izal Ltd in 1960, and in 1964, the businesses were brought together on the Chapeltown site. Known as Roncraft, it became a separate sales division of Izal in 1970 and was acquired in 1973 by the Sterling Drug Company.

In 1994, one of the most memorable and effective marketing slogans for a household product was coined for Ronseal by Liz Whiston and Dave Shelton at the London advertising agency, HHCL. David Cameron, the former Prime Minister used the phrase to sum up the state of the UK coalition government at its halfway point, saying 'it is a Ronseal deal – it does what it says on the tin.' He had used it previously in 2004 saying 'People are crying out for a kind of Ronseal politics – they want it to do what it says on the tin.' One wonders what Whiston and Shelton would have created for Izal, if it had survived.

Chapter Six

The Co-operative Movement

The Co-operative Movement is a complex subject because it is a philosophy, a political ideal and a philanthropic belief. Today it is also a major commercial activity which some would say has moved away from its nineteenth-century roots, and its principal purpose of giving the less fortunate in society the power to make changes to their lives. Brief character outlines of the most prominent pioneers can be misleading because of this complexity. Compared with the founders of many of the High Street brands we are familiar with today, who were focussed on making money by innovation, hard work and commitment, the co-operative pioneers held many other beliefs and principles which sometimes worked together, but were often in conflict. Religion, socialism, philanthropy and commercial entrepreneurial activities worked together to create something remarkable.

The Industrial Revolution provided employment for hundreds of thousands of unskilled workers, but as larger and faster machines were introduced into the mills and factories, the livelihoods of skilled workers and their families became threatened, with many suffering extreme poverty. The adjective 'extreme' is accurate. The 1840s became known as the 'hungry forties', partly because of the free trade policies of the British Government under Sir Robert Peel, and because of the consequences of potato blight which had caused this vital crop to fail across Europe. In France, it is estimated that 10,000 people died from famine. In Ireland, there were one million deaths and two million refugees.

Peel had promised 'modest' reforms. In 1844, the Factory Act became law, which moved some way to limiting the hours that children and women could work in factories, and it was his repeal of the Corn Laws which ended his tenure as Prime Minister; but the effect of his reforms did little to improve the lives of the working-class population.

In England, a large percentage of the population was living in conditions which would today be described as 'third world' with inadequate housing and no access to nutritious food. In addition, the mill owners and manufacturers had created a system designed to produce the largest-possible profits.

The 'truck' system paid workers in kind, so that many had to buy back the produce they had grown themselves at inflated prices. The health and well-being of the workforce was of little or no consequence.

The co-operative idea had existed long before the industrial revolution created the need for it to be put into practice. The Shore Porters' Society, which is a removals and haulage business based in Aberdeen, was founded in 1498 as a co-operative for porters working at Aberdeen harbour. Their records show that in 1666 the society set up an arrangement for providing for retired members and those in ill-heath. Since the middle of the nineteenth century, the society has been a private partnership controlled by six active members, six retired members and two widows. The Shore Porters was, until its demutualisation, a form of friendly society, rather than a commercial co-operative.

Arguably, the first of these in the UK, the Fenwick Weavers' Society, was also founded in Scotland in the village of Fenwick in East Ayrshire. The original purpose of the society, formed in 1761, was to foster high standards in the craft of weaving, but eight years later, it set up a consumer co-operative to enable the collective purchasing of bulk food items and books. After being dormant for many years, the Fenwick Weavers were reconvened in 2008 as an industrial and provident society so that its records and heritage can be researched and catalogued for the future. By the 1830s there were several hundred co-operative organisations, but most were short-lived. Of these early societies, the Lockhurst Lane Industrial Co-operative Society, which was founded in 1832 by ribbon makers in the Foleshill area of Coventry, is still trading, and is now the Heart of England Co-op. The Galashiels and Hawick co-operative Society, which was active by 1839, merged with others and is therefore still trading today as part of the Co-operative Group.

The Rochdale Pioneers

The principles of the Co-operative Movement were laid down by a group of twenty-eight workers in Rochdale in 1844, although other similar concepts were beginning to form elsewhere. Over a period of four months, each member contributed one pound to form the capital needed to start trading. Four days before Christmas, they opened a shop selling a small range of butter, sugar, flour, oatmeal and candles. Within ten years, nearly 1,000 co-operative stores were trading.

The key to the success of the Rochdale Pioneers, as they were to be called, was their clearly-defined set of co-operative principles which became the foundation for all such groups worldwide. These rules defined a 'co-operative' as 'an autonomous association of persons united voluntarily to meet their common economic, social and cultural needs and aspirations through a jointly-owned and democratically controlled enterprise.' The history of the Co-op is one of optimism, suffering, desperation and frequent failure. It was perhaps the first time that very high utopian ideology combined with the suffering of the impoverished working-class population of the British Isles. The result was a somewhat confusing mix of hope, aspiration and political pragmatism.

Robert Owen

Several key thinkers guided the concept of the Co-operative Movement in its earliest years. Undoubtedly the greatest of these was Robert Owen, although his philosophies were much wider than simply running shops in which customers could share in the profits. The son of a saddler and ironmonger in Newtown in Montgomeryshire, Owen began his working life in a drapery shop. In 1792, he became manager of a mill in Manchester at the age of just twenty-one years, and two years later set up his own Chorlton Twist Mill in partnership with other entrepreneurs. His intelligence and deep humanitarian convictions were already being recognised. In 1793, he was elected as a member of the Manchester Literary and Philosophical Society.

Owen was more than a skilled entrepreneur, persuasive speaker and successful manager. He was a man who genuinely cared for others and saw his workers as people who deserved the same quality of life as himself. He was also a practical man who could take philosophical theories and turn them into reality. It was at New Lanark in Scotland that he set about his task in the mills that had been built by the industrial pioneer Richard Arkwright. Owen had married Caroline Dale, the daughter of the owner of the New Lanark Mills. One year after his marriage, his dynamism meant he had made his home at New Lanark and was part-owner of the vast complex.

It was here that he could provide a better, healthier and more wholesome way of life for many hundreds of workers, and where he set up the first true co-operative shop. It was common practice then for workers to be paid in part or completely in tokens which could be exchanged only for goods purchased in the mill-owners' shops. This allowed mill-owners to sell shoddy goods at high prices. Owen paid his workers in ordinary currency, and opened a shop on site. He not only charged fair prices for goods – only just above the price he had paid for them – but also passed on to the workers the savings he made through bulk purchasing. Owen set the standard for all future employers with his fair-minded and practical policies. Of the length of the working day, he said that:

> Eight hours daily labour is enough for any human being, and under proper arrangements sufficient to afford an ample supply of food, raiment and shelter, or the necessaries and comforts of life, and for the remainder of his time, every person is entitled to education, recreation and sleep.

Owen was not always successful in the practical extensions of his philanthropic and socialist ideas, and he faced considerable opposition from many other businessmen; but his work at New Lanark became respected nationally and further afield. He was supported and respected by the greatest thinkers of his time and his concepts influenced later parliamentary social reforms. Some of his predictions have yet to be attained, such as his idealistic socialist world which he hoped was close to being realised, 'when man, through ignorance, shall not much longer inflict unnecessary misery on man; because the mass of mankind will become enlightened, and will clearly discern that by so acting they will inevitably create misery to themselves'. Although many of his grand ideas failed, and he may have lost faith in some of his utopian plans in later life, Robert Owen is still justly regarded as the father of the Co-operative Movement.

William King

Far away from the 'dark satanic mills' of northern England, William King lived in Brighton on the south coast. His was not a working-class upbringing. Born in Ipswich 1786, he was the son of the Master of Ipswich Grammar School. He trained as a physician and married one of the daughters of Dr Thomas Hooker, the vicar of Rottingdean in Sussex.

King took Robert Owen's co-operative ideas, and related his global concepts to the local situation. He could explain his own ideas clearly and in a relatively simple form:

> The key to economic prosperity is to store up enough capital to get control over our own labour, and then, possessing both labour and capital, we will be able to do without the capitalist altogether. But individual workers cannot do this on their own; there is too much risk, the process

of accumulating enough capital takes too long, and if we become ill or grow old there is nothing to fall back on. But together, if we learn to co-operate, we can do it.

William King is also regarded as Robert Owen's publicist, putting into printed words, the ideals of co-operation which he achieved by launching, in 1828, his own newspaper called *The Co-operator.* The first issue was published on 1 May 1828, providing a mix of co-operative theories and practical advice about running a co-operative shop. King encouraged working-class people not to withdraw from society, but to create societies within societies. He recommended that these co-operative groups should start by opening shops because it was a basic element of everyone's daily lives: 'We must go to a shop every day to buy food and necessaries – why then should we not go to our own shop?'

King was an intellectual but also a very practical man. He drew up simple and sensible rules based on common sense which included keeping a weekly financial record, appointing three trustees (so that majority decisions could be made) and refraining from meeting in public houses where there was a temptation that any profits might be lost through drink. The journal ran for only twenty-eight issues and each was only four pages in length; but it was read across the country, was very influential, and at one time achieved a circulation of 12,000.

It was largely because of William King that Brighton became a centre and early pioneer in the co-operative movement. He became known as the 'poor man's doctor' because although there were plenty of wealthy men and women who came to Brighton for reasons of their health, he treated poor people free of charge or asked them to contribute what they could afford. In 1837, he opened the Brighton Self-Supporting Dispensary for which he acted as physician, and in 1842 he was appointed consulting physician at the (Royal) Sussex County Hospital for 'the sick and lame poor of every country and nation'. He also supported the creation of the Brighton Institute which provided education for working-class people, and where he often lectured.

His most important legacy was his own co-operative shop called the Brighton Co-operative Trading Association which opened in 1827. At the time, Brighton was not the popular seaside resort of later years. In the early decades of the nineteenth century it was expanding but still had only two main streets. The advances in factory mechanisation had hit the area hard resulting in mass unemployment. These skilled workers, out of work and with little money became the nucleus of the new co-operative movement.

With a capital of only three pounds, they opened their shop selling basic foodstuffs. With the money that came in from sales, they acquired twenty-eight acres of land where the unemployed could cultivate crops. They also funded workshops where the redundant craft skills could be rescued and used once again to earn a living.

The Brighton and Hove bus fleet includes a double-deck vehicle bearing King's name following a campaign by David Lepper MP, who was the Labour Co-op member for Brighton Pavilion from 1997 to 2010.

Alfred Waterson

Retailing and politics have often been interwoven in the fabric of our society, but the relationship also produced a political party which was born on 17 October 1917. The Co-operative Party put up several candidates in the 1918 General Election but just one succeeded to Parliament. Alfred Waterson was elected as the Member for Kettering. He had been born in Derby and was a railwayman and a trade union activist. He lost his seat in the 1922 General Election and became the National Organiser of the party until 1945. He contested seats in Nottingham in 1930 and 1931 but failed to attract the support of the electorate. He died in Wood Green in the London suburbs in 1964.

The 1918 Election was significant for the working classes. It was the first general election to be held after the Representation of the People Act of the same year. It was therefore the first election in which women over the age of thirty, and all men over the age of twenty-one, could vote. Previously, all women and many poor men had been excluded from voting. It resulted in a landslide victory for the coalition government of David Lloyd George.

Waterson frequently took part in parliamentary debates on a wide range of topics that were relevant to the working classes. In one exchange across the House, in December 1919, he addressed the then Prime Minister David Lloyd George with an accusation so outrageous that the Speaker demanded he withdrew the remark:

Is the right honourable Gentleman aware of the fact that the co-operative movement was compelled to enter into politics because of the action of vested interests in this House; and, further, is he aware that over two-thirds of the questions submitted to him is a complete falsehood, from beginning to end?

Following repeated calls for him to withdraw the remark he agreed to substitute 'inexactitude' for 'complete falsehood'.

Ed Balls and his contemporaries

It may be a surprise to some to find that Edward Michael 'Ed' Balls, who was shadow Home Secretary in the Labour Party under Ed Miliband, is part of the history of the Co-operative Movement. Until losing his seat in the 2015 General Election, Balls was the Co-operative Party Member of Parliament for Morley and Outwood, which is located between Leeds and Wakefield in Yorkshire. He was first elected in 2005 to represent Normanton in Nottinghamshire. He went on to hold the post of Secretary of State for Children, Schools and Families from June 2007 to May 2010, then served as Labour's Shadow Chancellor from 2011 until 2015. He was a candidate to become leader of the Labour Party in September 2010, losing to Ed Miliband.

Former Prime Minister Gordon Brown, former First Minister for Wales, Alun Michael and Ted Graham (Baron Graham of Edmonton) have all represented the Co-operative Party in Westminster in recent decades.

The Evolution of Cooperatism

The success of the co-operative societies in the last half of the nineteenth century led to a steady increase in their numbers, and this in turn caused some private shopkeepers to view them as unfair competition. A small number of the more powerful shopkeepers even lobbied manufacturers and wholesalers to stop supplying to the co-ops. This very rarely happened in practice, but the threat was real enough to prompt co-operatives to work together to set up their own wholesale operation. In 1863, the North of England Co-operative Wholesale Industrial and Provident Society Ltd was launched in Manchester, serving three hundred separate co-operative groups across Yorkshire and Lancashire. It later became the now familiar Co-operative Wholesale Society (CWS). A similar Scottish Co-operative Wholesale Society was founded in 1868. The CWS grew quickly into a powerful and innovative organisation not only wholesaling but manufacturing as well. By 1890, CWS was making its own footwear, biscuits, soap and clothing. By the outbreak of the First World War, it had reached far beyond UK shores with activities across the world in Australia, Denmark, the United States, and even its own tea plantation in India.

Some of the co-operative retail societies saw the expansion of the CWS as a threat to their independence and strove to source stock from other suppliers, rather than allow CWS to become a monopoly. CWS responded by diversifying, creating other services which local societies needed. These included providing loans for new buildings and developments, insurance and legal services. The Second World War forced changes on all manufacturing, wholesaling and retailing operations, with CWS finding a role in sourcing overseas goods for UK consumers, and manufacturing items for military purposes. In the decades that followed, the co-ops failed to modernise, although many moved into self-service formats. In 1968, to address the trend of dwindling business which included much less member investment, the co-ops adopted, for the first time in their history, a national corporate branding: the familiar clover leaf. A period of mergers and reorganization followed in which there was little unified strategy, and in 1973, serious financial issues with the Scottish CWS led to its merger with CWS to form a single wholesale society.

Adding the prefix 'community' to the word 'co-operative' has created, in recent years, an entirely new concept. Away from the High Streets, in more rural areas where there are few amenities, community shops have opened, which are similar in their structure to food co-operatives. Over 400 of these small stores are now trading, with some providing healthcare and library facilities. Similarly, where pubs tied to brewery chains have become unprofitable, local communities have stepped in to rescue them under a provision of the 2011 Localism Act which allows for such amenities to be declared 'assets of community value'. Some of these community pubs also provide space for a shop, perhaps in a converted out-house or former stabling area. The latest co-operative concept is in community energy projects where small investors can own and operate small-scale renewable energy projects including wind farms or solar-power installations on village halls and other community buildings. The financing of these forward-looking initiatives harks back to the earliest days of the co-operative movement, with profits being returned to the community and to the individuals who committed the start-up finance.

Chapter Seven

On your feet

We all need footwear. There are many commodities on sale in the High Street that we would like to own but are not necessary; but protection for our feet is an essential item. By extension, it could be assumed that a company which could manufacture boots, shoes, sandals and trainers of good quality and at affordable prices would be guaranteed good business and sustainability. Yet the opposite became true in the British High Street when, over a remarkably short period of time, numerous long-established brands disappeared.

The history of Britain's boot and shoe industry is both illustrious and tragic. The once-prolific High Street names have all but vanished, although some have found reincarnation as niche franchises within larger stores. An industry which was one of the biggest employers in the East Midlands centres of Leicester and Northampton and their market towns, has virtually ceased to exist, a decline in fortunes which began in the 1980s when the massive and grandly-named British Shoe Corporation failed to respond to competition from the supermarkets and from niche brands.

Freeman, Hardy and Willis

One of the earliest High Street footwear brands, and one of the most familiar to many shoppers was Freeman, Hardy and Willis. The man who created what was to become the largest footwear retailer in the world was none of the three principals celebrated in the company's name, but a Leicester businessman and staunch Baptist, Edward Wood.

Wood was born in Leicester in 1839 and began his career as an errand boy and was then, at the age of eleven years, apprenticed as a printer to Thomas Cook, the founder of the holiday travel company, eventually going on to become Mayor of Leicester, serving in that role for four terms. By 1861 he was working as a hatter and hosier, and in 1870, he began manufacturing shoes under the name of Edward Wood and Company, employing seven men and one boy.

It was on 2 December 1876 that he appointed three directors, Arthur Hardy, an architect, William Freeman, his factory manager, and his travelling salesman, Frederick Willis, and launched the retail company as 'boot and shoe manufacturers and leather factors and leather merchants'. The venture lasted just one year, when it was dissolved and the company merged with Wood's own business, and began focussing on retailing rather than manufacture and wholesale. In that same year, Freeman, Hardy and Willis opened its first branch, in the Wandsworth area of London. The brand 'Freeman, Hardy and Willis' began appearing on signboards above shop frontages by 1879, and the company expanded rapidly. Some of the earliest branches were in Leeds, Lincoln and Leamington Spa. Transactions were strictly cash. Credit was not offered.

The company owned 460 shops by the outbreak of the First World War. The company advertised as 'The Boot Kings' and 'The People's Boot Provider'. Well before then, it was proclaiming itself to be 'the largest boot and shoe dealers in the world', and their shops had been laid out with separate rooms and repair departments for men and women. When Sir Edward Wood retired as Chairman in 1921, the company was operating from 428 shops.

Trueform

The boot and shoe manufacturer J. Sears & Co. (True-Form Boot Co.) Ltd. was founded in Northampton in 1891 by John George Sears (1870–1916), who was soon joined in business by his younger brother William Thomas Sears (1876–1950). The Sears brothers were following in their father's trade: John started out as a 'clicker' – cutting leather for uppers – then became a foreman. Their first factory was on Derby Road in Northampton, and the second on Gray Street in the town. In 1904, they moved to larger premises and modernised, on the corner of Stimpson Avenue and Adnitt Road. In 1908 a warehouse was built next to the factory to store goods prior to their distribution to retail branches. A stock room and packing department were added in 1910.

The first Trueform shop was opened in 1897 to give the Sears brothers a means of distributing goods without using other companies or travelling salesmen. Further shops followed in other towns. In 1912 Sears became a limited liability company. By this time, the company had forty-seven shops in London and thirty-three in other parts of the country, mostly in English cities but also in Edinburgh, Cardiff and Glasgow. Sears prided themselves on their window displays. Apparently describing a form of price maintenance,

The Times wrote on 21 February 1912: 'The boots and shoes are displayed in a novel manner, and their price in plain figures is not only stamped on the sole before leaving the factory, but is openly displayed to the possible customer who gazes through the shop window.'

The First World War brought many challenges to British manufacturers and retailers. Many of Sears' employees left to join the armed forces. Raw materials became difficult to source. The demand for army boots meant that the company found it difficult to satisfy their domestic civilian market. However, when hostilities ended, business began to boom, and in response, the company constructed two new factories, in Northampton and London.

Charles Clore and Sears Holdings

In 1927, Sears and Company took over Freeman, Hardy and Willis. The former had already acquired rival companies including Rabbits and Sons Ltd of Newington Butts in London, the Kettering Boot and Shoe Company Ltd., and the highly-respected Leicester business Leavesley and North. Together the two companies now had 722 shops, all in High Streets and other key retail areas in towns and cities across the country. Separately, Freeman, Hardy and Willis claimed to be the largest shoe retailer in Europe.

In 1929, a new chapter in the company's history began with the purchase of the business by Charles Clore. Clore was from a Lithuanian Jewish background. At one time, he owned Jowett Cars and the Lewis's department stores including Selfridges. He renamed the company Sears Holdings in 1955, and in the following year purchased two more shoe firms, Manfield and Dolcis. In more recent times, Clore, under Sears owned the bookmakers, William Hill, Wallis, Foster Brothers and Richards Shops.

British Shoe Corporation (BSC)

In 1956, Charles Clore brought together all his shoe companies under the name of the British Shoe Corporation. By 1962, these were joined by Saxone and Lilley and Skinner. The company became very large very quickly, and by the 1980s was selling 25 per cent of the nation's shoes: four million pairs of shoes every year from its combined High Street presence of more than 2,500 shops. The vast warehouse in Leicester was on the scale of later supermarket distribution centres. Its staff were issued with electric mopeds to convey them from one end of the building to the other.

Soon after this landmark decade, the British Shoe Corporation lost its way. In 1986, its head office in Leicester closed, and in 1996 the company, which had once owned Freeman Hardy Willis, Saxone, Trueform, Berties, Dolcis, Manfield, Curtess, Roland Cartier, Shoe Express, Shoe City and Shoe Connection ceased to exist. Several of the brands continued to trade after various purchases and deals, but the decline continued. In 2008, the Dolcis store group was placed in administration, making nearly 600 staff redundant and closing half of its stores. Stead and Simpson, which included Shoe Express and Lilley and Skinner, was put up for sale.

Dolcis, as a brand, dated back to 1863 when John Upson began selling his handmade shoes from a barrow on Woolwich Town Market. As his business and reputation grew, he opened his first store, still in Woolwich, and described both himself and his shop as the 'Great Boot Provider'. The business became a public company in 1920, and it was at that time that the brand name 'Dolcis' was added to shop frontages. Upton, it is said, took the name from a Swiss sock stamp. Dolcis was acquired by the British Shoe Corporation in 1966, and under the wing of the shoe giant, it prospered for some years. It was selected by BSC as the pilot chain to test EPOS (Electronic Point of Sale) systems in their stores.

The decline of the British footwear industry was not for the same reasons as the collapse of the British textile industry, whose decline was largely due to its failure to re-tool and modernise after the Second World War, thus allowing foreign manufacturers with modern machines and factories to sell attractive and quality garments at much lower prices. Most analysts and retail historians agree that the problem lay squarely with the management of BSC in the late 1980s failing to look ahead, not recognising changes in consumer demands, and not investing enough in their stores.

These well-known High Street names represented a 'middle market' in footwear retail, selling reasonably-priced shoes with designs that suited most consumers. By the 1990s there appeared new powerful competition, on the less-expensive side of the market from the supermarkets, with their power to import vast quantities of very cheap footwear which could be bought at the same time as the family's weekly groceries, and at the upper end by an increasing number of 'upmarket' niche designer brands. Thus, whilst their thousands of shops retained the décor and sales approaches of the 1970s, the British Shoe Corporation was faced with competitors with a fresh approach to retailing.

Quite simply, buying a pair of shoes, sandals or trainers was likely to be more exciting and glamorous, or easier and less costly, anywhere other than in the boring shops of the increasingly bland stalwarts of the BSC.

Cyrus and James Clark

A notable and remarkable exception to this sad history is the story of Cyrus and James Clark whose footwear company was founded in 1825 and is still largely in the ownership of the family today, trading worldwide through over a thousand branded outlets. The Clarks, from a Quaker family, joined with a cousin in the wool-staling and tanning industry in the small village of Street in Somerset, close to the more-famous Glastonbury. Their headquarters are still in the village today, and the local Clarks' shop occupies the site of their very first retail outlet. Initially, Cyrus Clark intended that his key product would be rugs made from sheepskins. He then began using the offcuts from the rugs to produce slippers.

Cyrus brought in his younger brother, James, as an apprentice, despite their parents wanting the boy to work for a pharmacist in Bath. He completed his apprenticeship in 1833 when Cyrus invited him to become an equal partner. Together, they developed a company which acquired lasting international markets, in Canada, Ireland and Australia, but not without financial difficulties. The business almost collapsed in 1863 because of a lack of business planning, but was rescued by the local Quaker community. As part of their bail-out plan, they insisted that William Stephens Clark, James's eldest son, took over the company.

William Clark set up arrangements that cleared his business of most of its debts. He began mechanising the shoemaking process, and was possibly the first shoe manufacturer in Britain to do so. He was forward-looking and innovative. In 1889 his younger brother Francis joined him as a partner, at the same time as James Clark retired. The Clarks' Quaker ideals guided them in how they treated their workforce. They founded a school so that their young employees could further their education, and they built a library, open-air swimming pool, low-cost housing and a theatre.

Despite the winds of economic change that have been the downfall of so many other footwear brands, Clarks have survived and prospered. By sales, it is one of the largest private companies in the United Kingdom, and in recent years, their long-established policy of seeking international trade has seen them break into the large Indian and Chinese markets. Eighty-four per cent of the company is still owned by the family, the remainder held by their employees. In 2013, Clarks enjoyed sales valued at £1,433 million and reported profits of £150 million.

Dr Martens

Although not of British origin, the iconic Dr Martens deserves an honourable mention, and most fans of 'docs' will know that they were created by a real doctor. The famous footwear was invented by a German military doctor during the Second World War.

Klaus Martens injured his ankle in a skiing accident and found his standard-issue army boots too painful to wear. He experimented in making a pair from vehicle tyres, adding air padding to the soles. After the war, he joined with an old university acquaintance from Luxembourg, Herbert Funck, and began producing boots using discarded rubber from former Luftwaffe airfields. Interestingly, 80 per cent of sales of his new footwear in the first ten years of manufacture were to women aged over forty years.

In 1959, Martens and Funck sought to market their product more widely. The rights to manufacture in the United Kingdom were acquired by the Northamptonshire-based footwear company R. Griggs Group Ltd. Griggs changed the design of the boot slightly, adding the familiar yellow stitching, and anglicising the name, and were successful in establishing the Air-Wair trademark for the soles. They began making the boots at their factory in Cobbs Lane, Wollaston, a village on the outskirts of Wellingborough. Both the style (known formally as Style 1460) and the factory, are still in production today. Due to financial problems, Griggs were later to transfer manufacture abroad, which resulted in more than 1,000 employees losing their jobs; but more recently, in 2007, the company resumed production in England in the original Northamptonshire factory where they were first made.

Wollaston is also the home of NPS Shoes Ltd., a footwear manufacturing company established in 1881. Their brand is Solovair and has some similarities to Dr Martens. In fact, when Griggs began manufacturing Dr Marten boots, they turned to NPS for technical advice. In 1960, they worked together. The Dr Marten boot as known in Britain, is a Solovair sole and a Griggs boot. NPS produced Dr Marten boots for Griggs for several years, and now make their own lines which found a niche with those who still wanted a British-made boot after Dr Martens had moved their production lines to China

Chapter Eight

Out of the box

Late in the evening of 20 July 1969, a small group of people, including the author, gathered outside the shop window of their local Co-op store. Inside the shop was a bank of television sets, and all three available channels, BBC1, BBC2 and ITV were featuring the same event.

We all missed the finale, the moment when Neil Armstrong stepped onto the moon because that took place at just before 4.00 am, but what we saw in those flickering images from so far away made for a very special experience, and a giant leap for the broadcasting industry. One channel – BBC2 – was broadcasting in colour, although a full colour service was still a few months away. Just seventy years before, the young Italian inventor Guglielmo Marconi had succeeded in sending a brief message in Morse code by wireless over the waters of the Bristol Channel; now we were watching live images from 384,000 kilometres away.

Broadcasting is about communication. Shopkeepers have always needed that ability to communicate with their potential customers through brand identity. The translation from the High Street and retail, to the internet and 'e-tail' is a phenomenon we shall investigate in a later chapter; but first we meet those men and women who enabled communication, in its widest sense, and the High Street brands that adorned the television set in the corner of the living room and the wireless set on the dresser.

International brands such as Samsung and Sony now dominate the market that began as the humble 'wireless set', to which the television was later added. Then came the transistor, and then the micro-processor, and with the invention of the internet, a whole new world of business opportunities that the nineteenth century retail pioneers could not imagine, and their successors in the twentieth century could, for the most part, only dream of.

With every innovation in broadcasting, there has had to be a close association between the broadcasters and the manufacturers of radio and television receivers. Colour television, teletext (CEEFAX and ORACLE), stereophonic sound and iPlayer are all technical innovations that depended upon the manufacturing and retail industries being able to supply the necessary equipment to listeners and viewers. Even today, 'on demand' television services require broadband services of a specific speed, and many software providers make the same demands upon the consumer's PC, laptop, or tablet. Conversely, none other than the biggest players such as Microsoft and Apple can commit the large investments necessary for a new product or means of communication without being assured that the manufacturers will follow suit – except of course if they are also the manufacturers.

Marconi and the BBC

On 13 May 1897, Marconi sent the world's first-ever wireless transmission across open sea from Flat Holm, a small island in the Bristol Channel, to the Welsh coast. He repeated his experiment five days later at 2.50 pm on 18 May 1897. For the experiment, Marconi moved his base across to a disused fort at the end of Brean Down on the mainland. The fort had been recently constructed as part of a plan instituted by Lord Palmerston to defend the country against a French naval attack. By the time it had been completed, the threat had evaporated, and the buildings had become known as one of 'Palmerston's Follies'. Brean Down is a promontory near to Weston-super-Mare on the English side of the Bristol Channel. It is the end of the Mendip hills. The relocation extended the distance of Marconi's transmissions to sixteen kilometres.

There followed two decades of committed development, and on Valentine's Day in 1922, the Marconi Company began broadcasting from a former army hut close to their base in Writtle near Chelmsford. The station's call-sign, 2MT, led to the creation of a sister station 2LO, and then the BBC. The 2MT station closed on 17 January 1923. By the following year, six stations were on the air, broadcasting under the name of the British Broadcasting Company. These were in London, Birmingham, Cardiff, Manchester, Newcastle and Glasgow. They were followed by stations in Aberdeen, Bournemouth, Sheffield, Plymouth and Belfast; and they came together under the BBC – the British Broadcasting Corporation – on 1 January 1927.

Except for Bournemouth, these city locations, with some additions including Norwich and Nottingham, formed the later BBC English Regions. In the 1920s the BBC operated both a National and Regional Service. Although it became possible, technically, for individual stations to broadcast the same programmes simultaneously, the GPO (General Post Office) discouraged the BBC from doing so because of the pressure it placed on their network.

At the outbreak of the Second World War, the National and Regional services were replaced by a single BBC Home Service broadcasting on two separate medium wave frequencies from transmitters across the country. Each group of transmitters was shut down during air raids to prevent their signals being used as navigational beacons, but the programme remained available on a very low-powered network. Three months after VE Day, on 29 July 1945, the BBC resumed the Regional Programme but renamed it the Home Service. The National Programme restarted as the BBC Light Programme. Under the *Broadcasting in the Seventies* plan, these became BBC Radio 4 and BBC Radio 2 respectively.

Television

Although the Scottish-born inventor, John Logie Baird is regarded as the father of television, it was Marconi who again created a system that had the potential for development. As early as 1929, only three years after the BBC was incorporated, Baird had transmitted images from the 2LO studios at London's Savoy Hill. The Baird system, based on a concept invented as early as 1884, was extremely complex and relied on mechanical components at the studio and in the receiver to be synchronised, which rarely happened. Yet, in July 1930, the BBC managed to broadcast the play by Luigi Pirandello, *The man with a flower in his mouth*, in its entirety, using the Baird method.

It was the combination of Marconi's genius and the resources of EMI that developed the system which would take television forward and make it available to the mass market, based not on complex spinning discs and wheels, but on the cathode ray tube, moving not pieces of metal but energy and light. The BBC dropped the Baird system, a decision which contributed to the financial collapse of Baird's company. In less than a year, his equipment was replaced by the Marconi-EMI cameras and receivers. Ironically, the first generation of video cassette recorders (the VHS or Video Home System) marketed by the Japanese JVC company from 1976 was a generic development of Baird's system, using a spinning drum to print the data onto magnetic tape. Sir Isaac Schoenberg, who led the EMI team, and was a brilliant project engineer and manager, made the wry comment after one of the earliest transmissions of his system: 'Gentlemen, you have now invented the biggest time-waster of all time. Use it well.'

Of great significance to the UK economy is the profusion of television services based in the United Kingdom which primarily target foreign markets. According to the European Audio-visual Observatory MAVISE database and research carried out for the European Commission in 2016, the

United Kingdom is home to by far the most television channels and on-demand audio-visual services compared with other European countries. In 2016, there were 1,389 channels established in the United Kingdom, representing one-third of the total across the whole or Europe. There were a further 747 on-demand services. By comparison, the country with the second highest number is the Czech Republic with just 91 channels. London is the commercial television hub for much of the Western world.

Rediffusion

Although mobile devices connect directly to transmitters, and almost all internet communication involves satellite technology at some stage, using the internet in the workplace or at home still depends on data being sent along cables. These may be fibre-optic, in which the information is carried on fluctuating light, but in most cases, at the point it enters your building, it still involves a pair of metallic wires.

The earliest mass provision of broadcasting was also a cable system, and it grew up alongside the development of the BBC's terrestrial transmitters. One such system, which relayed radio broadcasts to homes in Hull, is still a provider in the internet age, namely Kingston Telecom.

The most familiar name in this field of communication was Rediffusion. The company's origins date back almost as far as the BBC. It began as Broadcast Relay Service, and was founded in 1928. Its first cable relay service was introduced in Hull in the following year alongside what is now the Kingston Communications Group. Rediffusion mainly re-broadcast BBC radio in areas where reception was poor. The company prospered for several decades, their business boosted by the fact that their system was pre-installed in many new council houses, and by the advent of colour television. Their bright-yellow Morris 1000 vans were a familiar sight in many towns and cities. However, it was unable to compete with the modern digital cable networks which began being rolled out in the early 1990s. Eventually, the company was split into a retail division which was absorbed into Granada and the distribution system which was taken-over by Robert Maxwell's Mirror Group.

Radio Normandy

In theory, the British Broadcasting Company, in its early days before receiving its public charter, could have broadcast commercials. From 1922, it certainly

embraced commercialism by establishing financial arrangements with manufacturers of wireless equipment to enable receivers to be available to buy
in High Street shops, but with the formation of the British Broadcasting
Corporation in 1927 under the direction of John Reith, such tawdry matters
as advertising toothpaste and washing powder could not be considered; and
the corporation's charter then forbade it. The decision left the door open
for entrepreneurs to set up radio stations in Europe close enough and with
powerful enough transmitters to reach the British Isles.

The remarkable entrepreneur who filled the gap was an English former
Royal Air Force officer by the name of Captain Leonard Plugge who, in
1931, set up the International Broadcasting Company in competition with
the BBC. Plugge enjoyed motoring holidays in Europe and was a radio
enthusiast. On his travels, he would collect the schedules of European radio
stations and pass them on to the BBC who would publish them. On one
journey, he stopped at Fecamp in Normandy, and discovered that a member of the family who owned the town's Benedictine distillery had set up a
transmitter in his home, and that a local cobbler's business had increased
considerably after being mentioned on the air.

Plugge immediately contacted the young radio pioneer, and paid for some
airtime for broadcasts in English. A studio was constructed in a loft above
some stables, Plugge hired some staff, and persuaded the local branch of
the National Provincial Bank to pay for the first-ever commercial. Radio
Normandy was born. Over the years, Radio Normandy built up a large and
loyal listenership in England as far north as the East Midlands. It is even
claimed that John Reith 'lightened' his serious Sunday evening radio broadcasts because his audiences were deserting him in favour of the light music
and entertainment offered by Radio Normandy, and this departure from his
strongly-held principles ultimately led him to resign.

Radio Normandy prospered, and introduced several broadcasters who
were to become household names including Roy Plumley who later devised
and presented Desert Island Discs for the BBC, and Bob Danvers-Walker,
the announcer whose voice was heard on the narration of British Pathé cinema newsreels for many years.

The hostilities in Europe at the commencement of the Second World
War led to the closure of Radio Normandy. Plugge offered to broadcast propaganda into enemy-held areas of Europe, but his proposal was
turned down. The station was commandeered by German troops in 1939
who used it for their own propaganda before French resistance workers
sabotaged the studios and put it out of action. The Internal Broadcasting

Company's London headquarters, just a few buildings away from the BBC's Broadcasting House, was also bombed during the war, but rebuilt, and in the post-war period operated as a recording studio where artists and bands including Jimi Hendrix, The Who and the Rolling Stones recorded. It is claimed that the verb 'to plug' a record or a product derives from the amazing Captain Plugge, whose activities inspired another well-known commercial radio station that advertised British products to British people from the heart of Europe.

Radio Luxembourg

The station which beamed 'We are the Ovaltineys' and gave out Dan Dare hat badges, also brought the radio dramas of Perry Mason and Dr Kildare to an English audience. It advertised Horlicks and sold airtime to the Seventh Day Adventist Church and the Lutheran Church, and snapped up the long-running radio comedy series *Much Binding in the Marsh* when the BBC axed it, until the BBC reconsidered their decision. Even Dame Vera Lynn, arguably the most popular and sought-after British vocal star during the war years, signed with Radio Luxembourg for a series of forty-two shows because the BBC had asked her to brighten up her act!

The history of Radio Luxembourg dates to 1924, before the BBC became a corporation, when François Anen built a radio transmitter in Luxembourg, and began broadcasting military music. Inspired by Captain Plugge's activities, Anen convened a meeting of other mainly French businessmen and lobbied the Government of the Grand Duchy to award them a broadcasting license. Anen was successful, and in May 1932, Radio Luxembourg began test transmissions aimed at Great Britain and Ireland. For eighteen months, the British Government protested to the Luxembourg authorities, mainly because the transmissions – on Long Wave – were very powerful and of a higher quality than any radio signal previously broadcast towards the British Isles. The station finally commenced scheduled programmes in January 1934, their wavelength being formalised by the Lucerne Convention of the previous year.

In the years leading up to the Second World War, Radio Luxembourg gained a huge British audience for its sponsored programmes. It is estimated that its English Language reach was as high as 11 per cent of the UK population. Many British companies advertised on both Radio Luxembourg and Radio Normandy, their programmes and commercials having been recorded in London and then flown out to Europe because the GPO (General Post

Office) would not allow the stations to use their landlines. Hundreds of British companies and businesses, and millions of British people were exposed to commercial broadcasting for the first time, and the appetite for more was a prime mover in the decision to set up the Independent Television Authority in the early 1950s.

Although Radio Luxembourg successfully fought off the challenge of the pirate radio stations in the 1960s, it was unable to compete with the roll-out of Independent Local Radio in the UK which began with Capital Radio and LBC News in London, and the launch of BBC Radio 1 in 1967. The station attempted several relaunches on different media including satellite but closed at midnight on 30 December 1992.

In marketing terms, Radio Luxembourg defined a new approach to advertising by identifying specific markets. Over the years, it tailored its product to the teenage market, a specific consumer group which had probably always had a presence in the High Street but had been rarely considered. Print advertisements from footwear and fashion retailers had previously shown cute children in pretty frocks or sailor suits, and sophisticated women accompanied by suave handsome men. The teenagers, and the generation which had gone to war in their late teens, began to have a stronger cultural identity in the 1950s, and most certainly in the pop culture of the 1960s, and the commercial radio stations were a very important part of this revolution in the United Kingdom.

Perhaps the pivotal year was 1967, and the key event was the launch of the Beatles' *Sgt Pepper* album on 1 June 1967. From that moment, teenage styles, culture and consumerism became a worldwide phenomenon, and not simply a cult centred on London's Carnaby Street. It was to be a shift in attitudes that the big names and the traditional department and chain stores had to take notice of. The shop-girls in the 'fashion' departments of Littlewoods and Marks and Spencer, and the family-owned department stores realised increasingly that the products they were selling were for a certain generation of customers. They themselves found what appealed to them and their boyfriends in a new kind of retail establishment, small niche shops often away from the High Street where overheads were lower. Shops which teenagers wanted to be seen in, and would talk about to their friends. Shops which sold goods that were vibrant, different, and made a statement. It would take two decades before these concepts were fully adopted by the big players, and it was the rise of the shopping centres, precincts and malls which was to provide these businesses with a more up-market retail presence.

Independent (Commercial) Television

The BBC television service, which had closed for the duration of the Second World War, restarted in 1946 and gradually expanded its coverage, first to the Midlands and the North of England, and by 1953 to Scotland and Northern Ireland. One year later, the government passed the Television Act which paved the way for the introduction of independent or commercial television in the United Kingdom. This allowed the formation of the Independent Broadcasting Authority which began issuing franchises for regional services, and on 22 September 1955, the first commercial television station in the United Kingdom went on air, serving London, and provided by Associated-Rediffusion. Services for the Midlands and the North followed in 1956. Thus, a new era in advertising and marketing began which was to bring us such immortal lines as 'Beanz Meanz Heinz' and 'Don't forget the fruit gums, mum.'

The first television commercial was aired in the United States on 1 July 1941 by the radio station WMBT in New York. It was an advertisement for wristwatches, and the manufacturer, Bulova, paid $9 to have their commercial broadcast immediately before a baseball game. The concept of airtime placement, and the relationship between advertising charges and peak programme time slots had already begun.

The first commercial to appear on British television was for Gibbs SR toothpaste, and featured a tube of the toothpaste with a block of ice, and an out-of-vision voiceover proclaiming its 'tingling-fresh' qualities. At this early stage in the genre, agencies often used material on one or more media, so a frame from a television advertisement could be used in a newspaper, and vice-versa. The first commercials for Persil were lifted from existing posters with the addition of dancers dressed in various shades of white and the voiceover explaining that 'Persil washes whiter. That means cleaner.' These early commercials were produced with the deliberate intention of looking and sounding different from American material. So, the 'Englishness' was pointed up which meant a profusion of middle-class accents and values. They had little impact despite their message being projected slowly and with deliberation.

Celebrities, or at least, well-known figures, began to be used in British commercials, endorsing personally a product, usually extolling its virtues with the help of a chart or graph. There followed two further marketing approaches, the 'admag' and the 'time spot'. The former was a sequence of shorter commercials for various products linked by a familiar presenter.

They were designed for the smaller companies which had a limited budget for marketing. The 'time spot' was a very simple brief reference to a product during a continuity announcement such as 'It's [the actual time], and time to light a red and white.' The Independent Television Authority banned these in 1960.

The first generation of television advertising followed the approach of previous newspapers and shop window marketing, telling the viewer why they needed to buy the product. Concepts such as lifestyle and aspirations had to wait until the 1970s when the advent of 625-line and colour television gave advertising agencies greater scope for innovation. Competition in what became a decade of materialism, compared with the immediate post-war years, encouraged higher production values which resulted in much greater sophistication.

Commercials became more subtle and were often gently self-mocking, such as the Martians laughing at the inhabitants of earth for growing and peeling potatoes when they could be buying the powdered version called Smash, a campaign which gave viewers the unforgettable 'For mash get Smash'; and the iconic, almost psychedelic cigar advertisements which informed that 'Happiness is a cigar called Hamlet' using the Jacque Loussier Trio's jazz interpretation of J.S. Bach's 'Air on a G String'. The commercials were banned in 1991, but continued in British cinemas for several years until 1999.

Until the 1970s, there were very few commercials for motor vehicles in Britain due to a secret agreement between the four principal manufacturers, Ford, Vauxhall, Chrysler and British Leyland, not to use television advertising. It was the arrival of the Japanese car manufacturer Datsun which broke up the agreement, so, ironically, the first car commercials seen in Britain were not for British-made vehicles.

Two curious and short-lived innovations came in the late 1980s. The banking group First Direct booked the same transmission slots on ITV and Channel 4. Viewers who changed channels during the commercial could see a different – good or bad – outcome to the story. A commercial for Mazda cars incorporated several short-duration images which could be seen only if viewers recorded the advertisement and then played it back, frame by frame. By doing so, viewers could enter a competition to win a car.

Although television advertising in the United Kingdom has always been strictly controlled, with a ban on certain products and services, it has been a medium which has broadened in style and production concepts over the past fifty years. Commercials can be annoying, over-repetitive or simply boring in the eyes of the viewer, but the only measure of their success is the sales figures for the products they promote. Today, solicitors, funeral directors, cancer charities and even the National Health Service all embrace television advertising.

Television advertising is a major commitment for any business, and the stakes are high. The bill for one thirty-second commercial during Coronation Street broadcast nationally is about £50,000, not including its production. For the big players, the figures are very large indeed. The John Lewis 2016 'Buster the Boxer' Christmas television campaign cost in the region of £7million, including a production budget of £1million, but was expected to generate sales of £1.3 billon.

Alfred Charles Cossor

Alfred Cossor established a company in the Clerkenwell area of London in 1859 manufacturing scientific glassware, but it was his son, also named Alfred Charles, who founded the electronics company which became a household name. Cossor junior joined the business in 1875. Ten years later, the younger son, Frank Cossor also joined the family concern. The company developed an expertise in fine electrical glassware including cathode ray tubes, thermionic valves and x-ray tubes. In 1902, they produced the first-ever Braun (cathode ray) tube. It was this capability which led them to start making wireless and television receivers, and eventually to move into the electronics industry. Frank Cossor later took over the running of the original glassware business which is still in operation under the brand name Accoson or A.C. Cossor and Sons (Surgical) Ltd. Their main product was the sphygmomanometer which is the technical name for the familiar instrument attached to an arm with an inflatable rubber cuff, used for measuring blood pressure. The company, based in Harlow in Essex, still manufactures a range of these devices, in use in GP practices and hospitals throughout seventy-six countries. In 1966, Adrian Cossor joined Accoson, the fourth generation of the family to do so.

In the 1920s, Cossor launched their famous Melody Maker wireless receiver which quickly established itself as the centrepiece of the British living room. By 1936, the company became the first company in the United Kingdom to sell a television set.

During the Second World War, Cossor, with other British radio and television manufacturers such as Pye, worked on the emerging electronics technology of radar, setting up the country's Chain Home radar around the

British Isles. A.C. Cossor was chosen by the UK Air Ministry to build the receiving units and operator displays that made the Chain Home air defence radar network viable. At the commencement of the Battle of Britain, this was the first operational radar system in the world, with nineteen stations stretching from Land's End to the northernmost point of the Shetland Islands. These provided the RAF with a twenty-minute warning of an attack by the Luftwaffe, enabling Britain's defences to be scrambled and directed to their targets.

After the war, Cossor continued with their domestic production, and were absorbed by EMI. In the late 1950s this part of their business was acquired by the Netherlands-based Philips company. The technical expertise was acquired by the American company Raytheon, which still uses the Cossor brand today.

William George Pye

Like Alfred Cossor, William Pye's expertise was in the manufacture of scientific and optical instruments. He was born in October 1869 in Battersea and became a member of staff of the Cavendish Laboratory in Cambridge. His company was set up in 1896 as a part-time occupation, at the time that Cossor was experimenting in cathode ray tube technology, but it was not until after the First World War that the company began manufacturing parts for radio receivers, including glass thermionic valves.

By the outbreak of war, Pye was employing forty staff making instruments for research and teaching. The war increased the demand for such instruments and created a need for thermionic valves. In responding to this demand, Pye accrued valuable experience and knowledge which was used in peacetime to make radio sets soon after the BBC was formed in 1922.

Pye finally produced their own radio set. William's son, Harold John Pye, working with Edward Appleton, his former tutor at St John's College, Cambridge, was instrumental in developing a set which became so popular that the company divided into Pye Radio, which was taken over by Charles Orr Stanley, an external investor, and the former business which continued to make optical instruments. Pye Radio opened a chain of small manufacturing facilities across East Anglia to meet the demand for their products.

Charles Stanley could not receive the BBC's first television transmissions from its Alexandra Palace transmitter because even their most southern offices were outside the coverage area which was limited to about twenty-five miles. Stanley rose to the challenge and developed a high gain television receiver which would pick up the transmissions, therefore increasing the BBC's potential audience. By 1937, this was in full production, retailing at twenty-one guineas (£22.05). They sold over 2,000 sets in the first two years.

In 1947, Pye Radio and Harold Pye agreed terms that reunited the firms, and Harold then retired, taking up farming near Burnham-on-Crouch in Essex. His father died at Bexhill in Sussex in 1949.

In 1955, the company diversified into music production, creating the Pye Records music label, but the arrival of the Independent Television Authority in the same year gave the company a new challenge, of designing television sets that could switch between the BBC and the new channel. Pye was ready for the challenge, having already committed engineers to creating the necessary components, enabling the company to begin selling their new 'tunable' television set in March 1954.

Unfortunately, a later variant of this set was unreliable and damaged the company's reputation. It led Pye to be cautious when attempting to lead the market with new products, but continued to pioneer new electronic research, developing the first transistor in 1956.

The company also began making equipment, mainly television cameras but also sound studio mixing desks for the industry. Both the BBC and the ITV companies were supplied by Pye, and their equipment enjoyed a good reputation with engineers and operators.

However, with the advent of colour, the Pye company fell by the wayside. Financial difficulties meant they were unable to commit the resources needed to develop their own colour television camera, and an attempt to design a colour cine recorder was a failure for the same reason. The financial problems had been caused mainly by the introduction of products into the United Kingdom from the Japanese giants, Sony and Hitachi who were retailing colour television sets for less than £200. British companies, including Pye, were unable to compete because their manufacturing techniques were still based on concepts from the 1920s and their workforce was generally unwilling to accept change. With inflation and unemployment both rising fast, the company was selling less, stockpiling products they could not move, and suffering from a consequent lack of finance for investment. The company was bought by Philips in 1976. Pye's Lowestoft factory was later sold on to the Japanese firm Sanyo, and the manufacture of Pye products was moved to Singapore.

The brand enjoyed a brief revival in popularity with a design of music centre which incorporated a television receiver in the late 1970s and the 1980s which had a near-cult status with university and college students of that period. More recently, the brand resurfaced with new products including DVD recorders, and Pye remains one of only a few brands that have survived from the earliest days of the broadcasting revolution.

Charles Orr Stanley

Charles Stanley was a remarkable figure whose energies and diverse abilities spanned almost the entire twentieth century. He was the son of an Irish farmer from County Waterford, and was born in 1899. He became a school teacher and moved to England to take up a teaching post in Somerset whilst still in his teens. He joined the Royal Flying Corps in 1917 and served in the final months of the First World War, and then graduated in civil engineering at the City and Guild's School in Finsbury, joining Engineering Publicity Services, a London-based advertising agency set up by the radio and electronics pioneer Frank Murphy.

After a disagreement with Murphy, Stanley launched his own company called Arks Publicity, attracting some of Murphy's employees. They were successful in securing contracts with several leading companies in the radio industry including Captain Stanley Mullard's Radio Valve Company.

Less than a year later he was working with William George Pye, encouraging him to move into the radio manufacturing business, and in 1926, just as the BBC was forming itself into a corporation, he invented a wireless receiver in the form of a kit. The Mullard Company appointed him as their Sales Consultant, and Stanley then devised a marketing campaign to encourage people to build their own radio receivers at home, using Mullard components. He also built one of the first portable radios, and convinced a bank to loan him £60,000 to manufacture them, having demonstrated its capabilities to the manager. With the money, he purchased Pye Radio outright from William Pye. Although he was offered a large factory in Swansea, he chose instead to adopt outworking in a group of rural villages in East Anglia, employing in the region of 14,000 people in an area of high employment, but close to the cutting-edge research in Cambridge.

With the outbreak of the Second World War, Stanley was commissioned to design a 'radio proximity fuse', which he completed in 1941 and was subsequently used to destroy many German flying bombs. He also organised a convoy of trucks to rescue a stockpile of valves, vital for radar equipment, from a warehouse in Eindhoven. He managed to retrieve them before the

Germans invaded, and they were used in the first British airborne radar equipment.

His practical attitudes to challenges allowed him to think 'out of the box' and arrive at simple and successful solutions to a problem. The British military had given him specifications for the airborne radar kits which focussed on the need for them to be robust. Stanley chose instead to manufacture a lightweight design which used less power, was comparatively inexpensive, and could be moved and operated easily by troops.

After the war, he remained loyal to his native Ireland, creating the large Corran Works in Larne. In the 1960s, Stanley was the largest employer in the Republic of Ireland except for the Irish Government. He remained at the forefront of the broadcasting industry, forming the Associated Broadcasting Development Company which became ATV Ltd, specifically to provide a commercial television service in the English Midlands, and it is said he pushed the industry into developing 625-line UHF television sets when BBC2 was launched. He promoted independent local radio in England and even financed, secretly, some pirate radio stations, including Radio Caroline. Stanley was also the businessman involved in the marketing of the first colour television sets. Charles Orr Stanley died on 18 January 1989 at Lesselan in County Cork.

Frank Murphy

Perhaps not one of the major players in television retailing, Murphy is still a familiar name today. Murphy Radio was founded in 1929 by Frank Murphy, in partnership with E.J. 'Ted' Power as a mass producer of domestic radio receivers. Their factories were based in Welwyn Garden City in Hertfordshire. The company began with less than a hundred employees, and operated a manufacturing plant in Murphy's native country, at Islandbridge in Dublin.

Like other companies in this field, Murphy designed and supplied radio receivers for the British armed forces during the Second World War, and in the 1950s, developed these sets further for supply to the navies of the Commonwealth and to the British Army. The company moved into the television market, for which it became most well-known, and was amalgamated with Bush Radio in 1962 when Ted Power sold control to the Rank Organisation. The brand has survived, but is now owned by an electronics company in the far east. Frank Murphy left the company in 1937 to set up a new business called 'FM Radio'. It was not a success. He died in 1955.

E.J. 'Ted' Power

Another radio and television entrepreneur whose name did not become a High Street brand, but was responsible for significant developments in the technology, E.J. Power was born in Galway in 1899, the same year as Charles Orr Stanley, but spent his childhood in Manchester. He joined the Royal Navy as a wireless operator at the age of sixteen, and in the 1920s, launched his own business making crystal radio sets and transformers, but his main source of income was from repairing other retailers' products. In 1929, he renewed his acquaintance with Frank Murphy, a family friend, and together they launched the Murphy Company.

Power retired in 1962 after Murphy became part of Rank and merged with Bush Radio, and he committed the rest of his life to acquiring modern art and sponsoring other collections, notably the Tate Gallery. His very important collection is now the property of the nation.

His Master's Voice

One of the most iconic of all record labels, with a branding which has remained unchanged since the days of the wind-up gramophone, but which still has a powerful High Street presence is His Master's Voice or HMV, despite that company being forced into receivership in 2013.

The familiar image of Nipper the dog recognising his master's voice on a recording was painted by the English artist Francis Barraud who gave it the title that would become the name of the future business. The painting was of a real scene. Nipper was owned by Barraud's brother, Mark. When he died, the artist inherited the dog and a gramophone with recordings of his brother. He noticed that Nipper recognised his former master's voice.

The painting, and the title, were the subject of several copyright applications, including one from Emile Berliner who had invented the gramophone. The original image was modified by the artist at the request of the American-based Gramophone Company who acquired copyright and used it as the logo for the Victor Talking Machine Company. Victor was later to become the well-known RCA Victor company, and the Gramophone Company was absorbed into EMI. Therefore, the trademark is owned jointly by several very large companies which diminishes its value in the global music market.

The first HMV record shop opened in London in 1921, and by 2006, there were over 400 stores across the country. The chain entered receivership in 2013, but was relaunched shortly afterwards, and is now retailing in stores and on line.

Eric Kirkham Cole

His name is not familiar to many, but his initials are the clue. Eric Cole was the father of the familiar radio and television brand, EKCO. He was born in Prittlewell in the Westcliff-on-Sea area of Southend-on-sea near to the present London Southend airport. His father, Henry Cole, was a dairyman. After leaving Southend High School for Boys, Cole undertook a three-year apprenticeship and then went into partnership with his father as an electrical engineer. He set up a small business with his girl-friend, later his wife, Muriel Bradshaw, in Leigh on Sea, producing six radio receivers a week, which he sold, with batteries and headphones for £6.10s 0d. The EKCO brand name was created in 1926 when, in partnership with a former satisfied customer, the Coles established E.K. Cole Ltd.

Cole's major break-through and contribution to the industry, was to devise a radio set which could operate from mains power rather than from batteries. It was a step change, taking radio from being a complicated novelty needing a constant supply of heavy rechargeable batteries, to a modern household device which could be connected to the electricity supply of any home, and turned on, literally, at the touch of a switch.

The effect on Cole's business was phenomenal. From the first workshop in one small room above a confectioner's shop in Southend, EKCO was employing nearly 4,000 people in a factory covering almost a quarter of a million square feet in just twelve years.

In common with the other major British radio manufacturers, Cole worked with the British military during the Second World War. His manufacturing plants were dispersed to secret shadow sites to reduce the risk of being targeted by German bombers, and from September 1939 production switched completely to providing army radios and setting up night fighter radar. Much of this work took place in underground bunkers at Southend, and was to continue in peace time, through to the Blue Sky radio-controlled guided missile project of the 1950s.

In 1953, the company diversified into building television sets, and bought out Dynatron in 1954 and Ferranti in 1957. ECKO merged with Pye in 1960 to become British Electronic Industries in 1960. In 1958, Eric Cole was awarded the CBE. He died in a boating accident on 18 November 1966 in Barbados.

Sir Jules Thorn

The year of 1899 figures again in the biography of Julius Thorn who was born in that year in Vienna to Jewish parents. He gained a degree in business management at the business school of the University of Vienna, and became a sales representative for Olso, the Austrian manufacturer of gas mantles. His job later involved travelling to England to sell Olso's products. When Olso went bankrupt, Thorn was forced to seek a new career, and he chose to move from gas power to electricity. In 1928, he moved to England and within a short time established the Electrical Lamp Service Company, importing radio components and light bulbs from European manufacturers.

Thorn broadened the base of his business in 1932 when he purchased a controlling share of the Chorlton Metal Company, and he also set up a radio rental shop branded as Lotus Radio in the following year, as well as acquiring the Atlas Works which made electric bulbs called the Atlas Lamp. With the profits from these businesses, he bought the Ferguson Radio Corporation in 1936 which gave him the facility to manufacture radio receivers as well as selling them. In that year, he drew together all his business activities under the name of Thorn Electrical Industries.

His electronics empire prospered until the outbreak of the Second World War, when, as with so many other manufacturers of well-known domestic items, almost all the goods produced by Thorn became restricted by the Government's rationing programme; but when the war ended in 1945, Jules Thorn launched an ambitious expansion of his businesses, mainly through the acquisition of several well-known brands including Ecko-Ensign and Tricity Cookers. By the end of 1961, he had also acquired Philco and Pilot, and had major financial interests in Ultra Radio and Television, HMV and Marconiphone. In that year, Thorn Electrical Industries became the largest producer of radio and television sets in Britain. Thorn was knighted in 1964 in recognition of his contributions to the British electronics industry.

Additionally, the merger of Robinson Radio Rentals with Thorn's group of companies made the Thorn/Radio Rentals group the world's largest television rental company, controlling just under one-third of the 7.5 million televisions in Britain.

Jules Thorn was a practical man who remained involved in any facet of his business empire, sometimes to a degree that was overwhelming for his staff who could feel pressured by his dominating personality. However, he was also notable for his shrewd business decisions, and the introduction of colour television technology is an example of his ability to stay ahead of his competitors by making imaginative and somewhat daring decisions. The transmission of colour television programmes did not begin in Britain until December 1967. Thorn recognised that this development would dramatically increase demand for colour television sets, but the required technology and patents were difficult to obtain in the UK. Thorn, in a typical example of his lateral business thinking, imported blank television tubes from the United States and coated them with the necessary colour-sensitive pigments in his own manufacturing plants. In so doing, Thorn Electrical Industries could further consolidate its position in the British television market.

Thorn's largest takeover bid by far came in 1979 when an opportunity arose to purchase EMI, which was facing severe financial problems. Jules Thorn had retired earlier in 1979 and he died on 12 December 1980 at Westminster in London.

Chapter Nine

Being Friendly and Paying Up

T he High Street banks form a group of brands with which we have
a very particular relationship. Currency dates back in some form
through the whole of our history to the tribal groups who started to
replace the system of bartering goods by using a symbol, a token or a coin,
with a value allocated to them. Some 'goods' had different forms of value
over and above their intrinsic value or their usefulness or rarity, such as
spiritual and sacred, but money brought everything into a very physical and
pecuniary world. Some of the pre-Roman tribes in England minted their
own currency, such as the Corieltauvi in the Eastern area of the Midlands
who embossed the names of their leaders on their coins, and we are all
familiar with that much earlier record of coinage being exchanged – and
it would seem at high rates of interest – with the biblical account of Jesus
Christ expelling the money changers from the temple in Jerusalem. This is
recounted in all four New Testament gospels as well as some non-religious
texts, and would date to about 24–29 ad.

Today's High Street banks also have a long history, though mostly reaching back to the eighteenth century in England and Scotland. For many
years, the British banking industry, at least as far as domestic and personal
finance was concerned, was represented by a relatively stable grouping of a
small number of well-established names, but the worldwide financial crisis
of 2007 and 2008, commonly referred to as the 'credit crunch', sought out
those banks of least resilience and initiated a complex sequence of mergers,
takeovers and Government rescues. The present composition of all the big-
name banks in Britain today tell the same story of merger and acquisition
over a span of two centuries.

The structure of the present Lloyds Banking Group is an example of
how the industry has been reorganised. The Halifax Building Society (1852)
merged with the Bank of Scotland (1695) to form HBOS (Halifax Bank of
Scotland) in 2002. The Trustee Savings Bank (1810) and the original Lloyds
Bank, set up by a persecuted Quaker in Birmingham in 1765, merged in
1995 to become Lloyds TSB. HBOS and Lloyds TSB merged in 2009 to

form the present group. Scottish Widows (1815), an organisation whose founders include the great social reformer and thinker, Robert Owen, joined the Lloyds TSB group in 2000.

Hence, customers who bank with any part of Lloyds today are members of a banking dynasty which has its roots in Scotland in the late seventeenth century. The vaguely enigmatic black horse which is the present branding of the group dates back to 1728, when a goldsmith by the name of John Bland hung a similar sign above the door to his goldsmith's shop in London's Lombard Street. His business became Barnetts, Hoares and Company, and was taken over by Lloyds in 1884.

TSB has its roots in the trustee savings bank movement of the nineteenth century which was established under democratic and philanthropic principles. Their purpose was to encourage working-class people with a small income to be thrifty and to save, if only small amounts. Every penny saved was guaranteed by the local manager so that it could be withdrawn at any time, in full and with interest. These managers were therefore 'trustees', hence the name of the movement.

At a time when many banks would become insolvent due to bad decisions by their managers and owners, the funds in the trustee savings banks were made safer by the Saving Banks (England) Act of 1817 which required that all their monies were deposited in the Bank of England. The Act also set legal minimum standards of behaviour and actions for Trustee Savings Bank managers. By the middle of the nineteenth century there were over 600 such institutions in England. Each bank served a specified geographical area so did not compete, and by the outbreak of the Second World War their joint holdings exceeded £290 million which matched those of the major London-based clearing banks. By 1970 the number of banks had decreased through amalgamation and rationalisation to seventy-five, but their assets were more than £2.8 million.

The Trustee Savings Bank Act of 1975 led the way for the banks to merge and to be given the same financial status as the other High Street banks. Several decades of change resulted in the creation of a single bank which was floated on the stock market and later merged with Lloyds in 1995. After the 'credit crunch', when the UK Government undertook a rescue of Lloyds, TSB was separated off to satisfy European Union legislation. A new TSB was therefore formed in 2013.

It is not only the black horse which was born in London's Lombard Street. It was in the same street that Barclays Bank was formed, later to be established at 54 Lombard Street, beneath the sign of the black spread eagle.

The bank was created by John Freame, a Quaker, and his business colleague Thomas Gould, who began trading as goldsmiths and bankers in 1690. In 1736, the son-in-law of Freame, James Barclay, became a partner, and gave his name to the bank, although in its century of trading it was known by the names of all its partners. It must be noted that the Barclay family had derived much of their wealth from the slave trade until David Barclay, in the late eighteenth century, freed his slaves and acknowledged their equality with the white population.

Although the fiscal landscape in Britain and across the world has changed dramatically in recent decades, we still recognise the names and stylings of what became known as the 'Big Four'. These are now generally accepted to be, in order of holdings, Barclays, Lloyds, HSBC and NatWest, although behind those names and their present standing in the marketplace, there are complex and intriguing stories. All those big-name banks who constructed impressive cathedrals to wealth in England's High Streets have a similarly complicated genealogy, and in most cases, they reach back to single individuals, many of whom had genuinely philanthropic principles.

The image of the golden griffin surrounded by golden coins became familiar in the High Street in the 1960s as the logo of the Midland Bank. It was later animated in television commercials, with the griffin holding its arm to its ear with the phrase 'Come and talk, talk to the Midland. Come and talk to the listening bank.' Even after more than twenty-five years since it was last aired, the phrase and the musical jingle that accompanied it is familiar to many. The Midland was founded in Union Street in Birmingham in August 1836 by a former Bank of England employee, Charles Geach. In his later years, Geach became a prominent businessman, industrialist and politician, but it was when he was still in his twenties that he was sent to Birmingham by the Bank of England to open a branch. He settled in Birmingham, and went on to establish two new banks, but despite his hard work and commitment, he was not appointed manager. A group of Black Country businessmen then approached him, and invited him to set up a rival bank to the existing Birmingham Joint Bank and the Town and District Bank. The result was the first branch of the Midland. The choice of a griffin, a legendary creature, is obscure but appropriate. According to mythological experts, griffins were known to guard treasure and priceless possessions. In Roman and Greek texts, griffins were associated with gold, and later accounts suggested that griffins laid eggs which contained gold nuggets.

Birmingham became a prosperous and lively centre for business in the middle of the nineteenth century, particularly in the iron and steel trades and the activities they supplied, such as the burgeoning railway system and the various municipal corporations who were laying sewers and water supplies, and building public facilities including public bathes, libraries and museums. The Midland Bank grew quickly, acquiring other financial institutions, first in Birmingham and then reaching out to the West and East Midlands. A major milestone in its history was the acquisition in 1891 of the Central Bank of London, which provided the Midland with a seat in the London Clearing House. By the end of the First World War, it was the largest bank in the world with deposits of £335 million. The Midland Bank was the first in the country to abolish charges for operating a current account maintained in credit. The bold step was so successful in attracting customers who then made use of the bank's other paid-for services, that all the other banks followed suit, and current accounts in the UK remain free today.

In 1992, the Midland was acquired by the Hongkong Shanghai Banking Corporation, giving them a firm foothold in Europe. It was one of the biggest banking take-overs in history. The Midland continued with its traditional identity for some years, but was rebranded in 1999 when the friendly griffin was finally retired.

There are many other bodies which manage money, and as the industrial revolution began to affect people's lives, a wide variety of institutions were set up to help those who were destitute, and workers who needed immediate funds to respond to a family crisis. These became the friendly societies, and they came in all shapes and sizes. By the beginning of the twentieth century, the working classes in England were being given a voice through a surprising collection of organisations, each with its own agenda. There were the evangelical religious groups, the early socialist, labour and co-operative organisations, the philanthropists, and the enlightened businessmen. In terms of managing workers' money, this resulted in friendly societies who sometimes provided more practical support than simply handling people's money, and which at times seemed very like the emerging trade unions which also offered financial support to their members.

It also gave rise to societies such as the Rechabites, who looked to the tribes of Israel as the basis for their rules and constitution. The biblical clan called Rechabites descended from a man called Rechab, and were Kenites, a group which went with the Israelites at the time of the Exodus. They were forbidden to drink alcohol, and mainly occupied towns and cities rather than live a nomadic way of life, although the biblical account says that God commanded Rechab to live in a tent.

The Salford Unity of Rechabites was founded in August 1835 in Salford, near Manchester. Just four years earlier, the first Co-operative Congress had taken place, on 26 May 1831, in the *Spread Eagle* pub on Chapel Street in the town, and in the same year as the founding of the Rechabites, the Co-operative Movement in Salford opened a Social Institution located in Great George Street which could hold up to six hundred people. However, the Rechabites chose to be separatists. Each group or lodge was called a 'tent'. From the start, women and children from the age of five years could join, though they met in different 'tents'. Their activities, which could be accurately described as rituals and ceremonies, varied across the country, but always involved moving through three levels or 'degrees' of membership, these being Knight of Temperance, Knight of Fortitude, and Covenanted Knight of Justice. The Order was governed by a small group which travelled from tent to tent, and was therefore called the Movable Committee, meeting in a different town or city every two years. Membership was open to anyone who was willing to sign a pledge that they would abstain completely from alcohol for all religious and medical purposes. Members received death and sickness benefits, and could be buried in Rechabite graveyards.

Another section of the temperance movement was the Oddfellows, who were regarded as 'odd' because they refused to meet in licensed premises. This organisation, originally one of many, has been active throughout their history and is still thriving today. In the 2016–17 financial year, the Oddfellows reported funds of over £289 million. Established in 1810, they now operate as a friendly society, being a bank without shareholders, their profits being placed at the disposal of their 310,000 members. Despite their powerful fiscal presence, they work through small local branches, refer to their members as 'brothers and sisters', and still provide, at a very local level, grants for children to further their education and for members to buy spectacles. The local groups hold Christmas parties for their members, and do now meet in licensed premises. It is remarkable, and in many ways, reassuring to know, that such an organisation can not only survive but prosper in the twenty-first century.

The fascinating connections between the friendly societies and the working-class political movement of the nineteenth century produced many surprises. Brass bands were sponsored by the temperance movement, or by friendly societies, as in the case of the Ancient Order of Foresters. The Foresters was formed in Rochdale in 1834, and in 2016 had over 78,000 members. Their local branches are called 'courts' as distinct from the Oddfellows' lodges, and they acquired their name from the courts held in the Royal forests of England. Today, the Foresters sponsor a brass band, but also provide a range of social care support to its members and their children.

Alongside the friendly societies, whose prime purpose was to provide funds for welfare and education, were the building societies. The first English building society was founded in 1775 by Richard Ketley, who was the landlord of the *Golden Cross* public house in Birmingham. His members, who, like those of the friendly societies, paid a monthly affordable subscription, were very different. Birmingham was home to a new class of skilled and prosperous workers, businessmen and property owners. Ketley's purpose in setting up his society was to raise funds contributed by this group to fund the construction of homes for their workers. Originally, the building societies were 'self-terminating'. Once all their members had acquired a house, the society would be dissolved.

The Foresters and the Oddfellows may not be familiar names to High Street shoppers, but they form part of a colourful and complicated financial service industry which is closely linked to the High Street banks. One example from many is the present Santander Bank which uses premises formerly occupied by several different and familiar names from the past. The Bradford and Bingley Building Society was formed in 1964 with the merger of two well-established friendly societies, the Bradford Equitable and the Bingley Permanent, both dating back to 1851. In 2008, following the credit crunch, Bradford and Bingley's branches were taken over by Abbey National, which had earlier been acquired by the Spanish banking group, Santander. Previously, the 1990s saw a move towards 'demutualising'. Ten British building societies were floated on the stock market and became banks or were merged with existing banks. The Cheltenham and Gloucester was taken over by Lloyds Bank, and the National Provincial by Abbey National.

Abbey National is another former building society with a distinguished history, having been formed as the National Permanent Mutual Benefit Building Society in 1849 by two prominent members of parliament, Sir Joshua Warmsley and Richard Cobden, who were joined, one year later, by John Bright. Cobden was one of those dynamic individuals who reformed and innovated. He was a wealthy businessman who owned a very profitable business dealing in calico printing in Manchester. Yet he was also a liberal politician and statesman who held many radical ideas which included the concept of free trade. John Bright was a Quaker and another member of the free-thinking Liberal group of his time. He served as an MP for over forty years, campaigning for electoral reform and religious freedom. He opposed the Crimean War, virtually as a lone voice, and the privileges of the landed gentry. He can also claim a place in history for being responsible for the phrase 'mother of parliaments'.

The National Permanent Mutual Benefit Building Society later joined with the Abbey Road and St John's Wood Permanent Building Society, which had been founded in 1874. The headquarters of this society was a Baptist chapel (another example of the somewhat curious co-operation between religious political and financial groups in nineteenth century England) in Abbey Road in Kilburn, London. This is the same Abbey Road on which the famous recording studios are situated where many groups and rock stars of the 1960s and 1970s, including the Beatles, recorded their iconic albums.

Northern Rock, a building society which had a strong presence in the High Streets in the north of England, was nationalised in February 2008 after facing near-collapse following the credit crunch. They were bought by Virgin Money in January 2012.

Forty building societies in the UK have survived the turbulent financial times of the past decades and two world wars. By far the largest is the Nationwide with assets in the region of £208,939 million, and operates from 650 branches. The second largest is the much smaller Yorkshire Building Society with assets of £39,600 million. Nationwide is the result of over one hundred previous mergers, the most notable being the last two with the Anglia Building Society in 1987 and the Portman Building Society in 1987. This made Nationwide the second largest provider of household savings and mortgages in the UK. The two smallest building societies still operating are the Earl Shilton Building Society in Leicestershire, trading from two branches in the town of that name, and the Penrith Building Society in Cumbria, which has one branch and assets of around £106 million.

One further group of players in the complex world of banking and financial services are the credit unions. Existing for the mutual benefit of their customers, credit unions function in similar ways to building societies and other mutual organisations. They may in time come to represent the rebirth of the original friendly society concept, remaining small in scale and therefore able to provide a high degree of customer satisfaction and involvement. They stand independent of other financial institutions, generally providing smaller loans to customers who cannot meet the criteria required by banks. Although, in order to conform to legislation, they may appear to be very similar to other financial organisations, their total commitment to social responsibility sets them apart.

As the late Ronnie Barker's 'Arkwright' often said, the secret of a successful shopkeeper is forever inventing new ways of relieving customers of their cash. Little could the nation of shopkeepers, who Barker's character represented, have known that the age was approaching when our consumer society could be completely cashless. From cheque and PIN, to the ubiquitous plastic card and ETPOS (Electronic Transfer at Point of Sale), to card-less transfers of funds using smartphones and other mobile devices, all based on an internet technology which also enables customers to pay utility bills, order foreign currency, top up their mobile phones, pay a bus fare – on board the bus – and the postage required for parcel delivery services.

In one sense, coinage is itself an indication or representation of, or substitute for, an individual's wealth. Bank notes are promissory vouchers, in England still signed by the Chief Cashier of the Bank of England. The theories of economics and wealth are complex, but the invention of money was itself an inflationary measure. Support for this statement can be found in the way in which monastic establishments and then priests – rectors and vicars – were supported by their parish. The ancient system used the biblical concept of tithing, giving one-tenth of income to the work of God, and in Great Britain dated back to at least the eighth century. It became an annual enforced formality to contribute to the church the required 10 per cent of one's physical income, be it in corn, wheat or other crops, trees (timber), geese, lamb or other animals. Across the country, large tithe barns were built, many still standing today. In the gardens of monasteries, and later, rectories, ponds were dug and streams were diverted so that fish, ducks and geese could be kept.

Then, in 1836, the Commutation Act was passed. In very simple terms, it placed a monetary value on each item previously tithed, based on average prices over a seven-year period (itself a truly biblical measure of time!). Without exploring the consequences in detail, it is evident that if the rector's income was to remain steady from year to year, then the numbers of wildfowl or animals, or the weight of crops would increase or decrease, depending on their selling price. It was therefore affected by inflation. On a different plane, the ancient way in which the farmer or the villager who kept a few geese on the common, and gave of his property to support the church, became a mundane financial transaction which was, in the view of most parishioners, a tax bill. Before tithe commutation, some villages, particularly where the rector was resident, turned the act of tithing into one of celebration. In Norfolk, the Revd James Woodforde would provide a large dinner to all the farmers and other parishioners who had contributed to his wellbeing through tithes. In his diary for 4 December 1797, Woodforde, who had recorded earlier that he had been feeling unwell, wrote 'Hurried rather to day in preparing for my Tithe Audit to Morrow, which in my weak state will be a great Undertaking, but hope I shall be able to get thro' it.' On the following day, he recorded:

> This being my Tithe-Audit Day, the following farmers dined & spent the Afternoon & Evening at my House. [He then lists over twenty local farmers] I gave them for Dinner, two boiled Legs of Mutton and Capers, a very fine Surloin of Beef roasted, Salt fish with plenty of plumb Puddings &c, Punch, Port Wne & strong Beer. A very pleasing Tithe Frolic indeed, and all left me by ten in the Evening – very well pleased with their Frolic. Every thing went of harmonious & Noise.

Tithe commutation certainly diminished this ancient annual rite, even though it was becoming outmoded by the time of Woodforde and, in a country where the role of the church in local society was already being questioned, perhaps unsustainable. Less than fifty years after money had replaced property and physical assets in this context, the first 'card' to replace money was invented.

It was an English invention by the Provident Clothing Group which was formed in Bradford by Joshua Kelley Waddilove in 1880 for the sole purpose of providing credit. It was the first-ever credit card. Provident issued a card voucher to approved customers who could use it to purchase goods at selected retailers. The debt that accrued was paid off when a representative of the company came knocking at the door. Provident Clothing is now the Provident Financial Group. Surprisingly, this new idea, which Provident demonstrated could be very successful commercially, was not developed by other British businesses and entrepreneurs. It was not until 1963 that American Express brought their card to the UK. At first, it could be used only in about 3,000 retail stores in this country, and it was certainly not designed to help the more lowly-paid. Its annual fee was £3.12s.0d which is equivalent to £52.71 in 2017, and interest was added. To qualify, a cardholder needed an annual income of £2,000 (equivalent to £29,218.48 in 2017).

1966, when England won the World Cup, is the year that the UK also gained the first British credit card, launched by Barclays Bank. One year later, Barclays unveiled the first cash machine, or ATM (Automated Teller Machine) – or 'hole in the wall'. At first, the card was not plastic, but card, with the data recording the customer's name and account details, represented by a series of punched holes. The other three 'Big Four' banks responded by joining forces with the Royal Bank of Scotland to set up the Joint Credit Card Company (JCCC) which launched the Access credit card in 1972. In the same year, Lloyds rolled out cash machines that accepted plastic cards and were linked to the bank by computer technology.

Just when the Big Four thought they had the monopoly, with Access and then Visa and Mastercard, the other sector of the banking industries, the friendly societies, invented LINK, a network of cash-issuing machines across thirty-three different societies. This was followed by the Matrix network involving other societies such as Bradford and Bingley, and Alliance and Leicester. The two systems merged in 1989.

From this time, the technology allowed swift change and innovation. Debit cards, Switch cards, Maestro, affinity (or store) cards arrived within a short space of time. The pace increased with Electron, Egg, Smile and Marbles, the latter brand being cleverly reminiscent of the childhood pastime of exchanging marbles, each of which one had placed a value on. By 2004, more than half of UK retail spending was through payment cards with more than 100 million plastic card transactions enabled through online technology. The next big breakthrough was three years later when the first contactless payment was made, using, in the main, Radio-Frequency Identification (RFID). This is the same technology that prevents library books from being removed from libraries without being issued. The location and movement of the book, a parcel, a high-value item in a shop display or a patient in a hospital, can be tracked and recorded by sensors that pick up a unique electro-magnetic signal from a tag attached to the item or person.

Also in 2014, the first mobile phones capable of providing money transfer services were trialled in London, connected to the Oyster card transport service. To be precise, Oyster is a stored-value system. Stored-value cards are not linked to a bank account but can be 'charged up' with a sum of money. The take-up in the provision and use of contactless payment facilities took off dramatically. In this year Transport for London (TfL) recorded over sixty million journeys paid by contactless card in six months, and 30 per cent of all card payments in the London area were by this method. Today, tickets for any journey on any part of the British railway network can now be purchased on line, and printed on demand at any railway station of the customer's choice. The printed cards, carrying embedded digital information, can be used across the entire network, on trains operated by different companies and throughout the Transport for London system. Later in 2014, Apple introduced ApplePay, followed by Samsung's own version. Since then, almost every major retailer, service station, fast-food outlet, garden centre and many smaller shops have moved to accept contactless transactions. The Download music festival at Donington Park in the East Midlands in 2015 was the first 'contactless' event in UK history, with those attending wearing wristbands with the necessary technology built in.

Retail researchers have identified a psychology at work which the 'Arkwrights' of this world were probably already aware of. The easier it is to pay, the less pain is felt by the customer. Handing over cash or bank notes, or a written cheque, is a physical process. Showing a plastic card or a mobile phone to a card reader is quick, simple and less painful because it does not trigger the same activity in the pain centres of the brain. Because each transaction is restricted to relatively small amounts, customers regard them as less significant or important. However, the card providers have seen a dramatic increase in the number of card transactions. Mastercard saw an increase of 30 per cent in the first year after contactless cards were introduced.

Such technology can be adapted to many other purposes and situations. People attending an event who have pre-purchased tickets through online systems such as EventBrite need only show their smartphone to a scanner held by the door staff, a process which takes a matter of seconds thus preventing queues while tickets are checked. This is particularly useful at outdoor events where there may not be mains power supplies, or where many people need to be processed as quickly as possible. So long as there is a mobile phone signal, the system will work. Market and street traders can also use contactless systems.

With all new technologies, the risk of fraud is present. Some customers still feel nervous about the simplicity of contactless payment without the comforting verification of a PIN number, but more innovation is on the way. Zwipe uses fingerprint recognition, and Apple Pay is now making use of biometric verification on their iPhones and iPads. HSBC introduced a voice recognition system to their telephone banking service in 2017.

The underlying technology for all these systems is what we commonly refer to as 'the internet', although that is a very vague term for a massive concept. In very simplistic terms, the internet is a means of transferring and storing vast amounts of information. It does so by connecting together billions of devices which convert all the different forms of information and communication we use, including the spoken voice, images, sounds and text, into one universal 'digital' form, and it uses many different ways of sending that data around the world, from satellites, to light bouncing along the inside of cables, but also the pair of copper wires that is used by your landline phone, the latter being a communication system that was first laid out in the

Victorian era! Thus, in the moment that it takes to show your smartphone to a contactless terminal in a store, the information from both devices may travel half way round the world, to be matched against information stored in remote computers, and compared.

Of course, this information, which is ever-changing and updating, can be used by retailers to manage the movement of their products, and even to predict your future purchases. Scanning an item at the point of sale not only serves to define how much you are spending, but also feeds back to the store's stock control systems, so that more stock can be ordered from manufacturers or moved from warehouses to stores. By connecting this information to details on a store card or 'loyalty' card, the retailer also knows what you have purchased. This information can be used to tailor special offers to your circumstances, because it can be determined easily whether you own a pet, have a small child, follow a vegetarian diet, or have a food allergy.

It is not simply the amount of information about each of us that is stored somewhere in the internet, but the ability for organisations anywhere in the world to extrapolate that information and re-assemble seemingly unconnected fragments of data like a digital jigsaw puzzle which is of concern to many. Coupled with social media networks which track your location, software that can put a name to a photograph of any individual, and then connect that name with other data, together with a record of every transaction made electronically and CCTV systems recording activity on service station forecourts and shop counters, the level of surveillance – and the storing of the resultant information – means that there is no longer anonymity in the world of buying and selling. Yet the stakes for the retailers remain very high. Several well-publicised breaches have demonstrated that no online electronic system is totally safe. All have their vulnerabilities, as banks and some supermarkets have found to their cost.

The moment a transaction has been completed is the whole point of retailing. Of course, being a shopkeeper or store manager involves more, including providing the products that customers want or need at the right price, and in an environment that they are comfortable with; but everything is designed towards that moment when Arkwright's cash register would ring out loudly to record another sale, like the emphatic clatter of a gavel marking the completion of an auction, or the gentle reassuring ping that informs you that your contactless payment has been accepted.

Chapter Ten

Reading all about it

Newspapers have always had a presence in the High Street. Henry and Anna Smith created the W.H. Smith chain most often associated with the sale of newspapers and other reading matter on Britain's railway stations, and it was the decision by some of the railway companies to increase the rent that the Smiths paid for their presence on railway platforms that prompted the move towards the High Street. However, long before Henry Smith set up his first stall in Berkeley Square in the upmarket London suburb of Mayfair, in the major shopping streets of every sizeable town and city was an army of small boys, contributing to their family's often meagre income by being newspaper street vendors. These children were frequently under-nourished, and in some areas, charities were established to support them. At one seaside resort on England's east coast, camps were set up where boys could be given a week's free holiday away from the city. The original temporary accommodation was replaced in time by purpose-built hotel-like accommodation, and the Children's Holiday Centre in Mablethorpe is still providing these holidays for children from families that have a low income. When the age of the newsagent arrived, the street vendors remained, but the newspaper barons realised that paying for their name to be displayed prominently in shop windows was advantageous to their circulation figures.

The publication and distribution of material to the public dates from the 1600s and probably earlier, when ballads were sold on street corners, and religious tracts were printed, often in secret for fear of the consequences. Religious and political constraints remained until after the English Civil War, which had created an appetite on behalf of the British people to hear the latest news. In earlier centuries, news had been broadcast by the town crier, who either stood in the market place or followed a prescribed route around a town, proclaiming as he went, and sometimes accompanied by the leading figures of the corporation if the news was particularly sensational or important, such as the death of the monarch.

By the 1720s there were twelve newspapers being published in London, and twenty-four elsewhere across the country. The first English journalist to gain national recognition was the author Daniel Defoe, who launched *The Review*, a weekly newspaper, in 1704. It gained enough popularity to be printed three times every week and was the forerunner of *The Tatler* and *The Spectator*, journals that are still familiar today.

The newspaper business still faced many restraints, not the least being taxation. A duty on each printed copy was imposed in 1712 which gradually increased with the Stamp Acts, one effect of the increases in cover prices being that newspapers could not be afforded by those on lower incomes. However, many of those people were unable to read at that time. Despite such restrictions, newspaper sales continued to grow, as did the number of journals. In 1767, over eleven million newspapers were sold. Ten years later, the number of newspapers published in London had risen to fifty-three.

All duties on newspapers were finally abolished by 1855. This, and increased literacy because of compulsory state education introduced by the Forster Education Act of 1870, led to a massive growth in the newspaper industry. Improved transport and communications played their part in this expansion, taking newspapers from the printing presses in Fleet Street to the furthest towns of the country using the extensive railway network.

The newspaper boom was not limited to the national press. The abolition of tax led also to a profusion of 'penny dreadfuls', profusely illustrated with artists' impressions, mostly of gory crimes. In 1888, those based in London enjoyed increased circulations due to the Whitechapel Murders and the so-called Jack the Ripper crimes. One of the most notable newspaper editors of that time was William T. Stead, who had moved to London from north-east England where he had edited the *Northern Echo*. He used his journal, the *Pall Mall Gazette*, to campaign against inequality and corruption, the most famous of his campaigns being to uncover the traffic in child prostitution between London and the continent. His exposés, under the banner of 'Maiden Tribute to Modern Babylon' gained both massive support – George Bernard Shaw volunteered to stand on the streets of London to sell copies – and to outrage and condemnation, leading to Stead serving a short term of imprisonment accused of the same crime as the one he was attempting to stamp out. Stead also lobbied Members of Parliament in a way no former journalist had dared, standing outside the Palace of Westminster so that he could challenge members as they left. He even moved to a new house in nearby Smith Square so that he could be close to the heart of the British political system.

Except for *The Times*, the national newspapers we read today were founded in or after the first decades of the nineteenth century. *The Times* was founded on New Year's Day in 1785 by John Walter, but was called *The Daily Universal Register*. Walter was employed by an insurance company which had filed for bankruptcy because of large pay-outs to companies affected by a hurricane in Jamaica. He bought the patent of a new form of type-setting, opened a printing business and decided to launch a daily advertising sheet. It was successful and later carried news, but Walter was sentenced to sixteen months imprisonment in Newgate Jail because of a libel case. In 1803, his son, also named John, took over the paper.

The *Manchester Guardian* was launched in Manchester in 1821 by a small group of businessmen holding non-conformist beliefs. Over half a century, its most famous editor, C.P. Scott, turned *The Guardian* into a journal of world renown and respect, and had set up editorial offices and printing presses in London. The *Daily Telegraph* appeared on 29 June 1855, initially under the ownership of a British army officer and travel writer, Colonel Arthur Sleigh, who transferred it to Joseph Levy, the newspaper's printer because he was unable to pay the printing bills. English-born Levy had learned the printing trade in Germany, returning to London to establish a printing press in Shoe Lane off Fleet Street. His son, who assumed the name of Edward Lawson, took over the editorship and steered the newspaper to become the voice of the middle class, adhering to a Liberal political view until it chose to oppose William Gladstone's foreign policy, when it adopted a Unionist slant. The *Daily Mail* was first published in 1896 by Alfred Harmsworth, the 1st Viscount Northcliffe. It became the country's second biggest-selling daily newspaper, the first journal of its kind to target the newly literate lower-middle class market, using a combination of a low cover price, competitions, prizes and promotional campaigns. It is the only newspaper in Britain read by more women than men.

With Stead, who is recognised as the 'father of tabloid journalism', Harmsworth was a leading pioneer of popular journalism. He bought several failing newspapers and made them into an enormously profitable chain because he could appeal to popular taste. Harmsworth also founded the *Daily Mirror*, first published in 1903, rescued both *The Observer* and *The Times* from financial collapse, and acquired the *Sunday Times*, as well as holding a portfolio of book publishing concerns. In the 1950s and 1960s, the *Daily Mirror* was noted for its clear reliable journalism which explained sometimes complex news stories concisely and accurately.

Alfred Harmsworth justifiably deserves the popular title of being a Baron of Fleet Street. He died in August 1922 in a shed on the roof of his London residence at 1 Carlton House Gardens, after undertaking a world tour to shrug off a period of ill-health. In his will, he gave three months' pay to every one of his 6,000 employees. He was buried at East Finchley cemetery in North London.

There remains a curious connection between several of the leading newspaper publishers of that era. In his youth, Harmsworth was employed by another major newspaper editor, George Newnes, the founder of *Titbits*. Harmsworth's first published piece of writing was apparently an article on butterflies. Newnes, Harmsworth and Stead all became spiritualists. Stead lost his life on board the *Titanic* in 1912, and it has been claimed that he foretold the nature of his death.

The later and maybe greater of the British press barons was Max Aitken, otherwise known as Lord Beaverbrook. Born in Canada in 1879, Aitken seems to have had an innate ability to make money which enabled him to become a millionaire before his thirtieth birthday. He became a leading businessman, politician, and newspaper publisher, and used each of these roles to be an influential figure in British society in the earlier decades of the twentieth century.

After the Second World War, his principal business focus was the *Daily Express* which he redesigned to become an attractive, sometimes witty and entertaining reflection of life, purveying an editorial expression of optimism at a time when his readers were still suffering from the trauma and consequences of war. His magic touch had already improved the paper before the onset of war. By hiring the best writers, photographers, cartoonists and journalists, he increased the circulation, which for many years had been in the doldrums and numbered in the tens of thousands, to over 2 million a day in 1937, and by the late 1940s, almost 4 million, making it the best-selling newspaper in the country. The *Daily Express* brought Aitken great wealth, but by then he was already so wealthy that he found it unnecessary to take a salary. He had already launched the *Sunday Express*, just after the cessation of military action in the First World War, and had acquired both the *London Evening Standard* and the *Glasgow Evening Citizen*. Later, he launched the *Scottish Daily Express*.

Aitken was regarded by some historians as the first 'baron of Fleet Street' and one of the most powerful men in Britain, whose newspapers could make or break the most prominent figures in the country. He used his papers – and enjoyed doing so – to attack anyone who opposed his political views.

In 1919, he launched a sustained attack on David Lloyd George which lasted over three years. He campaigned for fifteen years to have Stanley Baldwin removed from the leadership of the Conservative Party.

Max Aitken, Lord Beaverbrook, died in Surrey in 1964 at the age of 85 years. He was a figure who was both admired and despised. The author H.G. Wells once commented of him: 'If ever Max ever gets to Heaven, he won't last long. He will be chucked out for trying to pull off a merger between Heaven and Hell after having secured a controlling interest in key subsidiary companies in both places, of course.'

Not only is the High Street a place where newspapers are sold, but it has also been a rich source of revenue through advertising, but written advertising, sometimes called 'advertorial' has been with us for a very long time. A celebrated example, because of its heritage, and the nerve of the writer, comes from Thebes in Ancient Egypt, where Hapu the Weaver was posting a request for anyone who had seen his escaped slave. He wrote: 'For his return [of my slave] to the shop of Hapu the Weaver, where the best cloth is woven to your desires, a whole gold coin is offered.'

In more modern times, in London in 1657, an advertising periodical was launched called the *Publick Advertiser*. It consisted entirely of advertisements divided into various categories that included shipping, stagecoaches and lost and stolen. Houses for sale were also advertised, the cost being one pound to advertise a property valued at £240. It may be, according to research, that this was the first printed journal to promote chocolate in England, in June 1657, a promotion that doubles as a very early advertisement for a takeaway! The advertisement read: 'In Bishopsgate Street, in Queen's Head Alley, at a Frenchman's house, is an excellent West India drink called chocolate to be sold, where you may have it ready at any time, and unmade at reasonable rates.'

In 1652, the first fully-illustrated advertisement in an English newspaper appeared in *The Faithfull Scout*, picturing two lost jewels. In the following year, another journal, *The Perfect Diurnall*, was publishing up to six advertisements in each issue for new books, patent medicines and 'lost and founds'. Each advertisement cost one shilling. The first known advertisement for tea was published in a journal titled *Mercurious Politicus* on 30 September 1658:

That excellent, and by all Physicians, approved China drink, called by the Chineans, Tcha, by other nations Tay alias Tee, is sold at the Sultaness Head Cophee House in Sweeting's Rents, by the Royal Exchange, London.

The same journal was later to publish the first advertisement for beer, but it was not until the 1830s that the first household product was advertised nationally. It was for Robert Warren's Patent Shoe Blacking. The advertisements used different printing designs to create impact, such as bold type, capital letters and italics, and many of Warren's texts were in the form of rhymes. These advertisements were so poetical that it was thought, wrongly, they had been composed by Lord Byron.

Newspaper advertising largely held its own when commercial television was launched in the UK but in recent years, British newspapers have struggled with declining circulation. Much of their advertising revenue is now dependent on their online presence, and in some instances, the 'journalism' found online is written as 'click-bait' to encourage readers to move on to view advertising material. Regional newspapers have suffered a massive drop in their sales figures, with almost all regional daily newspapers seeing a steady year-on-year decline, but their names, some of which have appeared on shop frontages for more than a century, are still prominent in shops, stores and service stations across the country.

Chapter Eleven

Wrapping it up and delivering the goods

Customers tend to take packaging for granted, but each time we make a purchase, in a store or online, we make use of products in a wide-ranging variety of shapes and materials which are the result of a design industry with a long history. The tins, bottles, cartons, carrier bags and boxes of today's retail industry are sophisticated and costly items that protect the product from contamination, enable it to stay fresh and so have a longer shelf life, allow manufacturers to transport their goods over very long distances without damage, and at the same time, use colour, printing and design to act as a powerful brand identifier.

Packaging was first needed in pre-history when people began to exchange goods, particularly food, and transport items from tribe to tribe. Containers made from natural materials such as coconut shells, gourds, hollowed-out wood from trees, and woven bamboo, have been found by archaeologists. Their main purpose was to facilitate transport, and for containment and storage, and most could also be used to mix different foods and to eat from, thus doubling up as the first kitchenware.

The pattern of the seasons was vitally important, with entire villages pre-occupied in harvesting crops before the winter storms arrived, and storing them to use over the winter months. In medieval times and later, as well as barns being used, cottages would have wooden containers in which to store grain which could be dismantled when not required. Techniques for extending the life of food such as smoking, salting and pickling were refined.

It was the industrial revolution that changed these age-old practices. Mechanisation made mass-production possible. The canals and, later, the railways, allowed goods to be transported so it was no longer necessary for the manufacturers and suppliers to be close to the consumers; but both these innovations required another component, the packaging industry. The industrial revolution also provided the new materials for packaging such as glass moulded into shapes, metal cans, cardboard and cellophane. None of these were possible, or could be produced in quantity, until the age of the steam engine.

Most packaging obscures the contents, so there was an obvious need for the printed identification of what was contained in tins and boxes, or inside a sweet wrapper. With such simple concepts as a tin containing a liquid, a piece of paper wrapped around a small item of confectionery, or a plastic or paper bag used to carry vegetables, came the merger of numerous sophisticated and innovative processes which could promote the product, catch the attention of a customer, make the contents look bigger or better than they were, and in more recent times, allow the contents to be cooked within its container. Paper and card that could be waterproofed and shaped into boxes in which liquids could be stored, metal cans which have lids that can be removed without a can opener, and widgets in beer cans that release gas when the can is opened, are all part of this fascinating industry.

Until the 1960s, in the UK groceries were handled only by shopkeepers and their staff, and many food items such as bread were displayed without packaging. Refrigeration had been introduced, as had glass-fronted counters as a means of protecting fresh food and dairy products from contamination. It was the rise of the self-service store that made it necessary for foodstuffs to be packaged in a way that protected the contents from clumsy customers, maintained a degree of hygiene and alerted customers to a potential special offer.

Nicolas Appert

From prepared fruit and vegetables to soup and beer, cans made from tin revolutionised the grocery trade. It is claimed that tin cans were invented in Bohemia as long ago as 1200 but that the process was secret until refinements in the production of steel in the United States in later centuries. The concept of putting food into containers which could preserve and maintain freshness arose from military needs. Food preserved in tin cans was used the Dutch Navy as early as 1722, and by 1800, there was already a small canned salmon industry operating in the Netherlands. Fresh salmon were cleaned and boiled in brine, and then smoked before being packed into tin-plated iron boxes. However, in this early process, the food was already preserved before being packed. The invention of a container which facilitated the preservation came in 1809 in response to a call from Napoleon Bonaparte for a means of protecting and transporting his army's food supply. He offered an award of 12,000 francs as an incentive. It was Nicolas Appert who provided the solution.

Appert was a confectioner and chef, working in Paris at the end of the eighteenth century. To maintain the freshness of his ingredients, he experimented in ways to preserve foodstuffs and initially used glass jars that he sealed with cork stoppers and sealing wax before immersing them in boiling water. He called his invention a 'canning jar'. This process, he found, was successful for a range of items including milk, butter, jellies, jams, soups, vegetables, juices and syrups. Appert won Napoleon's award, but it was conditional on him making his invention publicly available. Appert did so in what is regarded as the first-ever cookbook to explain modern food preservation methods.

Appert's work continued. He patented his canning jar and set up a factory in Massy, near Paris, as the world's first food bottling plant, pre-dating the work of Louis Pasteur which, provided the scientific explanation for Appert's discovery. Strictly-speaking, Appert was not 'pasteurising' or 'sterilising', but cooking the food within the container.

Peter Durand

The man who is generally credited with obtaining the first patent for preserving food in tin cans was a British merchant of French origins, Peter Durand. He was based in Hoxton Square in Middlesex, from where he travelled widely, and it is known that he credited a friend in France as being the inspiration for his invention, and it seems likely that this was Philippe Henri de Girard, an engineer and inventor of the flax spinning frame, who had also responded to Bonaparte's call.

Durand's technique was to fill a container with food and then seal it. Vegetables were put in raw, and meat could be raw or partly cooked. The container was then heated, preferably by being immersed in water that was brought up to boiling point. Immediately cooling, the container was then sealed to be airtight. Durand used tin cans. To demonstrate that his technique was successful, the Royal Navy carried several of his sealed cans on manoeuvres for several months and then invited members of the Royal Institution and Royal Society to examine the contents. The food was confirmed by these men to be preserved and wholesome.

Bryan Donkin and John Hall

Durand did not develop his invention further but sold the patent to a mining engineer, Bryan Donkin, and his former employer, John Hall, an iron-master from Dartford in Kent. Donkin was looking to find markets for tin products in the food industry, and in 1813 they constructed the first commercial canning factory in Bermondsey, London, manufacturing canned goods for the British Army. Five years later, Peter Durand took his invention to the United States by re-registering his original patent there. The Bermondsey-based business of Donkin and Hall was later merged with the soup manufacturer Crosse and Blackwell. Donkin was a remarkable inventor, and was associated with the construction of Thomas Telford's Caledonian Canal, Brunel's tunnel under the Thames, and Charles Babbage's original computing machine. He advised the British Government and was one of the leading figures in the development of industry and mechanisation in the Victoria era.

However, the tin-canning industry was not an immediate success, either in the UK or USA, because of one design flaw. Each tin of preserved food required a hammer and chisel to open it before its contents could be used. The big boom time for the tin can had to wait until the invention of the tin opener in 1855 by Robert Yeates, who was a cutlery and surgical instrument maker working in Trafalgar Place West on the Hackney Road in Middlesex.

John Kilner

Yeates, Donkin, Hall and their contemporaries are names from the past, but one pioneering inventor of storage methods from that time created a product which is still on sale today with a design that has not changed fundamentally in over 170 years, although it is no longer manufactured in the UK. John Kilner established his business in 1842 producing glass jars and bottles, and after several decades of development, invented the original 'Kilner Jar' as a reusable air-tight storage container. Kilner's invention was simple, robust and unique, giving him the right to proclaim in advertising that his jar was 'the original and the best, all other brands are substitutes'.

Despite the success of his jar, Kilner's business encountered many crises in its history. In 1871, legal action was taken against the company over excessive coal smoke emanating from the factory's chimneys in Thornhill Lees near Dewsbury in Yorkshire. Kilner was forced to close down all production until he had converted his power from steam to gas furnaces. The loss in trade led to cash flow problems and 3,000 redundancies. In 1937, Kilner became bankrupt. The assets of the company were sold, including the patent for the Kilner Jar which was bought by the United Glass Bottle Company. It was sold on in 2003 to the Rayware Group which makes and sells the jars today, using John Kilner's original design patent.

Ermal Cleon Fraze

This son of an Indiana farmer invented a mechanical process which is now one of the most often used devices in the world, examples of which can be seen in every supermarket in the world in vast numbers. Ernie Fraze invented the ring pull or pull-tab can opening system. Fraze began his engineering career in the 1940s in Ohio, working as a machine tool operator. With money loaned to him by his wife Martha, he set up his own business, the Dayton Reliable Tool and Manufacturing Company in 1940, producing, in time, tools and machined products for several major industries including the Ford Motor Company, General Electric and NASA.

It was his desire to enjoy a can of beer while on a family picnic which led Fraze to devise a can which could be opened without the need for a can-opener. Indeed, because he had forgotten to bring an opener with him, Fraze used a combination of brute force and the bumper of his car to get at his beer, and stayed up the whole of the following night to invent a solution, which he patented in 1959.

Fraze's solution was a small metal tab which could be peeled away from the top of the can to reveal a triangular hole which had been pre-scored. The ingenious solution was immediately a success, but in time created social and environmental problems. As each 'pull-tab' was detached from the tin they were frequently discarded thoughtlessly, causing littering. Also, there was a possibility that the small pieces of metal could drop into the can creating a choking hazard. The Coors Beer Company provided the answer with a redesign with a raised aluminium 'blister' which was simply pushed down, but remained connected to the can. These 'pop-tops' solved the litter and choking problems but provided a new one, namely that fingers and thumbs could be trapped in the opening, causing injury.

It was not until 1975, and the inventive genius of Daniel F. Cudzik, who worked at Reynolds Metals in Richmond, Virginia, that today's safe aluminium lever system was introduced, which opened the can by being lifted, with all components remaining connected, and no risk of an injury arising from clumsy use.

The ubiquitous metal can is produced in its millions, but it is a complex product, with the lid being thicker and stronger than the sides and the integral base. Its shape at the top and the bottom provides strength without additional weight. The design also enables them to be stacked for purposes of display and storage. Some are lined with a form of plastic to prevent the aluminium from tainting the contents. Others contain a small hollow plastic sphere which releases carbon dioxide gas, triggered by the reduction in the internal pressure of the can when it is opened. This was developed by Guinness to provide canned versions of their draught ale with the traditional head. Most importantly, all tin can be recycled in its entirety.

Cardboard packaging

Cardboard in its commercially-manufactured form, more accurately referred to as paperboard, was invented 200 years ago, probably by M. Treverton and Son in England. A report in a later trade paper refers to Treverton's having in 1817 'placed on the market in London, a small box which was made of chip wood and covered both inside and outside with paper, the whole thing being something similar to our present matchbox.' It is said that Treverton received the idea from a French inventor. There is a record of another London maker of cardboard boxes in the following decade by the name of William Austin, who reused discarded ledger paper to form paper tubes from which he made pill-type boxes.

The pre-cut cardboard box which could be manufactured and supplied flat and then folded into a box, is credited to Robert Gair, a Scottish-born inventor living and working in the Brooklyn district of New York. The invention, in the 1870s, was by accident. Gair was a printer and manufacturer of paper bags. Whilst printing an order of seed bags, a metal rule that was used to crease the bags slipped out of position and cut them. Gair realised that by creasing and cutting card in one operation, a prefabricated box could be made. Thirty years later, when corrugated cardboard had been produced, the operation was easily transferred, and the box that is now used universally to pack and store goods during transit was born. One of the earliest manufacturers to use card boxes was the Kellogg Company. Their cornflakes were first sold in boxes with a plastic bag on the outside to prevent moisture from affecting the contents. Later, the flakes were packed into plastic or waxed bags, sealed and then placed in the card boxes, as they are to be found in supermarkets and grocery stores today.

The plastic bag

The plastic bag is probably not the most celebrated of inventions but is one of the most often used, despite legislation in recent years to limit its distribution and inconsiderate disposal. The modern supermarket plastic bag, lightweight and easily folded and stored, was invented by a Swedish engineer Sten Gustaf Thulin in the early 1960s for his employer, Celloplast. All modern plastic bags are based on his design which is, essentially, a plastic tube, sealed at the bottom and with an open top. It became known as the T-shirt plastic bag, and is made of the same type of plastic as is used to manufacture plastic bottles.

Celloplast held the patent and monopoly for some years until the American Exxon-Mobile petroleum group overturned the American patent, and, in the late 1970s, introduced their bags to stores in the United States. However, it was not until 1982 that shoppers began using them in quantity, when Kroger, one of America's largest grocery chains, adopted them, followed almost immediately by Safeway.

The bags also became a powerful marketing tool, as they made every shopper who used one a mobile advertising facility, adding to brand identity by taking supermarket logos into streets, homes and even rival stores across the country, at little cost to the supplier.

In 2014, the seven largest UK supermarket chains handed out 7.64 billion plastic carrier bags, each bag having consumed energy in their manufacture and the printing process which placed the company's logo on each of them. Most were disposed of at landfill sites, although some companies had switched to plastic which biodegraded over time. Many bags were discarded inconsiderately, creating a lasting danger to wildlife. A report in the journal *Science* in 2015 had estimated that 8 million tonnes of plastic was dumped in global waters every year. In the first six months of 2016, after the UK Government introduced a levy of 5p for every bag provided by large retailers, the usage has dropped by 85%. Worldwide, the figures are truly vast, with estimates by environmental groups of the number of bags being used ranging from 500 billion to one trillion every year.

Tetra Pak

A further major worldwide development in grocery food packaging came in 1951 with the work of the Akelund and Rausing food carton company based in Malmo in Sweden. Reuben Rausing had studied in New York in the 1920s and had noted how self-service grocery stores were struggling to display and sell their food products in hygienic ways whilst allowing customers to self-select. He acquired a run-down packaging plant and with the support of an industrialist, Erik Akerlund, launched a dry food carton manufacturing plant.

Rausing's stated aim was that packaging should not only achieve high standards in food safety, hygiene and distribution efficiency, but that the package should save more than it costs. In 1943, he turned his innovative skills to devising a carton that could safely contain liquids such as milk. It took the rest of the decade for his company to refine his initial idea of a tetrahedron-shaped package, and how production lines could be developed so that the pack could be filled efficiently and hygienically whilst preventing oxygen from entering. Further research was necessary to produce a strong card-based material coated with polyethylene, and capable of being sealed by heat. A production version was distributed, but met with numerous technical problems which took a considerable amount of money, time and resources to address. It was not until the 1970s that the company began reaping the financial rewards of such a prolonged and costly development programme.

The internet has changed the way in which many of us make purchases, as has home delivery services being provided, in the main, by the major supermarket chains, but new technology has led to an even greater demand for similar advances in the packaging industry. Next-day deliveries of almost any product needs packaging that will protect the contents as they move through complex distribution and delivery arrangements. Many products are now supplied direct from the manufacturer, or from large regionally-based warehouses and may be transferred through several 'hubs' and carried on a variety of different vehicles. The consumer expects a perfect product in prime condition when it is delivered to the doorstep, and at the agreed time. Such demands can be fulfilled only because of two centuries of intensive and inventive designing.

Eddie and Edward Stobart

Completing the complex process which connects the point of manufacture to the delivery of products to the supermarket, corner shop or the door step, is a major and vital industry on which every aspect of the retail trade depends. Supermarket stock control is so refined and precise, that one delayed delivery of produce would result in empty counters and dissatisfied customers. That industry is the backbone of the UK economy and involves hundreds of thousands of drivers in command of a vast fleet of heavy goods vehicles that travel the motorway and trunk road network every day. It is an industry which now relies on complex computer software to ensure maximum efficiency and reliability, and is more commonly known as 'logistics'. It is extremely sophisticated, allowing for road closures, vehicle breakdowns and weather-related problems; and one company has become the most prominent deliverer of what we have purchased, or intend to purchase. So identifiable is the brand, that people collect scale models of their lorries, and their drivers have starred in 'fly-on-the-wall' documentaries on British television.

Edward Pears Stobart was born in 1929 and began an agricultural business in the 1940s in a remote corner of the Lake District in the village of Hesket Newmarket by the side of Skiddaw, the sixth-highest mountain in England. The company developed into Eddie Stobart Ltd in 1970, and the Stobart group in 2007. Edward was born to John and Adelaide Stobart in July 1929 and he married Nora Boyd on 26 December 1951. His first lorry was a Guy 'Invincible' four-wheeler truck which he bought from a local garage in 1960, repainting it in his favourite colours of Post Office red and Brunswick green. His first significant contract was transporting slag from steelworks to be reused as fertiliser. He purchased two Ford Thames Trader trucks and added a logo to the side of the driver's doors. In 1963, he secured a contract with ICI which gave him the financial resources to expand further. In November 1970, his operation became a limited company with a share value of just £10,000.

It was Eddie's third child of four, always known as Edward to distinguish him from his father, who developed the business, having taken over the transport management in 1976 at the age of twenty-one. Edward left school at the age of fifteen, with a speech impediment and a poor school report. He joined his father's company and demonstrated an aptitude for business, and a willingness to work hard. As a teenager, he showed interest in organising the drivers and making the most out of the loads that his father's small vehicles were handling. So, in 1976, Eddie set up Eddie Stobart Trading as a separate firm to continue the agricultural business, and installed his son as the head of the other company.

Eddie and Nora's strong Christian principles have permeated their business to the present day. Their motto was 'always the best'. Edward, born into that family structure, used his talents to develop Stobart along the same ethical lines. In the first years, he often polished his vehicles himself when the drivers had gone off duty, to ensure they were smart and presentable for their next journeys. He would sleep on site, in the office, and would happily turn out to collect a late load. When lorries needed replacing, he bought new vehicles, often paying for them out of his own pocket. He instilled pride into a previously rather dowdy and down-at-heel form of work. Lorry drivers had little self-esteem and even less recognition by other road users. Edward turned his drivers into smart, uniform-wearing knights of the road. By the 1980s, Edward's drive and inspiration had achieved a yearly growth of 25 per cent, and by the millennium, he was managing over 800 vehicles operating from twenty-two depots.

As 'Stobart Spotters' will know, each of their red and green vehicles has a female name. It was Eddie senior who began the tradition. The first lorries were named after Twiggy, the famous model of the 1960s, and the American country and western performers, Dolly Parton and Tammy Wynette. The tradition continues to the present day. This identification of each vehicle encouraged the formation of a fan club which has 35,000 members, keen to report sightings of the vehicles on their own website. The enthusiasm has been harnessed with a separate company, worth more than £3.5 million, manufacturing and selling miniature replicas of the fleet, and additionally, a series of children's books which tell the adventures of Steady Eddie, the big-hearted lorry, and an Eddie Stobart rail service powered, not by Thomas the Tank engine, but Eddie the Engine, operating between the Midlands and Scotland.

Edward, a shy and retiring man had a business philosophy which remained simple and true to his father's beliefs. He said that:

> We never turn any customer away, and we always do it at the right price. We are always smart, tidy – the best at everything. We have the smartest drivers and the smartest trucks, and we do our job well, which is why people notice us, and why we are a success.

He died in Coventry in 2011 of a heart attack at the age of fifty-six. Later, it was revealed that he was personally bankrupt. At the time of his funeral at Carlisle Cathedral, Richard Butcher, chief executive of Stobart Group, said of his former boss:

> I worked with him for a number of years and he was an absolute gentleman. A very generous, a very kind man. A very shy man in some respects. He demanded the best from everyone who worked with him, but he was loyal to those who worked with him throughout his time at the business.

Chapter Twelve

The checkout – the lost brands

There is something comforting and nostalgic about walking in one's mind along the High Street of a past time, remembering the names above the shops where your parents bought their weekly provisions, or those establishments where you worked as a Saturday boy or girl. The sense of comfort comes largely from the reassuring longevity of some brands, but the construction of out-of-town shopping centres in the last three decades of the twentieth century, and the rise of internet shopping in the present century, meant dramatic and destabilising changes to the High Street of our memories.

Even after a well-known shop closes, the brand lives on. In my hometown, one end of the High Street is still referred to by the name of the department store which occupied the site until it was destroyed during the Blitz. On a broader canvas, the international confectionery manufacturing giants of today gain much of their income from selling the chocolate and sweet lines of the past, many now more than a century old. They don't always taste as they did when their inventors mixed the ingredients by hand, but just the familiar wrapping is enough to activate the taste buds.

F.W. Woolworth

One of the most destabilising events of recent years was the collapse of F.W. Woolworth, the famous retail chain that everyone knew, and needed to 'pop into', because it sold products that everyone needed, and at prices that we all could afford. In towns and cities, and in relatively small market towns, 'Woolies' was at the heart of the weekly shopping experience. For many, shopping started at Woolworths and extended outwards, so the value of retail properties near a Woolworths store were often higher than those further down the High Street. It was never an 'up market' store, and value came before quality; but until the 1970s, almost every family in England had items in their home bought from Woolworths, in the kitchen, the wardrobe, or the bathroom. The Woolworths brand names, Winfield, Ladybird (for children's clothing) and Chad Valley (toys) are still familiar today.

To some extent, it was its dependence on volume sales of small basic items which played a significant role in Woolworths' downfall. In the immediate post-war years, austerity lingered, and many families had to 'watch the pennies'; but by the 1960s, shoppers were starting to buy so-called luxury goods, and for the first time for many, items that they desired, rather than needed. Design, rather than utility came to the fore with the rise of retailers such as Habitat. By the time that Woolworths went into receivership it had many powerful competitors, such as Wilko, BHS, Dunelm, and to some extent, NEXT, as well as the supermarket giants, which were selling products with a high design factor (and which therefore had a good profit margin because people are willing to pay for what they perceive to be good design) alongside the basic lines. Another major factor in the company's decline was the development of new recorded music technologies. The 45 rpm single, the mainstay of the pop revolution since the rock and roll era, gave way to the CD single and eventually to the download music market.

Woolworths attempted several projects to address their financial problems, but all failed. The construction of large out-of-town stores under the Wilco brand was tried, but these were never successful, most being sold on to Gateway and later acquired by Asda. They tried reducing the size of their estate, selling off larger stores and moving to sites with much smaller sales floors, and in the last decades of their existence, they introduced their 'Big Red Book' which was intended as a direct challenge to Argos.

The British Woolworths brand began when Frank Winfield Woolworth arrived in Liverpool from America. He claimed English ancestry, stating that his family had its roots in the village of Woolley, a very small hamlet close to the A1 and near Huntingdon in what is now Cambridgeshire. The present population of Woolley is about the same as recorded in the Domesday survey. The first store was opened in Liverpool on 5 November 1909, occupying a site between Church Street and Williamson Street. Whether the date was deliberately chosen by Woolworth is not clear, but the opening ceremony was accompanied by fireworks, as well as an orchestra and circus acts. The launch was very successful, with shoppers queuing at the entrances. By closing time, almost all the counters had been cleared of stock.

By the outbreak of the First World War, forty stores were operating. Sadly, many of the store managers who left the company and went to fight never returned. Nevertheless, expansion continued in peacetime with the 400th store opening in 1930, and by the time of the company's collapse, this had increased to more than 800.

British Home Stores

British Home Stores, more familiarly known as BHS, was founded in 1928 by four American entrepreneurs, and was based on the successful trading model created by F.W. Woolworth. The company shied away from direct competition with Woolworths, and so set their highest price for any item they sold at one shilling, although this was raised to five shillings within a year so that more expensive goods could be sold, including home furnishings, and to give BHS its own brand identity. The highest price in Woolworths at the time was sixpence, which was half of one shilling.

The first store opened in Brixton, and the company then expanded steadily. Each shop included a café and a grocery section. After the Second World War, responding to the growth in consumerism when rationing ended, BHS continued to develop, so that by the end of the 1960s there were ninety-four stores nationwide with 12,000 employees, and at the time of its collapse into administration it was trading through 165 outlets. For fourteen years from 1996, BHS was part of Sir Terence Conran's Storehouse Group, which included Habitat and Mothercare, and it was then sold to retail billionaire Sir Philip Green. Overwhelmed by debt and sharply falling sales because of new competition from stores such as Primark, BHS was sold to Dominic Chappell's Retail Acquisitions for just one pound in 2015, and one year later with debts of £1.3 billion, it was placed in receivership. All 164 stores closed, making 11,000 people redundant.

Fine Fare

The history of the Fine Fare supermarket chain is part of the much longer and fascinating story of Canadian entrepreneur, Willard Garfield Weston. He was born in 1898 in the apartment above his father's bread factory. It is said that shortly after his birth, his father carried Willard down to the factory so that he could be exposed to the smell of the bread.

He served as a sapper during the First World War, on the front line in France, and then returned to his father's company. In due course, he took over from his father and became general manager of the family's biscuit business. He persuaded his father to import high-quality biscuit-making equipment from England and even relocated English workers to Toronto. To ensure the highest-quality of taste, he then set up his own dairy to provide the butter for his production lines.

Weston moved with his family to England in 1935, by which time he was operating fifteen bakeries and employing 15,000 people across the country under the Allied Bakeries brand. In just two years, he doubled the number of bread-making plants, making his operation the largest bread producer in England.

It was after the Second World War that Weston diversified into supermarkets, He was already a successful retailer, having acquired several very distinguished brands including Fortnum and Mason, and he had continued to acquire highly-successful lines such as Ryvita.

Initially, Fine Fare was not successful, but Weston had the resources to stay with his enterprise and make it work. After sustaining steady losses for nearly a decade, he decided on a strategy of fast and major expansion. Starting in 1961, he opened 130 stores in just fifteen months. By the end of the 1960s, this had grown to more than 1,000 stores, making Fine Fare the largest supermarket chain in Britain. In 1986, Associated British Foods sold the Fine Fare chain to the Dee Corporation, which later became Somerfield. The larger and most profitable stores were rebranded as Gateway. The others were closed.

Garfield Weston died in October 1978. For more than fifty years, he had led his business and developed it into one of the largest bakery operations in the world. When he handed over the day-to-day management of his businesses to his son, he was rated as the second most profitable merchandiser in their world. He had fought in the First World War and was a Member of Parliament in England during the second conflict. His legacy continues in the form of the charitable foundation which he set up with his wife.

Of the many brands that Garfield Weston acquired, Burton's Biscuits is one of the most historical. George Burton was born in Leek in Staffordshire in 1829, and by the 1950s was manufacturing his own biscuits. The company remained a family business for five decades. It went through several mergers and acquisitions, including being part of Associated British Foods, and was ultimately sold to the Ontario Teachers' Plan in 2013. Its successor, the Burton Biscuit Company, is the second-largest biscuit manufacturer in the UK, and is responsible for well-known lines including Jammie Dodgers, Maryland Cookies and Wagon Wheels.

Somerfield and Gateway

The history of these two former giants of British food retail can be traced back to several pioneering grocers, including James Harding Mills who opened a grocery and hardware shop on Radcliffe Hill in Bristol in 1875. By 1900, his business had expanded to more than twelve shops, and it became a limited company. In 1950, the company which then had fourteen shops, was taken over by the Bristol-based Tyndall Finance House, which renamed it 'Gateway', referring to Bristol being the gateway to the West Country. The shops were converted into supermarkets, the first opening in 1958.

On the east coast, another supermarket chain which had begun as a single grocer's shop, was emerging. Frank Dee opened his first shop in 1933 at 773 Hessle Road in the Gypsyville area of West Hull, overlooking the Humber Estuary, and close to where the Humber Bridge now stands. Dee was a pioneer of self-service, and in the 1950s opened six shops in Hull, laid out in what would become the familiar supermarket format.

In time, and having made several acquisitions, including the S&H 'pink stamps' operation, Gateway was taken over by Linfood Holdings, which already owned the substantial Frank Dee supermarket chain. By acquiring rival operations including Fine Fare and Keymarkets, the Dee Corporation were operating over 1,100 supermarkets, almost as many as Sainsbury's and Tesco at the time. In 1988, the Dee Corporation was renamed Gateway Corporation, with Frank Dee as a non-executive director, but its diverse operations led to financial difficulties and the beginning of the Dee empire's break-up.

In brief, during a period of extensive and complex re-structuring and reorganisation, some Gateway stores were sold to Asda, and the Somerfield brand was launched, with the remaining Gateway stores rebranded. The former Kwik-Save shops were sold off, and other Somerfield-branded stores were also sold to chains, including Sainsbury's. Finally, in 2008, Somerfield was taken over by the Co-op with some of its stores being bought by Morrisons. Somerfield also operated stores at over a hundred Texaco service stations which the Co-op has gradually sold on, some now trading as SPAR stores.

Over a relatively short space of time, some stores saw their names change many times while continuing to trade throughout financial upheavals. If different decisions had been taken along the way, Frank Dee could still have been a big name in the supermarket world. As it is, it is the Co-op that consolidated its long-standing place within the top five food retailers in Britain.

Sir Joseph Nathaniel Lyons

For many families, a Saturday morning shopping spree along the local High Street involved, sometimes as a special treat, a visit to the local Lyons Corner Coffee House. However, Joseph Lyons, who was born in London in

December 1847, had no experience or background in catering. His father was described as 'an itinerant vendor of watches and cheap jewellery'. He himself was apprenticed to an optician and became very competent in designing small useful gadgets such as a combined microscope, binoculars and compass which he sold from a stall at the Royal Jubilee Exhibition in Liverpool in 1887.

Lyons became involved in catering because of a family connection. He was distantly related to the fiancée of Isidore Gluckstein, a member of the Gluckstein family of tobacco merchants. Salmon and Gluckstein were a British tobacconist company that had been founded in London by Samuel Gluckstein and Barnett Salmon in 1873. They decided on an aggressive expansion plan and within a short span of time established themselves as the largest retailers in tobacco in the country, operating from more than 140 outlets. They claimed to be the largest tobacconist in the world. The family decided to move into catering but did not want to use their family name, believing that the catering trade was beneath them. Instead, they invited Lyons to join them and to use his name.

The Glucksteins initiated a strong, dynamic strategy for their new project. At the same Jubilee Exhibition in 1887, they set up a tea pavilion which was very successful. They became an incorporated private company and appeared at further major exhibitions in Glasgow and Paris before taking over the entire catering franchise for Olympia, Crystal Palace and White City in London. J. Lyons and Company Ltd was formed in 1894 and the first Lyons teashop was opened in Piccadilly later in the same year, as the first-ever Lyons Corner House. Joseph Lyons became Chairman of the company, a role which he retained for his entire life. He died at the Hyde Park Hotel in Knightsbridge on 22 June 1917.

Timothy White

Until 1968, High Street shoppers in most towns and cities could choose between Boots the Chemists and Timothy Whites for their pharmaceutical products. In some locations, the two stores were neighbours, resulting in fierce competition. Timothy White was a shopkeeper who first traded in ship chandlery in Portsmouth. He opened his first shop at the age of twenty-three years, and was described as being in an 'an oil dry saltery business'.

The history of chandlery is fascinating, originating in medieval households where the vital work of maintaining and storing the candles for lighting was carried out in a room close to the kitchens. Candles and wax are closely associated with soap, so the chandler's role widened to include other essential household supplies, and was later applied to the hardware required by ships. The B&Q DIY chain has its headquarters at Chandler's Ford near the port of Southampton. Chandlery therefore developed into general hardware supplies, which was Timothy White's main business. In the 1920s, the company was marketing as 'cash chemist and household stores'.

White qualified in pharmacy in 1869 according to the records of the Pharmaceutical Society. His business expanded with the purchase of a retail property on Commercial Road, Portsmouth followed by a warehouse in adjoining Chandos Street and a further shop in Southsea. By 1890 he was managing a chain of over ten stores selling both hardware and pharmaceutical products. The business grew, merging with Taylors, another pharmacy chain, in 1935 until, by the 1960s, there were more than 600 branches across the country.

The Taylors Drug Company was formed in 1888 as a limited company, but had been founded by a W.B. Mason many years before. He named the stores after his wife's maiden name. Crucial to Timothy Whites was that Taylors were based in the north of England with branches in Leeds, Bradford, Bingley and Shipley, later developing a stronghold further north in Lancashire, Durham, Northumberland and the Lake District. When acquired by Timothy Whites, whose trading area was still the south of England, Taylors had 373 stores north of the Pennines.

Timothy White's personal history is difficult to clarify in detail. He was born in Hampshire in 1824 and married Emily. He also, allegedly, had a mistress, Jane Curtis, with whom he fathered five children. He died in 1908, which is when his son Woolmer White, who was also a qualified chemist, took full control of the company.

One of Timothy White's young employees in the late 1920s was James Kemsey Wilkinson. The training and experience he gained whilst working with Whites on the south coast gave him the practical knowledge he needed to open his own hardware shop in 1930 and to found the Wilkinson store group, now trading as Wilko from over 400 stores with an annual turnover more than £1.5 billion. The mix of pharmacy and chandlery is still, to some extent, apparent in the lines that Wilko sell.

In 1968, Timothy Whites (and Taylors) were taken over by Boots. In more than one location where the two shops were side by side, the stores were merged using the simple measure of opening interconnecting passages between the two buildings. In other areas, some of the shops were rebranded as Boots and sold only pharmaceuticals, leaving 196 shops retaining the

Timothy Whites name selling only hardware. These were all closed or converted to Boots by 1985. The Timothy Whites brand lives on in the form of an online pharmacy based in Surrey.

Lewis's

Shopping was a wonderland experience at the Lewis's stores belonging to retail entrepreneur, David Lewis. Many children remember the exciting Christmas grottoes and window displays at the home store in Liverpool, or the exhilarating experience of riding in lifts controlled by lift operators to roof gardens high above the city, such as at the Bristol Broadmead store. The concept of making the shopping experience totally inclusive, providing entertainment – even a ballroom in one store – and services in addition to retailing, was David Lewis's over-riding motivation.

He was born David Levy, of Jewish parentage, in London in 1823 but settled in Liverpool. At sixteen he became an apprentice at Benjamin Hyam and Company, who were tailors and outfitters. In 1856, he opened his first shop in Bold Street in the city, selling menswear and boys' clothing. He diversified into women's clothing in 1864. To this core sales base he added shoes and tobacco, and in 1879 created what is regarded as one of the world's first 'Christmas Grottos' at his store in Church street, Liverpool, advertised as 'Christmas Fairyland'.

From Liverpool, Lewis started to build his impressive landmark stores across the country, starting with Manchester in 1877, and Birmingham (Corporation Street) in 1885. The Manchester store accommodated a multi-purpose space on its fifth floor which was used for exhibitions and as a ballroom.

David Lewis died in December 1885, just as the Christmas decorations and tableaux were being erected in his stores. His business was acquired by the Cohen family, initially Louis Cohen and later Harold and Rex Cohen, who expanded the company, constructing new stores in Glasgow, Leeds, Stoke-on-Trent and Leicester. In each location, the Lewis's stores were landmark buildings, often the largest stores in their areas. When the very large Leeds store was open on 17 September 1932, over 120,000 people went through the doors on the first day of trading. The building was forty feet higher than any other retail store in the city, and the largest ground area of any department store outside London. It was faced with more than 40,000 cubic feet of Portland stone and over 21.5 million bricks.

The 'home' store in Ranelagh Street, Liverpool, was badly damaged in the Blitz, and rebuilt in the early 1950s to a design by architect Gerald de

Courcy Fraser. Like the Leeds store, it used Portland stone façades at the front and brick at the back, supported by a steel frame. True to the spirit of David Lewis, the building was designed to impress and dominate, and still achieves that aim today. There is a giant bronze statue of a nude man by Sir Jacob Epstein, Festival of Britain motifs in the former fifth floor restaurant and marble staircases. It is now a listed building, a rare achievement for a retail building. The final Christmas Grotto displays in this splendid building covered over 10,000 square feet of retail space.

The Leicester store, another building predominantly of Portland stone which towered above the city centre, incorporated a remarkable tower which still stands. Surprisingly modernistic in its design, it is very much in keeping with the twenty-first century city landscape. It was used as to receive radio transmissions from the home store in Liverpool and included a small studio. Each morning before the doors were opened, the shop assistants, standing by their counters, would receive a broadcast message of encouragement from the senior management.

The Glasgow store in Argyle Street was another vast art deco building which claimed to be the largest purpose-built department store in the UK when it was built in 1929. In the 1950s, the company opened a menagerie on the top floor, with parrots and other small animals. The six-storey Bristol store dominated the Broadmead Shopping area and included a roof garden which gave customers an open-air panorama of the city, except in inclement weather when it was closed to customers for reasons of safety.

The company continued to grow in the post-war years, acquiring Selfridges in London in 1951, and becoming part of the Sears Group under Charles Clore in 1965. Changing trends in consumerism, the failure of the business to keep ahead of the retail game, and the emergence of new niche retailers began to eat away at Lewis's market share, and the company went into administration in 1991. Several stores were sold to the Owen Owen group, a powerful competitor, some stores, including Birmingham, closed, and the Leicester store continued for a short time under a management buy-out. The last store to trade as Lewis's was the home store in Liverpool. Operating independently, it went into liquidation in February 2007 and closed permanently on 29 May 2010 after the management confirmed that the lease on the building could not be renewed.

David Lewis was a great philanthropist. Early in his business career, he donated £1,000 to support persecuted Jews in Russia. For many years, he was the warden and treasurer of the Old Hebrew Congregation in Liverpool to which he gave substantial sums of money. In his will, he bequeathed nearly

£500,000 to several philanthropic institutions and for the construction of a hospital in Liverpool. The David Lewis centre, located in the Cheshire village of Warford near Alderley Edge, was set up with funds from Lewis's estate. It provides residential facilities, education, medical and therapeutic support for people with learning disabilities, epilepsy and autism. David Lewis lies buried beside his wife Bertha in the Kensington Deane Road cemetery in Liverpool.

Comet

The one significant retailing innovation that Michael Hollingbery from Hull is recognised for is the concept of the discount warehouse. Hollingbery, whose father created the electrical retailer Comet, took advantage of the 1964 Resale Prices Act which made all resale price agreements illegal, unless it could be proved that they were not against the public interest. The freedom to set its own prices turned Comet from a relatively small retail chain covering Yorkshire to a national discount retailer. It was in Hollingbery's home town of Hull in 1968 that he owned the first out-of-town discount warehouse, with a range of fifty radio and television products. It was to change the face of retailing.

Initially, most sales were by mail order, with Comet advertising prominently in selected magazines and newspapers, listing their prices and illustrating their stock in full colour. Comet's prices were set at 15 per cent lower than the manufacturers' recommended retail prices, and some of the discounts were as great as 45 per cent. Customers could also visit the store and buy items in person. It is claimed that one advertisement in the *Yorkshire Times* resulted in customers 'queuing round the block'. It was a new dynamic and tough retail strategy which the small independent electrical shops were not able to compete with. In 1969, Comet opened a second discount warehouse, in Leeds, and the company rebranded itself as Comet Radiovision Services. In just eighteen months from February 1971, Hollingbery opened seven further warehouses with another nine planned for the following year. Comet took off, and sales soared, from just over £300,000 in 1968 to more than £5 million, three years later.

Comet had begun in 1933 as the Comet Battery Stores, and was one man's response to the growing need for batteries to power wireless receiving equipment. As radio listening became a habit rather than a novelty, many households needed a service whereby the large wet-cell batteries could be recharged on a regular basis. Hollingbery, with one assistant, provided it. Batteries were charged in a small workshop in Hull and then delivered to customers. The constant need for replenishment guaranteed a steady trade. By the end of the 1930s the business had grown to about 2,500 customers which had meant Hollingbery acquiring a fleet of vehicles to handle the deliveries. He also offered to replace wireless sets that had broken down or were becoming out-dated, and opened his first retail shop in the appropriately-named George Street in Hull, with two more stores following, in Driffield and Bridlington. When George died in 1958, aged just 55 years, his son Michael took charge of a flourishing business.

Michael Hollingbery continued to innovate, taking full advantage of the technical developments in broadcasting such as colour televisions and VHF radio sets, making these products more easily available to those customers who saw them as desirable products but did not have the buying power. He continued to discount his prices, offered hire purchase facilities and rental services. He set up an after-sales service and a twice-weekly delivery service for larger products, and most of his goods were sold with a year's free servicing, including parts and labour. The popularity of washing machines, tumble driers, freezers and fridge freezers and audio–visual equipment during this boom period added to the company's popularity.

It was a retail model which was unmatchable at that time, but it was also a precedent which forced all other white and brown goods retailers to move towards or risk annihilation. Its outstanding success meant that rival businesses had to adopt a similar model to survive. The notable brand to mount a challenge in later years was the one that would out-survive Comet and take over its dominant position, namely Currys PC World. The brand identity of these two businesses, and their locations, often close to each other in out-of-town shopping centres, in similar buildings, were so similar, that a significant number of customers began to believe them to be the same business, often buying from one store and returning goods to the other.

Comet's marketing concepts also attracted growing criticism from consumer-protection groups which criticised the 'hidden' charges of extended warranties, and the encouragement by sales staff to purchase unnecessary accessories at unnecessarily high prices. Thus, customers were being informed that their brand-new DVD recorder would produce a better picture if a certain high-quality cable was used with it. After numerous takeovers and mergers, Comet went into liquidation in November 2012. All 236 stores were closed by the end of the following month.

Maypole

The history of the former Maypole grocery chain is the story of the battle for the margarine trade in the UK. Margarine was invented in France in 1869, when Emperor Napoleon III demanded a cheaper substitute for butter that could be supplied to the military and to the 'lower classes'. Its name comes from Margaric Acid, which had been discovered by chemists as early as 1813. Instead of using buttermilk fat, as in butter, the earliest margarine used beef fat. It was later that vegetable oils and other animal fats were used. The first margarine did not have the yellow colour of butter, and looked more like lard, until manufacturers began adding yellow dye.

The forerunner of the Maypole shops was a small grocery business owned by a family by the name of Watson which began trading in Birmingham in the early years of the nineteenth century. The business was acquired by a George Jackson in 1859 who adopted the name Medova Dairies. Three members of the Watson family, all brothers, worked for Jackson as apprentices.

The debate about margarine caused a rift between Jackson and the Watsons. George Watson could see the potential of margarine as an affordable product for the working classes in the large and growing Birmingham and Black Country conurbation. George Jackson did not want his reputation as a purveyor of high quality dairy provisions damaged by being associated with the product. A three-way division took place. Jackson continued to trade as Medova Dairies, George Watson left and set up his own business, opening his first Maypole Dairy Shop at 67 Queen Street in Wolverhampton in 1887, and his brother Charles Watson opened a dairy dealing in Danish dairy products in Wednesbury before moving his business to the Manchester area in 1889.

The split appears to have been amicable because the Watson brothers, including Alfred, the third brother, reached a trade agreement with George Jackson. Clearly, all four men were convinced that their businesses were to flourish. The Watsons specialised in butter and margarine. Jackson focussed on butter and milk, and they agreed not to compete in the same towns. Charles opened shops across the north of England, Alfred created a chain in the Midlands, and the Medova company developed its trade in the south and east.

In a matter of a few years, it also became clear that it was the Maypole group which was leading the way and becoming a household name. Jackson's Medova chain had begun to fade by this time, and it was the dynamic Watsons who were determined to dominate. By 1915, Maypole had 985 shops, supplying five key products: eggs, tea, condensed milk, butter and margarine. Such was their dominance in the market that they were by this time supplying a third of the entire UK margarine market. The Watsons had also forged strong business links with several Danish dairy suppliers, and even set up warehouses in Denmark to handle the butter which was being manufactured for them.

However, the Watsons also faced strong competition from Home and Colonial and Liptons over the import and sale of margarine. Sir Thomas Lipton's chain of stores, which were supplied by Van de Burgh, the same Dutch company as Maypole, became the Watsons' strongest challenger, prompting a fierce price war. Margarine was also to cause the demise of the Maypole empire. The general economic slump in the 1920s led to foreign margarine being cheaper than the British-manufactured product. The Watsons had invested heavily in sourcing ingredients and making their own margarine, but were unable to match the price cuts of their competitors. In 1924, the ownership of Maypole, still based in Wolverhampton, was transferred, along with its share capital, to Home and Colonial. Forty years later, they were trading as Allied Suppliers and had joined forces with their other chief rivals, Liptons and Pearks, in the same London headquarters.

Home and Colonial

Julius Charles Hendicott Drew, the man who founded Home and Colonial, was from a very different family background than most of Britain's pioneer grocers, and one with different priorities and interests. He was born near Ampthill in Bedfordshire. His father, the Revd George Drew served as the rector of Avington, near Winchester and was also a published author. His mother, Mary Peek, was a French-born artist. Julius had seven siblings, all of whom were to travel widely and settle elsewhere including in the colonies and North America. Possibly his only connection with retailing was through the Peek family which owned a ladies' fashions store in Paris. Drew went to the prestigious Bedford School and, still in his teenage years, began his working life in China as a tea buyer. He returned to England and opened his first shop in Liverpool in 1878 when he was twenty-one years old. Here he sold tea as a drink, and it was this commodity that formed the mainstay of his business. Five years later he moved to London to develop his business, which he named Home and Colonial Tea Association. His first store was on the Edgware Road, followed by shops in Islington, and then expanding north to Birmingham and Leeds.

He and his business partner, John Musker, retired from active participation in the business when they were still in their early thirties, by which time they had both amassed fortunes. They sold their shares in 1919 for £3.5 million, equivalent to about £195 million today, by which time the business was operating over 500 stores.

In 1924, Home and Colonial acquired the rival Maypole Dairies chain by buying out the financial interests of the Watson family. There followed a series of mergers, the most significant being with Sir Thomas Lipton's grocery stores, which also had their roots in the importing of tea, creating a grocery retail empire with over three thousand stores. Home and Colonial set up a separate company, Allied Suppliers, to handle the buying and sourcing for the whole group.

With its own factories in both the UK and overseas, wholesale and distribution operations, and a major presence in almost every main shopping area in the British Isles, Home and Colonial and its various retail brands were a major player in the grocery trade until the mid-1960s. The rapid growth of the supermarkets forced a re-grouping of much of the grocery trade, and Home and Colonial, then trading overall as Allied Suppliers, was acquired, first by Caversham Foods and then, in 1981, by Argyll Foods which later merged with Safeway, the supermarket chain. At the time of merger, Allied Suppliers had an annual turnover of £800 million.

Julius Drewe - he added the 'e' to his surname in 1913 - died in 1931. Perhaps his most substantial gift to the country was Castle Drogo near Drewsteinton in Devon, which he commissioned. It was designed in 1911 by the eminent architect Edward Lutyens and was completed in 1930, being the last 'castle' to be built in England. It took many years to build and underwent several changes to Lutyens' original design. Drewe moved in during 1925, but died only a year after its completion. The castle was a vast austere structure with walls up to six feet thick but containing all the comforts of the time including electricity generated locally by his own hydro–electric generating facility.

His wife Frances and her son Basil continued to live at the castle, and during the Second World War, Frances and her daughter Mary opened the castle as a home for babies made homeless during the London blitz. Now owned by the National Trust, together with an estate covering 1,500 acres, the building is Grade I listed, and the gardens have a Grade 2 listing. It was the first property built in the twentieth century to be acquired by the Trust, which in 2011 began major restoration work.

Aspirations and motivations

Castle Drogo is an appropriate metaphor and symbol with which to con-
clude this account of the aspirations, fortunes and failures of the men and
women who created this country's most familiar retail brands. Julius Drewe
had a strong sense of history and sought to prove long lineage, displaying his
own coat of arms at the castle which he paid for. After the birth of his third
child he began to research his family tree, hoping to find a distinguished
heritage. His painstaking and costly research, long before the days of internet genealogy websites, discovered a Norman baron from the Crusades
called Drogo, and known as Drewe de Teine. Hence his decision to settle
in Drewsteignton, and to build Castle Drogo. Of his own dynasty, there
was sadness. Albert Drewe died at Ypres 1917 having suffered a fatal mus-
tard gas attack. Neither of his other sons, Basil, who became a barrister, and
Cedric who served as an MP, wanted to be involved in either the business
or to regard Castle Drogo as their family home. Perhaps, by the time he
withdrew from the day-to-day running of Home and Colonial, Julius Drewe
knew that retailing, like the Britannic rule of colonies and empire, was but a
transitory activity, even for the most prosperous and profitable companies.
On that realisation, he turned his attention to creating something that he
believed would last long after his death. There was, in his intentions, certainly a sense of England still being a dominant power and influence across
the world. A belief in Empire, but also a personal conviction, in common
with many of the early retail entrepreneurs, that he could achieve what he
wanted. Perhaps the records we have today did not include the periods of
self-doubt which he may have experienced, but possibly there may not have
been many such moments.

The story of Home and Colonial could have been so different if decisions
at board level had taken the company in other directions. By the time it lost
its identity in the sequence of mergers in the 1980s, it was equal in trading
stature to several of the businesses that would become the top supermarket groups of the present day. Alongside the former grocery businesses that
became Tesco, Sainsbury's, Asda and Morrisons, we could now be shopping
at 'Drewes' or perhaps 'H&C'.

The steady increase in car ownership which began in the 1960s led in
part to the construction of larger supermarkets which, by necessity, had to
be located where there was adequate space. Some towns and cities were able
to redevelop redundant cattle markets and factory premises near to their
traditional shopping centres, giving rise to shopping 'precincts', the UK

equivalent of the American 'mall'; but these have always been limited by the amount of land available, and the very high price placed on that land. The space for one of the first post-war shopping precincts, in Coventry, had been created by wartime bombing rather than by town and country planning. Inevitably, everything began to get bigger. Supermarkets grew into superstores and even hypermarkets, and the 'out-of-town' shopping centre appeared.

Consequently, a major debate which began in the 1990s and is continuing, is whether the High Street has reached the end of its useful life. Many town and city shopping centres started to slip into a period of decline because of several different challenges. Small independent retailers found they could not compete with the low prices offered by the big chains, and were unable to afford the high rents charged by landlords and landowners. Several well-established chains collapsed, for reasons already discussed, not the least being the massive switch to internet shopping. The simple challenge of driving to and parking near to High Street shops led many families to take the easier option of going out of town, where the extra space made shopping easier, and the scale of the shopping areas brought back that sense of occasion and fun which many of the retail pioneers had worked hard to create.

However, despite years of gloom and boarded-up shop fronts, the High Streets are still with us, and in many places have entered a new era of activity, if not full prosperity. Prompting this new movement has been the pedestrianising of many central shopping areas which has, in turn, encouraged the 'coffee culture', when the British weather permits. Many of the old defunct brands have been replaced by new names and logos which are as innovative and appealing as those of the nineteenth century pioneers, and scale has been replaced by a sense of uniqueness with smaller shops targeting in their design and décor, very specific sectors of the consumer market. Where this movement will take the consumer is a matter for debate, but there are indications that we are turning away from the large-scale supermarkets, and becoming more subtle – and demanding – in our shopping habits. We may still look to the big supermarket chains for the essentials that we need every week, but we are also patronising the smaller independent stores, enjoying a new sort of High Street experience and culture.

The town markets and squares are still with us. Many still convene in the open air, and others are now held inside purpose-built market halls with air-conditioning and lighting powered by solar panels. The old market squares are still used as they have been for centuries, as focal points for the community. Where town criers once proclaimed the news of the day, community radio stations now set up their outside broadcast units; where traders once sold their wares from barrows, charities now raise money for a variety of local good causes. Voluntary groups care for the flower planters and hanging baskets. Surrounding the square, the austere and grand Georgian and Victorian buildings which, until recent times, were branches of the big four banks or the larger building societies, are now home to coffee shops and restaurants that spill out into the public space. In the summertime, some of these areas are covered with imported sand to create a seaside atmosphere, and Christmas is celebrated, not only as a commercial opportunity, but as a time when every aspect of the local community is recognised and can take part.

The one lesson which all the pioneering shopkeepers and market traders learned at some stage in their careers was that nothing stands still in the world of retail and consumerism. Turn your back on the customers for a moment, and they will go elsewhere. If you miss your pitch on the market for just one day, someone will take your place.

Acknowledgements

No history is the province of one person or one author. All the men and women in this book have their own histories, and many have commissioned writers to record the rise, and sometimes the fall of their businesses and their dreams. I must therefore acknowledge the work of all who have previously written about the great names in British retail. My mission has been not to copy or to repeat, but to tell the broader story by placing the great retail brands and the pioneers and innovators who created them, in the context of history, including the events and inventions that challenged them.

In my research, I have benefitted from advice, guidance and information offered by many individuals and organisations. Some have simply confirmed a date or an address, while others have checked facts and figures, or have told me stories from their own knowledge of a former business. I would especially like to thank the Willenhall History Society for confirming details of the Rushbrooke family, and Tony Wilkinson, former Chairman of Wilko, for allowing me to visit the company's headquarters to hear his reminiscences about his father. I must also recognise the work of the archivists and historians who have preserved their companies' histories, and made their work available on the internet, and the journalists of the nineteenth and twentieth centuries who recorded events in the High Streets of Great Britain. Finally, and importantly, my grateful thanks to Chris Wood who scrutinised my text and offered many sensible and valuable comments.

Bibliography and references

Harry Lerner, *Currys: The First Hundred Years*, Woodhead-Faulkner, 1984.

Keith Jopp, *Corah of Leicester 1815–1965*, Newman-Neame, Leicester, 1965.

Alcwyn B. Jones, *The Story of Halfords*, Published by the author, Llandudno, Gwynedd (printers), 1981.

Cynthia Brown, *Wharf Street Revisited*, Living History Unit, Leicester City Council, 1995.

Robert Ingle, *Thomas Cook of Leicester*, Headstart History Publishing, 1991.

Helen and Richard Leacroft, *The Theatre in Leicestershire*, Leicestershire Libraries and Information Service, 1986.

Piers Brendon, *Thomas Cook – 150 years of popular tourism*, Secker & Warburg Ltd, 1991.

Johnston Birchall, *Co-op, the People's Business*, Manchester University Press, 1994.

Edward H. Milligan, *The Biographical Dictionary of British Quakers in Commerce and Industry 1775–1920*, Sessions Book Trust, York, 2007.

Robin Harrod, *The Jewel of Knightsbridge: the origins of the Harrod Empire*, The History Press, 2017.

George Davies, *What Next?*, Arrow Books, 1991.

Maurice Corina, *Fine Silks and Oak Counters*, Hutchinson Benham, 1978.

Keith and Susan Snow, 'John Frederick Marshall and the British Mosquitoes' in *The Bulletin of the British Museum of Natural History, Vol 19, No 1*, 1991.

M.C. Barres-Baker, *An Introduction to the Early History of Newspaper Advertising*, Brent Heritage Services and Brent Museum, 2007.

Frances Spalding, *Roger Fry, Art and Life*, University of California Press, 1980.

James Woodforde, *The Diary of a Country Parson, Vol V (1797–1802)*, Oxford University Press, 1931 (First Edition).

John Grenville Corina, 'William King (1786–1865), Physician and father of the Co-operative Movement', *The Journal of Medical Biography*, Sage Publications, August 1994.

Index